India's Preferential Policies

Migrants, the Middle Classes, and

Ethnic Equality

Myron Weiner
and
Mary Fainsod Katzenstein

With K.V. Narayana Rao

The University of Chicago Press · Chicago & London

THE UNIVERSITY OF CHICAGO PRESS,
CHICAGO 60637
THE UNIVERSITY OF CHICAGO PRESS,
LTD., LONDON

Publication of this work has been made possible
in part by a grant from the Andrew W. Mellon
Foundation.

MYRON WEINER is Ford Professor of Political
Science at the Massachusetts Institute of Tech-
nology and the author of *Sons of the Soil:
Migration and Ethnic Conflict in India* and
*India at the Polls: The Parliamentary Elections
of 1977.*

MARY FAINSOD KATZENSTEIN is an
associate professor of government and women's
studies at Cornell and author of *Ethnicity and
Equality: The Shiv Sena Party and Preferential
Policies in Bombay.*

Library of Congress Cataloging in Publication Data

Weiner, Myron.
    India's preferential policies.

    Includes index.
    1. Manpower policy—India—Addresses, essays,
lectures. 2. Discrimination in employment—India—
Addresses, essays, lectures. 3. Social classes—
India—Addresses, essays, lectures. 4. Pluralism
(Social sciences)—India—Addresses, essays, lec-
tures. I. Katzenstein, Mary Fainsod, 1945–
II. Title.
HD5819.W44   331.13'3'0954   81-7523
ISBN 0-226-88577-1   AACR2

Contents

CONTENTS

List of Maps

List of Tables

Acknowledgments

We wish to express our appreciation to the Ford-Rockefeller Foundation Research Program on Population and Development Policy and to the National Institute for Child Health and Human Development for funding this study. We are also grateful to the Center for International Studies at M.I.T. and the South Asia Program at Cornell for their assistance.

We also wish to thank Bertram F. Wilcox for his comments on the chapter on residence requirements and the law, Martin Slater and Robert Berrier, former graduate students in the Department of Political Science at M.I.T., for preparing the preliminary statistical analyses for the chapter on Assam, Carolyn Elliot for her comments on the chapter on Andhra Pradesh, and Harold Isaacs, Joshua Cohen, and Michael Lipsky for their suggestions on the concluding comparative chapter. We gratefully acknowledge the able editorial, secretarial, and typing assistance provided by Roberta Ornstein.

Sections of chapter 6 are published by permission of Transaction, Inc., from *Patterns of Policy: Comparative and Longitudinal Studies of Population Events*, edited by John D. Montgomery, Harold D. Lasswell, and Joel S. Migdal (New Brunswick: Transaction Books, 1979) and sections of chapters 3 and 4 are published by permission of Cornell University Press from Mary Fainsod Katzenstein, *Ethnicity and Equality: The Shiv Sena Party and Preferential Policies in Bombay* (Ithaca: Cornell University Press, 1979).

The Bombay case study was prepared by Mary F. Katzenstein; Andhra Pradesh by K.V. Narayana Rao; and Assam by Myron Weiner.

One
Introduction

This book describes and assesses India's efforts to use preferential policies to achieve greater equality among ethnic groups. It focuses particularly on those preferential policies intended to improve the position of the local population in relation to migrants from other cultural-linguistic regions of the country.

By preferential policies we mean laws, regulations, administrative rules, court orders, and other public interventions to provide certain public and private goods, such as admission into schools and colleges, jobs, promotions, business loans, and rights to buy and sell land on the basis of membership in a particular ethnic group. These policies—called in the United States "affirmative action" by supporters and "reverse discrimination" by detractors, and, in India, "protective discrimination"[1]—have led to considerable controversy. Central to this controversy is the question of whether the goal of equality between ethnic groups—as distinct from the goal of eliminating discrimination and equalizing opportunities for all individuals—should be an objective of government. By giving preferences to some people on the basis of the ethnic group to which they belong, is the government discriminating against those who do not belong to the preferred group? Precisely what kind of equality is produced by such policies, and do preferential policies actually increase equality or do they merely reassign resources from one group to another without reducing the existing differences between rich and poor? Finally, what are the consequences of such policies? Do they achieve the objectives for which they are intended, and are there other unintended, less visible effects? Who gains and who loses as a result of preferential policies?

These questions are hardly confined to any single country. Few Americans are aware of the extent to which other multiethnic societies have their own form of preferential policies. Indeed, in Malaysia, Indonesia, Sri Lanka, India, and other multiethnic countries in the less-developed world, governments have adopted policies—often very different from one another and from American ones—to achieve greater equality between ethnic groups. The goals of these governments have been to raise education, income, and occupational levels of some ethnic groups in relation to—and sometimes at the cost of—other ethnic groups.

1

This study began as an inquiry into the efforts of India's state governments to control migration from one state to another. But like many policies to place restrictions on where people shall live or work, it was clear that these were intended to increase the educational and employment opportunities of some ethnic groups in relation to others. Thus, what might be seen by some observers as internal migration policies could be seen—and were so defined by most Indians—as preferential policies. Indeed, there was no attempt to disguise the purpose of this legislation and these administrative rules, as is the case in many societies where zoning regulations and other restrictions intended to keep out some ethnic or class groups are justified on the often spurious grounds of environmental protection, water conservation, or other "quality of life" considerations. To the contrary, Indians defined these policies as part of an explicit effort to achieve ethnic equality by providing greater access to employment to some groups, and less access to others.

India has two types of preferential policies. One provides special benefits and exclusive preferences to members of scheduled castes and scheduled tribes; these policies are analogous, though not identical, to affirmative action programs for minorities in the United States. These communities are given preferences in admission to schools and colleges (and special stipends), and in recruitment and promotion in government employment. They are also given reserved seats in state legislative assemblies and in parliament. Some of these preferences (not including reserved seats in legislative bodies) have also been extended by many state governments to a list of disadvantaged "backward" classes.

Another set of policies provide preferences to *local* ethnic groups in competition for higher-status, higher-salaried jobs with migrants from outside the state. There are domicile rules for employment by government, and the private sector is also "encouraged"—the pressures are often acute—to hire locally. In addition, preferences are also provided to local people for admission into educational institutions, especially into engineering and medical colleges. To the extent that the local ethnic group is disadvantaged in relation to outsiders, it is argued, they too deserve preferences. Both sets of policies share common assumptions about the responsibility of the state for the achievement of ethnic equality. They differ in that the first set of policies is intended to provide preferences to minorities, while the second provides preferences to a majority which considers itself educationally and occupationally subordinate to a minority.

Since this study grew out of an examination of internal migration policies, its focus is on preferential policies to achieve ethnic equality for the local population in relation to migrants: the history of such policies, the political process that produced them, their assumptions in the context of Indian values, and their effects. Though these policies have points of convergence with preferential programs for scheduled castes, scheduled tribes, and other backward

2

classes, and where appropriate we have related them to one another, a full-scale assessment of the preferential policies for the disadvantaged castes and tribes remains to be done. We can only lament that a subject of such importance to India, and of such obvious comparative value, remains in search of an author.[2]

The chapter that follows provides an overview of preferential policies for local people: how the migration process created ethnic inequalities, why the demand for preferences arose, the arguments employed, and the political forces at work. The third chapter reviews the legislative history, and then focuses on the way in which the judiciary has attempted to resolve the clash between preferential policies and the principles they embody, and some of the "liberal" provisions of the constitution which ensure India's citizens the right of free internal migration and freedom from discriminatory policies on the basis of religion, caste, tribe, and place of birth.

Chapters 4, 5, and 6 provide a history and analysis of policies in three of India's states: Maharashtra, in western India, whose government intervened in response to demands in Bombay city for preferential treatment in employment for local people; the southern state of Andhra Pradesh where there is a long history of government efforts in the Telangana region to reserve positions in the universities and in public employment for local people; and Assam, in the northeast, where a hundred years of in-migration have so transformed the social structure that how to cope with the resulting ethnic inequalities has become the central political issue.

Though these are by no means the only states in India which have adopted preferential policies—such policies exist now in virtually all of India's states—there are at least three reasons why these cases were chosen for study.

The first is national prominence. In all three the demand for preferences took a political form that commanded national attention. In Bombay, the nativist Shiv Sena party won considerable electoral support in a city that is well attended to by the nation's press; and in both Assam and Telangana the demand for preferences became so violent that the central government called in the army. In the case of Andhra Pradesh, decisions by the state and central government led to court rulings with implications elsewhere. All three localities have been widely regarded as pacesetters for state and local legislation.

A second reason is that these three examples provide the reader with some sense of how preferential policies work in states where they have a long history. In Telangana preferences date back to the early 1920s; in Assam, the state government has been giving preferences to Assamese in state employment since the 1950s; and in Maharashtra legislation was passed in 1969. We are thus also in a position to make an assessment of the effects of policy interventions in states where considerable time has elapsed.

A third and perhaps the most important reason is that each of these cases illuminates a different dimension of the problem of preferential policies. Bombay provides us with an opportunity to examine the policies in India's most industrially advanced region, an educational center, a magnet for Indians all over the country, and by any criteria one of India's most modern centers. Bombay has also been a growth center where competition for education, jobs, and promotions is as fierce as in any place in the country. Bombay thus enables us to see how the demand for preferences arose and how they have worked in an economically dynamic setting.

In contrast, Assam is one of the more backward regions of India with almost no industry, a less-developed educational system, and a relatively small modern sector. Yet its local population has been overwhelmed by an influx of outsiders who have taken visible positions in the modern occupations—in administration and in salaried positions in whatever there is of a modern sector. Assam, with its reserves of timber and oil, has a considerable growth potential, but thus far it has progressed slowly. Here the demand for preferences often borders on a demand for exclusion. It is a far more central issue than in Bombay, and the demands have taken an acute form accompanied by sharp political cleavages and violence.

The demand for preferences in the Telangana region within the state of Andhra raises still another issue: what is local? The state? A region of the state? A district? A city? The question of preferences for whom has nowhere taken such a perplexing form.

In all three cases we shall describe the policies that have been adopted to expand the educational and employment opportunities for the local majority community, to reduce the opportunities for migrants and descendants of migrants living within the state, and to slow or halt the flow of migrants from other states or regions of the same state. In each of the cases we shall first show how the government attempted to restrict population movements for the achievement of educational and employment objectives. Then, secondly, we shall examine and where possible measure the effects of these policies, whether unintended and indirect or intended and direct. In all three cases we shall explore as a central theme of this book the political logic of preferential policies: how those who make policy weigh the costs and benefits of preferences as they respond to demands by the educated sections of the local population in competition with middle-class groups from outside.

In chapter 7 we draw from the case studies to comment on the political calculations that policymakers must make as they deliberate over preferential policies and we assess the impact of those policies. Preferential policies are, as we shall see, largely intended to provide benefits to the middle classes within disadvantaged social groups. Whether they do so, and with what other consequences, are what we mean to investigate. We consider, thus, the effects on local employment and on migration, on relations among ethnic groups, and, more broadly, on the politics of the state.

INTRODUCTION

Though the book is neither prescriptive nor explicitly comparative, readers will find much to support or undermine their own beliefs concerning the merits and demerits of preferential policies in countries other than India. That is, we must admit, what we intend. To look at others is to see oneself. To study policy is to be engaged in applied social philosophy.

It seemed appropriate, therefore, that the final chapter consider India's preferential policies in comparison with at least our own country. A more comprehensive comparative study, drawing from the experiences of Malaysia, Sri Lanka, Nigeria, and other countries that have some form of preference, is clearly desirable, but we have confined our own comparison to the country of obviously greatest interest to our readers. To make the policies more comparable we have broadened the discussion of Indian policies in this last chapter to include the full range of preferential programs, including those intended to benefit the scheduled castes, scheduled tribes, and other backward classes. The apparent differences in values, social structures, and politics notwithstanding, we suggest that the policies pursued by the two countries have had a number of similar consequences.

Of the many consequences of these policies for India, there are four that emerge from this study as particularly important.

The first is that preferential policies in India are primarily directed at expanding educational and employment opportunities for the middle classes within each ethnic group that considers itself "backward." Members of these middle classes have been the primary beneficiaries of preferential policies, although we suggest that there is at least some evidence that the position of these groups might have improved even in the absence of such preferences.

Second, the extension of preferences to local ethnic majorities has meant that an ever-increasing proportion of the middle classes in almost all ethnic groups is assured of a "share" (though often an unequal share) in education and employment. What is thus emerging in India is a government-regulated labor market in which various ethnic groups are given a reserved share of that market. Competition for employment is thus not among all Indians, but within specified linguistic, caste, and tribal groups.

Third, various ethnic groups, therefore, politically fight for a share of that labor market. The major political struggles are often over who should get reservations, how the boundaries of the ethnic groups should be defined, and how large their share should be. There are also political struggles over whether there should be reservations in both education and employment, in private as well as in public employment, and in promotions as well as in hiring. The preferential policies themselves have thus stimulated various ethnic groups to assert their "rights" to reservations.

Finally, we emphasize in this study that the response to demands for preferential treatment and the incorporation of preferences within governmental

5

policy must be understood in terms of political logic: we thus attempt to identify how those who make policy perceive the costs and benefits of preferential
treatment. We look not only at the social and economic linkages between policy makers and ethnic claimants, but also, even more important in our view,
at the political gains and losses which policy makers must attempt to calibrate
as they react to demands for preferences.

Readers of this volume are not likely to agree on the question of whether
the state should provide assistance and preference to individuals not because
of their individual characteristics but because of the ethnic group to which
they belong, or whether assistance for one group is discriminatory for another,
or when support for an individual on the basis of the group to which he belongs erodes equality of individual opportunity, or whether preferences for
some interfere with the opportunity of others to advance on the basis of merit, or whether preferences for ethnic groups are necessary to stabilize the social
order, or whether preferences are themselves determinants of ethnic conflict.
The authors themselves are often in disagreement on these questions demonstrating if not our resistance to being influenced by empirical evidence, then
suggesting how many of these issues are at bottom moral questions that go
beyond weighing, as social scientists do, the costs and benefits of government
policies. But whatever viewpoint one takes it is important to understand what
the consequences are of these policies, the unintended and the intended, the
indirect and the direct, the less visible as well as the apparent.

Two
Preferential Policies and Ethnic Equality

Migration, Modernization, and the Growth of an Ethnic Division of Labor
The shift from colonial to independent status of many of the developing world's multiethnic societies often proved most disruptive for the very groups that had been receptive to the educational and economic opportunities created by the imperial rulers. Among the first to be both modernized and westernized, these ethnic groups tended to send their children to the new educational institutions created by the Europeans, where they acquired the skills, the work habits, and the languages that eased them into the newly created industries and made it possible for them to man the European-created administrative system. Many took the initiative themselves in creating new industries, establishing banks, opening new marketing networks, and in other ways playing a role in the creation of the institutions of modern society.

Unfortunately for them, and for their societies, these groups often belonged to an ethnic minority. In many instances they were migrants from other countries or from other parts of their own country. The rulers of the newly independent states, and the social classes which supported them, usually came from the majority ethnic communities, and they viewed the migrant minorities as interlopers who stood in the way of the full expression of the cultural and economic aspirations of the majority communities. Since the minorities were typically educators, businessmen, administrators, professionals, and middle-level clerks, they threatened the new middle classes emerging within the ethnic majorities.

In Sri Lanka, for example, the Sinhalese majority turned against educated Tamils. In Malaysia, the Malays, declaring themselves "Bhumiputras" ("sons of the soil"), legislated job preferences for themselves over the local Chinese population. In Nigeria, the Hausa and Fulani turned against the Ibos. And in Uganda, President Amin expelled Pakistani and Indian settlers. In country after country migrant minorities were expelled, abused, or discriminated against—not because they had failed to contribute to the country's economic life, but rather because they had been successful. They were resented not because they were unemployed and imposed a burden on the country's social and welfare services, but because the dominant ethnic majority, and particularly the edu-

7

cated section of that majority, saw them as barriers to its own aspirations for jobs, status, and wealth.

The ethnic majorities that dominated the new governments pursued a variety of policies intended to increase their own share in the economy. When the ethnic minorities originated from outside the country, governments often expelled the migrants—or their locally born descendants. Several West African government expelled migrants from neighboring countries. Both Uganda and Burma expelled Indians and Pakistanis. Sri Lanka followed a more gradual course by negotiating a treaty with India for the repatriation of part of the Tamil population. In both Indonesia and the Philippines, and more recently in Vietnam, violent attacks against the Chinese led many Chinese to flee the country. Similarly, protectionist policies for the Malays in Malaysia have led some Chinese to move to neighboring Singapore.

When the ethnic minorities originated from areas within the same country, the matter was more complicated. The Ibos, for example, are resented in northern Nigeria, though they are after all Nigerians, entitled to the same rights as other Nigerians. Throughout much of Africa—indeed, in many of the multiethnic countries of the third world—the desire of local ethnic groups to dominate their own turf leads them to challenge the ethnic minorities from other regions of the same country who, by virtue of their education, skills, motivation, and the opportunities made available to them earlier, hold important positions in the local economy and status system.

This tension between the local majority ethnic community and what Donald Horowitz has called the "achieving minority" ethnic community, often of migrant origin,[1] involves not just a clash of cultures, but rather is rooted in the country's history, economy, polity, and social structure.

Nowhere are these relationships revealed on such a grand scale as in India, the world's largest multiethnic society. Though India's many linguistic communities are territorially rooted, even before the Europeans arrived an intermingling of ethnic groups had taken place through the process of migration. We know, for example, that as a result of warfare entire communities were uprooted and moved from one section of the country to another to form a new ethnic enclave.[2] Rulers sometimes invited priests, administrators, and merchants from other regions—a particularly common practice among many Muslim rulers who recruited not only from other parts of India but from Iran, Turkey, and the Arab countries.[3]

But from the middle of the nineteenth century onward, migration played an even more important role than it had earlier, transforming the ethnic composition, social structure, and economy of a number of regions within India. The unification of India under a single ruler and the termination of internal warfare facilitated the movement of merchants, traders, and bankers from one region to another. The establishment of institutions of higher education in Bombay, Calcutta, and Madras attracted students across long distances. New occupations emerged—law, medicine, journalism, university teaching, the higher levels of the civil service—whose English-speaking members moved freely across linguistic lines.

The investment of British (and later Indian) capital also created new industrial, agricultural, and plantation occupations. There were tea plantations in Assam, coal mines in southern Bihar, textile mills in south India, Gujarat, and Bombay, jute mills in Bengal, and many new industrial enterprises of all kinds in Bombay and Calcutta. In time there emerged a dual economy and a dual labor market encompassing on one side a modern sector and on the other an agricultural sector with its traditional technology.

The concept of a dual labor market has recently been developed to characterize a market divided into a primary sector and a secondary sector of low-paying, unskilled jobs that are low in status and typically dead end. In the United States and in Western Europe the notion of a secondary labor market helps us to understand why migrants were needed and for what kinds of jobs. In advanced industrial countries this labor intensive sector initially recruited migrants from the countryside, and, when that supply dwindled, migrant laborers were imported from Mexico and Puerto Rico in the case of the United States, and from Algeria, Yugoslavia, Greece, Portugal, and Turkey in the case of the countries of Western Europe.

But in India, as in other developing countries, migrants were recruited not only for the bottom of the labor market, but for the top as well. The reason is that in many regions the "modern" sector—and here we include recruitment into the modern professions, not simply into the modern industrial sector—often grew too rapidly to be adequately manned by the local population. Often the new modern occupations were recruited prior to the creation locally of a modern educational system—with the result that lawyers, doctors, teachers, and administrators were recruited from other regions of the country.

In some regions there thus emerged an ethnic division of labor in which modern jobs were held by ethnic minorities who came from outside the region, while the local population remained on the land in traditional occupations. The ethnic division of labor took a variety of forms. In some regions, almost all jobs in the modern sector were held by migrants. In Assam, for example, the professions and administration were largely in the hands of Bengali Hindu migrants, transportation was run by Punjabis, trade and commerce were controlled by mercantile communities from Rajasthan, and tea plantation workers came from the tribal regions of Bihar. In Bombay, the local Maharashtrians did seek and find employment as workers in the new industries, but the higher-status, better-paid jobs that required more education were more often taken by Tamils, Malayalees, Gujaratis and others.

Not every ethnic division of labor put the locals on the bottom and the migrants on the top. In Calcutta, for example, where the level of education was high, positions requiring education were taken by the local Bengalis, while it was the manual jobs in industry, construction, and in the port that attracted the migrants from the rural areas of nearby Bihar and Orissa. Nor did the emergence of a modern sector necessarily create an ethnic division of labor. In the city of Ahmadabad, for example, the textile industry was locally developed, financed, managed, and staffed. Owners, managers, and workers were all Gujaratis. Similarly, in Madras industry tended to recruit manpower locally, and the modern occupations of law, journalism, medicine, and administration were also locally recruited. Madras and Ahmadabad did attract migrants, but the migrants were from the nearby countryside rather than from distant cultural regions. Even now Ahmadabad and Madras remain more linguistically homogeneous cities than Calcutta and Bombay.[4]

Why an ethnic division of labor emerged in some regions but not in others, and why a migrant minority is on the top of the labor market in some instances and at the bottom in others, are matters rooted in local circumstances. Factors involved include the rate of investment in local education versus the rate of industrial and mercantile development, and the capacity of local communities (and the incentives available to them) to take advantage of new educational and employment opportunities in relation to the capacities, incentives, and opportunities of potential migrants from other regions.

The Demand for Restructuring the Ethnic Division of Labor

In those regions and urban areas of India in which migrant minorities were educationally and occupationally more advanced than the local population, the expansion of local secondary schools and colleges subsequently created an aspiring middle class that was dissatisfied with the existing ethnic division of labor. As the local community, or at least the educated portions within it, felt blocked by migrants and descendants of migrants, they sought state intervention to provide job reservations for the local population.

The demand was not simply for equality of income—there was no demand, for example, for more equitable income tax policies—but rather for equality of employment *in the modern sector of the economy*. Newly educated natives, seeking jobs in the modern sector, viewed the successful migrants from other cultural-linguistic regions as barriers to their own social and occupational mobility. The demand for ethnic equality was not a demand for state-subsidized assistance to compete in the labor market, or for the elimination of discrimination in employment, but for a set of policies that would restrict or even exclude migrants and their descendants in order to improve the position of local ethnic groups. In other words, the demand was that the state intervene *to restructure the ethnic division of labor.*

One argument for intervention is that the existing division of labor is the result of a historical set of policies adopted by the British rulers that made it possible for outsiders to take the best positions in the modern sector and in administration. In the Telangana region of the southern state of Andhra Pradesh, it was argued that while they had lived under the "backward" rule of the Nizam, the people of the delta districts in the eastern part of the state had had the benefits of British education. In the state of Assam in the northeast, the Assamese argued that they had in effect lived under a double colonialism; by incorporating their region into the presidency of Bengal, the British had made it possible for the more educated Bengalis to take control of the administration and to occupy positions in the emerging modern sector of the economy. The state should intervene to remedy what the state had itself created. To permit equal competition for positions would not reverse this historic division of labor since the two groups, the natives and the migrants, continue to be unequal in education and skills. Only a system of preferences in employment, it is argued, can change the existing division of labor.

A second argument is that local people have a right to employment in the modern sector created within their territory. They are entitled to whatever benefits modernization and industrialization bring to their region, since the region provides the resources which make development possible. Hence, it is only right and proper that the tea plantations in Assam be managed by Assamese, and that industrial houses in Bombay be staffed by Maharashtrians. Moreover, it is further argued, the children of migrants have no claim to employment locally since they have no proprietary rights in the soil; unlike the local ethnic group, they cannot be, in a cultural sense, "sons of the soil," for they have their cultural roots elsewhere. After all, the descendants of migrants can "return" to their native province for employment; the local people should not be required to look for jobs outside the region without first having an opportunity to take employment within their native place.

A third argument is that social justice requires that all ethnic groups share equally in the benefits of modernization. According to this argument, all ethnic groups—and by ethnic is meant linguistic, tribal, religious, and caste groups —ought to have the same internal division of labor that exists in the society as a whole. Thus, according to this argument, each ethnic group ought to have its share of positions in the modern sector of the economy—in administration, in the professions, in the factories, and so on. If, to place a numerical value on the principle, ten percent of the jobs are in the modern sector, then ten percent of each ethnic group ought to be employed in this sector.

Such numerical quotas were initially established for the employment of scheduled castes and scheduled tribes in the state and central administrative services. Under government law, each state has a list or schedule of local tribes and what were once called untouchable castes. Members of scheduled castes and tribes have reservations for seats in the state legislative assemblies and in the national parliament, admissions into colleges and technical institutes, and jobs in the central and state administrative services. These reservations or quotas are in proportion to the population of the scheduled castes and tribes within each state; in a state where ten percent of the population belongs to scheduled castes and another five percent to scheduled tribes, ten and five percent respectively of political offices, college admissions, and civil service appointments are reserved for these communities.[5]

A number of state governments also provide preferences for a category known as "other backward classes." A Backward Classes Commission established by the central government in 1953 presented a list of 2,399 groups entitled by its criterion to government benefits, totaling 116 million members, or about thirty-two percent of the total population of India.[6] According to the commission, in Mysore the OBCs (as they are often called) constituted sixty-six percent of the population, in Uttar Pradesh forty-three percent, in Bihar thirty-eight percent, and in Madhya Pradesh thirty-seven percent. Were preferences extended to the OBCs in proportion to their population as in the case of scheduled castes and scheduled tribes, then there would hardly be a state in which preferential reservations in education and employment fell below fifty percent. (Nationally, the scheduled castes, scheduled tribes, and other backward classes together total fifty-four percent of the population.) In fact, as we shall see later, the courts prevented an extension of preferences to OBCs in proportion to their population when the combined preferences in a state exceeded fifty percent.

The demand by other local groups for reservations was thus a logical extension of the system of reservations for the scheduled castes, tribes, and OBCs—with one significant difference. While reservations for scheduled castes, tribes, and OBCs were intended to benefit disadvantaged minorities (though collectively they may form a majority), the demand by local people for preferences against migrant communities was a demand on behalf of a disadvantaged majority. Moreover, while the case for preferences for the scheduled castes and tribes in part rested on the argument that they suffered from social disability as a consequence of their place in the Indian social order and the discriminations which they experienced, the case for preferences for the local population did not rest upon the notion of discrimination, but rather on the argument that for one reason or another they had been left behind. The principle was thus argued and accepted that disadvantaged groups—that is, those that have a disproportionately small share of jobs in the modern sector—irrespective of the cause and irrespective of their size, are entitled to preferences.

It is in this context that we can understand the claims by local people against minority migrant communities. The demand for preferences for the local population comes primarily from those who do not receive them as members of scheduled castes, tribes, or other backward classes. This explains in part why the political movements for local preferences have their social base among caste Hindus and particularly among the more "advanced" higher castes within the local community (approximately 34% of the Indian population). In every state these are the groups that would otherwise receive no preferences and hence no protection in the competition for admission into colleges and universities and in employment.

In the city of Bombay, the Shiv Sena, a local political party, demanded that special job rights be given to the local Marathi-speaking population (42% of the city) in preference to middle-class migrants from south India. In Andhra, the Telangana Praja Samiti, a local regional party, demanded special job protection for people living in the western districts of the state who faced competition with migrants from the eastern districts. And in Assam, the local Congress party demanded special employment rights for the Assamese-speaking people (76% of the state in 1961) in preference to Bengali-speaking migrants and settlers.

Preferences for Whom?

Strictly speaking, the preferential policies adopted by the state governments refer to "local" people, not an ethnic group; the preferential laws and administrative rulings specify that preferences will be given to "local" people as defined by their place of birth and/or duration of residence. It is generally understood, however, that the intent of these policies is to give preference to the "indigenous" ethnic group to the exclusion of those who may have been born in the locality but who are, ethnically speaking, "outsiders." Thus, government directives in Bombay say that preferences shall be given to those born in the city or those resident in the state for ten or fifteen years, but in fact employers are told by government officials that "local" means Marathi speakers. Similarly in Assam, local means Assamese speakers though there are many locally born non-Assamese. And in the Telangana region of Andhra, the Urdu word *mulki,* which distinguishes the people of Telangana from those who originate outside, has taken on ethnic overtones.

Policy clearly means more than the laws and regulations alone; it includes the intent of government and the implementation of government actions. From this point of view the preferential policies are clearly directed at the achievement of greater equality between *ethnic* groups.

Underlying the various arguments for preferential treatment on the basis of ethnicity is the assumption that the position of an individual in India's hierarchical society is largely shaped by the position or rank of the ethnic group to which he belongs. Hence, any effort to improve one's position rests upon changing that of the group as a whole. This is a different argument from one which says that one's position is affected by the prejudice of society. Although many Indians recognize that there is prejudice, especially against scheduled castes, the argument for preferences rests more broadly on the notion that individual success requires an improvement in a group's standing.

The struggle for positional change on the part of caste groups is an old one in India. As M. N. Srinivas has often noted, castes have frequently sought to change their ritual standing through the adoption of the rituals of higher-status groups, a process called Sanskritization. While there are many instances of individual social mobility, often an individual's social standing changed because of positional changes on the part of his group.

The familiar distinction between ascription and achievement seems appropriate here. India's traditional system of social stratification rested upon a caste division of labor; with the intrusion of the British and the beginnings of modernization, the division of labor broadened to incorporate other ethnic categories. British recruitment into the military was based upon a theory of "martial" races; Gurkhas, Punjabis, Rajputs, Coorgis, and Marathas were thought to be particularly qualified for military service. Racial Eurasions—Anglo-Indians—were hired by the railway service. Harijans were recruited as municipal sweepers. Both private and public employers continued to use ascriptive criteria for hiring. Hardly anyone questioned the notion that it was appropriate for the state itself to support the ethnic division of labor. The state, no less than private employers, hired on the basis of ethnic membership since it was considered fitting and proper for occupational stratification to be based upon ethnic stratification and for ascriptive criteria to exist side by side with achievement criteria. The "best" might be recruited for the military, but the best, by definition, came from specified ethnic groups.

The question of what constitutes an ethnic group remains as unclear in India as it does in so many other multiethnic societies where ethnicity itself is in a state of flux. Indians belong, of course, to a wide variety of groups simultaneously: religion, sect within the religion, caste, linguistic group, region. Given the subjective character of ethnicity—you are what you call yourself as well as what others call you—individuals and the groups to which they belong may change their identity. The choice of an ethnic identity is often political; it is by no means a given in any immutable sense.

Ethnic claims have a long and controversial history in India. Under the British virtually all types of ethnic groups had a legitimate status. The British provided separate political representation to a variety of ethnic groups—tribes, castes, religious and racial groups—on the grounds that their minority status, their economic and social backwardness, or their relationships to the British warranted special protection. Ethnic groups, along with a variety of economic interest groups and institutions, were given formal representation in a political system that became increasingly corporatist in its organizational structure.

When India became independent, some of these special rights were incorporated into the constitution, and hence declared legitimate. Scheduled castes and tribes were given explicit recognition in the 1950 constitution. In 1953 a government States Reorganization Commission was appointed to consider the demand that state boundaries be redrawn so as to approximate the country's linguistic boundaries—thereby constitutionally establishing the principle that India is a multilingual society with each regional language group possessing political power in at least one state. The commission gave a qualified acceptance to the linguistic principle, and shortly thereafter the boundaries were redrawn to accommodate linguistic claims.

But while caste, tribe, and language were given legitimate status, religion was not. Since Indian nationalists believed that the British policy of reserving constituencies for Muslims provided the impetus for the Muslim League's demand for partition, the postindependence government viewed claims on the basis of religion illegitimate—and they were derogatorily labeled "communal." Several Muslim political groups continued to function and to make claims as Muslims, but in time most other religious groups redefined their identity in an effort to find some nonreligious basis for making community claims. Thus, the Sikhs, a religious community in the Punjab eager to create a state of their own, put themselves forth as Punjabi speakers when the central government made it clear that it would never authorize state formation along religious lines but would accept a linguistic claim. Similarly, in the hill regions of northeastern India some of the Khasi, Garo, and Naga tribesmen asserted their identity as Christians; then, realizing the political unacceptability of a religious claim, emphasized their tribal identities and successfully demanded the creation of tribal states.

An interesting example of the illegitimacy of religious claims is given by some scheduled caste Hindus in Maharashtra, who converted to Buddhism, thereby ending their self-defined status as Hindu untouchables. The "neo-Buddhists" demanded that they receive the same special benefits provided scheduled castes (including separate representation in elected bodies, reservations and scholarships for colleges and universities, and quotas for government jobs), but the central government took the position that while benefits were provided to them as members of castes that suffered from certain disabilities, they could no longer receive these benefits as members of a religious minority.[7]

Though religion thus far remains excluded from the category of ethnic groups entitled to preferential help,[8] the ethnic categories that are used as the basis for preferential treatment remain very broad. "Scheduled castes" refers to dozens of untouchable castes, with considerable variations in incomes within and between them; similarly, "scheduled tribes" refers to a large number of tribes at various levels of development, further divided between Christians, who are often better educated, and non-Christians. The category "other backward classes" is particularly ill defined and improperly labeled, since the "classes" that are so designated by state governments are always *castes*, not *classes*, chosen because in education and employment and in the social hierarchy they are "backward." As for the "local" linguistic groups, or, as they are called in India, "sons of the soil," they include, of course, a vast array of local castes and religious groups among whom there are educational, occupational, and income differences.

The Debate on the Use of Ethnic Criteria
Some Indians have argued against the use of any ethnic categories in employment on the grounds that within each of these ethnic groups there is a wide range of educational achievement and that preferences simply give jobs to those most qualified to compete while doing nothing for those who are the least qualified. Some critics have also argued that it is unfair to treat locally

born descendants of migrants as "outsiders" simply because they belong to another ethnic group, and that it is also unfair to give preferences to a local person (or to a member of a scheduled caste) from a well-to-do family while those who are excluded from the preferred groups may come from a less-advantaged background. Finally, some have argued that industry and government need the most qualified individuals without regard to ethnicity or place of birth, especially for managerial personnel and for the more technically sophisticated jobs.

The objection to preferences by ethnic criteria thus has two possible grounds: rights and justice, and efficiency. In this debate both the state governments and the central government have rejected the rights argument, concluding that the disadvantaged ethnic groups have legitimate claim for preferences, but accepted the efficiency argument. Thus, the laws and administrative regulations were written in such a way as to minimize the impact of preferences on employment where a high level of skill is required or where efficiency seems essential for the work of others. The central government, for example, declared that local people would be given preference in employment in centrally run public sector firms, but that technical jobs and senior administrative positions—an arbitrary salary level was defined—would be recruited nationally on merit alone. Similarly, private employers were informed that they might make a similar distinction; national recruitment (hence merit) for some categories of jobs, local recruitment (hence ascription and ethnicity) for others. However, state governments were generally reluctant to accept what they viewed as a dangerous loophole, so they have preferred to hire local people for all categories of employment.

Thus we can characterize India's policies in terms of their objectives; their criteria for choosing beneficiaries; and the justifications they use.

1. The central objective of preferential policies, whether for scheduled castes and tribes, backward classes, or "sons of the soil," is to expand educational and employment opportunities for what in India are described as the middle classes. In this context "inequality" refers to a group's disproportionately small share of positions in the modern sector of the economy rather than to any average income level of the community in relation to other communities. The "modern" sector is generally understood to include all positions in government, both central and state, from the clerical ranks upward; it includes all white-collar positions in industry and factory jobs above the menial level. And it includes employment in salaried positions in the urban services (ushers in movie houses, for example, but not rickshaw pullers; clerks in department stores, but not street vendors).

2. Preferences are on the basis of group membership rather than individual characteristics. Preferences are given to those who belong to the

"local" community, with "local" understood as referring to the numerically dominant linguistic group in the locality, though for constitutional reasons the law may refer to residence and birthplace as the criteria. Preferential claims on the basis of membership in a linguistic community, a tribe, a regional group, and a caste are considered legitimate, but preferential claims made on the basis of religious affiliation are, for historical reasons, generally considered illegitimate.

3. The justification for preferences is based neither upon minority status nor upon past discrimination, though both justifications are employed with respect to scheduled castes and tribes. The demand for preferences for sons of the soil is made by a majority in relation to a minority. The primary justification is the group's unequal status—in education, employment, and income—in relation to other groups within the urban locality or the state as a whole and is not linked to the question of *why* the group is economically, educationally, or occupationally behind.

When exceptions are made, they are not on the basis of any rights claimed by migrants but on the basis of the need by employers to recruit people who are more skilled than those who are available locally from among the linguistic majority. It is on this basis that certain jobs, in both the public and the private sectors, are recruited exclusively on merit. Merit—that is, open recruitment on a national basis—is thus justified primarily by the need for efficiency rather than any legal or moral rights.

The Political Logic of Preferential Policies

It would be a mistake to assume, however, that preferential policies in India are based upon a clear set of logical, consistent principles which make it possible to determine who should and who should not be given preferences, what kind of preferences, and for how long. Preferential policies have been adopted in India, as elsewhere, because of political pressures. There is in fact a political logic to preferential policies which accounts for the many inconsistencies and ambiguities in the policies themselves.

The initial constitutional decision by the Constituent Assembly to provide preferences to scheduled castes and scheduled tribes proved to be the critical turning point that was to have a decisive impact on the subsequent creation of preferential policies for other ethnic groups. Once the principle was established that the state should provide preferences to some ethnic groups because they were disadvantaged minorities, it became only a matter of time for other disadvantaged ethnic groups to assert their claim even when they were very numerous (as in the case of the other backward classes), or a majority, and even when their economic and social position was only remotely related to discrimination. As so often happens in policymaking, a decision creates a precedent which predetermines subsequent policy options.

Moreover, once the preferences were constitutionally mandated and further sanctioned by legislation and the courts, they became a permanent feature of social policy, though their original supporters envisioned them as a temporary measure. Certainly, none of the present beneficiaries views the policies as temporary. Scheduled castes and tribes, for example, are now resistant to any proposals to end preferences on the basis of ethnic membership. Similarly, when the courts ruled that preferences in Telangana could no longer be given on the basis of birth in a region of the state, Telangana produced a political movement that demanded separation from the state in order to preserve the system of preferences. So many individuals now benefit from preferential policies, and they are so well organized to protect their interests, that it would be naive to view these policies as merely temporary measures to achieve equality.

Once preferential policies for the local population were in place, the state governments themselves became interested parties in their maintenance. The main reason, of course, is that the state governments became dominated by the very ethnic groups that demanded the policies, a process accelerated by the policies themselves. The result is that the state governments—the bureaucracies as well as elected officials—have become advocates of the policies and wish to see them extended; from public employment to private employment; from the lower to the higher categories of employment; and from employment and education to housing and other public benefits. For this reason it seems unlikely that the tendency to extend preferential policies can be brought to an end by the political process within a state. They can be arrested only through intervention by the courts or by the central government, if at all.

Support for preferential policies is widespread within the beneficiary ethnic groups in spite of the evidence that the benefits are largely limited to only one stratum, the most educated and enterprising who have the requisite minimum skills and motivation to enter the modern sector. The vast majority who remain in the countryside or live at the bottom of urban society do not gain; nonetheless, they provide electoral support to political parties that advocate such policies. In Bombay, for example, the Shiv Sena won electoral support from Marathi voters across educational and class lines. Similarly, the Telangana Praja Samiti won the support of a majority of the voters in Andhra's western districts in the parliamentary elections of 1971. Given the narrow class benefits of the policies, why do the masses provide electoral support?

One answer lies in the familiar force of ethnic solidarity. By rallying the voters behind a demand made on behalf of an ethnic group, the middle classes are able to win the support of the lower-income groups from within their own ethnic community. This is apparent in all three cases analyzed in this book, though how the ethnic group was defined differed in each of the cases. In Maharashtra, the ethnic group was defined as Marathi speaking. But in Assam, Assamese was redefined by the Assamese Hindu leadership to include Bengali-speaking Muslim and Bihari tribal migrants who had learned to speak Assamese, a redefinition that gave the Assamese the political clout they needed to pass legislation over the objection of other ethnic groups in the state. And in Telangana, an effort was made to give the concept of *mulki*—the word for local people of diverse ethnic backgrounds—a distinct character that would distinguish between the people of the Telangana region and the people from elsewhere in the state.

Another reason is that many members of the lower-income groups believe that there are potential material benefits, not simply vicarious ones. If their ethnic group is in power they are in a better position to make claims, since government benefits—jobs, tube wells, roads, loans, etc.—are allocated on a personal basis, or so it is widely believed. It is critical then to have one's own patrons, the upper and middle classes of one's own ethnic group, in positions as administrators, teachers, bank officers, even clerks. It is, after all, the modern sector that determines how most resources, public or private, will be spent, and to the extent that one's own ethnic group controls the modern sector, the more likely or the less likely it is—or so it is believed—that the entire ethnic group will benefit.

We have already suggested one basis on which preferential policies have been challenged: efficiency. The central government and many of the "national" firms—i.e., those not owned by local people and that have offices in various parts of the country—would prefer to hire the most able without regard to caste, linguistic group, or place of birth. They have succeeded, thus far, in excluding certain categories of employment from preferential policies; but there are pressures to drop these exempt categories, since they are viewed locally as loopholes in the system of preferences. As for the future, it seems more likely that preferences will be extended into these job categories than that efficiency and merit criteria will be extended.

A challenge to the policies may also come from the local minorities who originate from outside the region, or are of local origin but do not belong to the numerically dominant local group. But their numerical status gives them little political clout except in one or two urban centers like Bombay, where the numbers in combined population of nonlocal ethnics give them some capacity to resist what they view as discriminatory policies. In Bombay opposition takes the form of demanding that preferences be given to the locally born, not simply to the Marathi-speaking population, rather than that the preferential system be dismantled altogether.

To the extent that preferential policies succeed in eliminating or reducing competition for employment *among* ethnic groups, it is inevitable that competition will take place *within* ethnic groups. Much of this competition will be among individuals competing for places in college, for jobs, and for promotions. Some of the competition may create social and political cleavages within ethnic groups. Beneath the ethnic solidarity that has united groups behind preferential policies often lie a variety of ethnic groups who may be divided as competition increases. This has already taken place among the scheduled tribes. Since, as noted earlier, the Christian tribals have more education and have been better able to take advantage of preferences in employment, the non-Christian tribals have been demanding that "converted" tribals be excluded from the system of preferences. Among the *mulkis* or local people of Telangana, the Muslims believe that the generalized preferences for *mulkis* have not provided them with an adequate share of employment. Similarly, among the Assamese, there are cleavages between Hindus and Muslims since some Muslims believe that they are not getting their share of employment. Thus, one can anticipate that within the preferred groups there may be demands for the exclusion of some, or for systems of preferences within preferences.

Thus, the political pressures in India are for maintaining preferences as a permanent feature of labor force recruitment, for extending preferences to the private sector and to the more skilled positions, for including religious as well as linguistic, tribal, and caste groups, and for more refined quotas for smaller groups. Opposition comes from groups who feel the brunt of the policies and from those who fear a loss of efficiency. Very little opposition, as we have noted earlier, comes on the grounds of rights, in contrast with the United States where nineteenth-century British liberal ideas continue to hold a central place. India's constitution and all the major political groups are committed to the principle that equality as a social goal should be given precedence over individual rights. In a society so ridden with inequalities—so India's opinion makers argue—the goal of greater equality ought to be given the highest priority. The instrument for the achievement of this objective—preferential policies —builds upon the tradition of judging people on the basis of the ascriptive group to which they belong. Here again, as in other areas of Indian policymaking, we see contemporary policies for the achievement of modern social goals built upon traditional values and relationships.

Three
Residence Requirements
and the Law

In New York City recently, Mayor Koch reacted with alarm to the announcement that the U.S. Supreme Court had upheld a law that set aside a quota of government funds for minority contractors. "I don't think it's unconstitutional...," he told legislators, "I just happen to think it's wrong. Where does it stop? Should the United States be like India with quotas for this group and that?"[1]

It is not surprising that a New York City mayor might allude to India's experience with quotas. Recent Supreme Court decisions have moved government policy somewhat closer to the practice in India of setting aside reservations for disadvantaged groups. In the United States, until recently, court-ordered quotas intended to assist minority groups were infrequent and were limited to instances where there had been a court finding of previous discrimination. Thus, where a particular employer, typically state trooper, police, or fire fighter division, had been found to have discriminated in past hiring, a court might order that future recruiting meet a given ratio of minority to non-minority employees.[2] But, generally, the U.S. courts were reluctant to countenance minority quotas. In 1974, for instance, a much-heralded case came before the Supreme Court concerning separate admissions procedures for minorities and nonminorities at the University of Washington Law School. The case was held moot, with one of the court's "liberals," William O. Douglas, writing a separate opinion declaring that any state-sponsored preference for one race over another was "invidious."[3] In recent years, however, the court has viewed race conscious policies with greater sympathy; race-specific preferences (but not quotas) in medical school were held constitutional, even in the absence of a specific finding of past discrimination (1978);[4] race preferences in job-training programs were deemed legal (1979);[5] and in the most recent decision, a ten percent set-aside for minority contractors as legislated by Congress was upheld (1980).[6] Such decisions indeed appear, as Mayor Koch intimated, to bring the United States closer to India's experience, where the issue has been not so much whether preferences are acceptable but more how they should be used—for whom, for which jobs, and for how long.

21

In India, extension of special protection to disadvantaged groups is explicitly prescribed within the constitution itself. Enacted in 1949, the Indian constitution provided through articles 330–34 that seats in parliament and the state assemblies would be reserved for scheduled castes, tribes, and Anglo-Indians. Article 335 provided for the reservation of government service appointments to the extent that such reservations would be consistent with the maintenance of administrative efficiency.

Based on the premise that legal equality is meaningful only in the presence of social and economic parity, the guarantee of equality of opportunity and the proscription of discrimination in the Indian constitution are modified by stipulations which permit extension of preferential treatment to disadvantaged groups. Thus article 15 declares as fundamental the right to equal treatment by the state: "The state shall not discriminate against any citizen on grounds only of religion, race, caste, sex or place of birth." This right, however, is modified by a clause which states: "Nothing in this article ... shall prevent the state from making any special provision for the advancement of any socially and educationally backward classes of citizens or for the Scheduled Castes and the Scheduled Tribes."[7] Similarly, article 16, which guarantees equality of opportunity in state employment, is modified by article 16(4): "Nothing in this article shall prevent the state from making any provision for the reservation of appointments or posts in favour of any backward class of citizens." Reflecting on the logic of such preferential policies, former Supreme Court Justice A. N. Ray observed: "Equality of opportunity for unequals can only mean aggravation of inequality. Equality of opportunity admits discrimination with reason."[8]

Although the basic principle of providing reservations in state employment and university admission has found a secure constitutional niche, the issue of who should be eligible for what reservations continues to be intensely debated. Sons of the soil claims that seek to establish ethnic preferences are one constituent part of this debate.

The Issue of Residence Requirements

Although the special protection of scheduled castes, tribes, and backward classes is directly mandated by the Indian constitution, the reservation of places in jobs and universities for "local persons" is on a less sure constitutional footing. Most articles in the constitution which relate to residence or place of birth *prohibit* discrimination. Among the fundamental rights enumerated in the constitution are the rights (article 19) to move freely throughout the territory of India and to reside and settle in any part of the country. As we have seen, article 15 bars discrimination on grounds not only of religion, race, caste, and sex, but also of place of birth, and article 16(2) states that no citizen shall on grounds only of religion, race, caste, sex, descent, place of birth, residence, or any of them be ineligible for or discriminated against in state employment. The only constitutional provision[9] which implies possible scope for the preferential treatment of local residents is article 16(3): "Nothing in this article shall prevent Parliament from making any law prescribing in regard to a class or classes of employment or appointment to an office under the Government of or any local or other authority within a State or Union territory any requirement as to residence within that State or Union territory prior to such employment or appointment." Article 16(3), which provides for an exception to the ban on discrimination based on residence, thus gives *parliament alone* the right to enact such an exception and only with respect to positions within the employ of a state (as distinct from the national) government.

The constitution thus provides an exemption to the ban on discrimination based on residence where parliament has approved such policies and in state government services; policies of localism, however, are in fact widespread and persist in the absence of parliamentary action. State domicile restrictions existed both before independence and in the 1950s.[10] In recent years, as pressure on employment and university admissions has heightened, state governments have exhorted both public and private employers to hire from the local labor force. In the late 1960s and '70s, these policies became more explicit, bringing a wave of state directives which urged employers and universities to favor applicants who resided in the local area for periods of ten and fifteen years.

The political logic of preferential policies is such that the state governments have a strong interest in the maintenance of preferences. Dominated often by the economically weaker but numerically stronger ethnic communities, the state governments are sought out by sons of the soil claimants as allies in the effort to establish protection. Pressure to inhibit the spread of sons of the soil preferences is, thus, more likely to emanate from other arenas of the government—from the central government and from the courts. This chapter examines the present status of residence requirements and explores the role which the different institutions of government—the central government, the states, and the courts—have pursued in their efforts to advance or curtail the promulgation of preferential policies.

Residence Requirements: The Constituent Assembly Debates

Sons of the soil claims for constitutional recognition were debated in the Constituent Assembly in 1947–48, and evoked a mixed reaction among the assembly delegates. Initially, there was considerable opposition to residence requirements, and the draft constitution barred any preferential treatment of sons of the soil. Article 10 of the draft constitution explicitly proscribed discrimination based on place of birth. During discussions of the draft, Jaspat Roy Kapoor of the United Provinces sought to strengthen the stricture by adding "residence" to the grounds on which discrimination would be prohibited. According to Kapoor's amendment, article 10 was to read: "No citizen shall on grounds only of religion, race, caste, descent, place of birth or residence or any of them be ineligible for any office under the state."[11]

Alladi Krishnaswami Ayyar, however, contended that residential qualifications should be allowed under some circumstances and sought to amend the article to permit parliament to set residential requirements for state employment.[12] Dr. B. R. Ambedkar, charged with the major responsibility for drafting the constitution, successfully urged the acceptance of both the Kapoor and the Ayyar amendments. The relevant clauses of the final constitutional provisions read:

1. There shall be equality of opportunity for all citizens in matters relating to employment or appointment to any office under the state.
2. No citizen shall, on grounds only of religion, race, caste, sex, descent, place of birth, residence or any of them, be ineligible for, or discriminated against in respect of, any employment or office under the state.
3. Nothing in this article shall prevent Parliament from making any law prescribing in regard to a class or classes of employment or appointment to an office under any State specified in the First Schedule or any local or other authority within its territory, any requirement as to residence within that State prior to such employment or appointment.

A number of different arguments were advanced in support of extending preferences to local persons. One position stated by Mahavir Tyagi cited the sovereign impulses of the separate regions. Tyagi proposed that residential qualifications were not an unreasonable concession to the desire on the part of the states to be self-governing: "If there are open chances for the residents of one province to serve in another, it means that the residents of that province shall not be able to enjoy self-government." The absence of residential requirements, Tyagi argued, "will go against the real spirit of Swaraj."[13] A second argument took a simple pragmatic stance contending that such preferences were then widespread and that their abolition would be "impracticable."[14]

A third argument, submitted by B. R. Ambedkar, made reference to the inequalities of the different regions and the need to protect the job interests of people from the less-advantaged states. Although Ambedkar conceded that residential qualifications detracted from the value of a common citizenship, he urged the assembly to recognize that: "At the same time ... you cannot allow people who are flying from one province to another, from one State to another as mere birds of passage without any roots ... just to come, apply for posts and so to say take the plums and walk away." Moreover, Ambedkar observed, "We are merely following the practice which has been already established in the various provinces."[15] Permitting the parliament rather than the different states to lay down residential requirements had at least the advan-

tage, Ambedkar noted, of imposing a uniformity on the highly disparate policies of the various states.

Present Policies

The uniformity of which Ambedkar spoke, however, has remained elusive.
Despite the constitutional stipulation that only parliament can set residential
requirements, the past thirty years have seen states enact laws and issue resolutions and directives setting their own preferential policies for state residents.

The states have assumed an important role in determining residence requirements in part because of the difficulty the central government has had in formulating policies that will prove satisfactory to all its varied constituencies.
Just as Ambedkar's constitutional formulation represented a compromise between protagonists and opponents of preferential policies, the central government responded to similarly conflicting pressures. On the one hand, it is cognizant of the view articulated most commonly in Delhi and within the all-India
services in the states that preferential policies introduce inefficiencies. On the
other hand, it is sensitive to the high-pitched demands which have fulminated
in the states out of the sense of inequalities suffered by local ethnic groups.

The government's policy, formulated by the National Integration Council
which met in Kashmir in 1968, reflects the effort to heed ethnic claims without doing damage to meritocratic principles. The committee urged that high-
level jobs be recruited on an all-India basis and that lower-level positions be
filled through local channels. Acting on the committee's recommendation,
the prime minister (then, Indira Gandhi) wrote to the minister of industrial
development and the minister of labor and rehabilitation directing them to
implement the National Integration Committee formula. The minister of industrial development in turn issued instructions to public sector undertakings
that recruitment to posts carrying a basic salary of not more than Rs. 500 per
month should be made through the National Employment Service (i.e., the
local employment exchanges which are reputed to favor local applicants). The
minister of labor and rehabilitation also issued appeals to the (private sector)
All-India Organizations of Employers to adhere to the same policy.[16]

The formula advocating an all-India employment competition for higher-
level positions and a localized selection procedure for less-skilled jobs sought
a balance between the desire to further national productivity and the need to
respond to claims for regional equality. As Mrs. Gandhi explained, preferential
policies were promulgated by the central government with reluctance:

> This is a matter in which one has to have a certain balance.
> While we stand for the principle that any Indian should be
> able to work in any part of India, at the same time, it is true
> that if a large number of people came from outside to seek
> employment...that is bound to create tension in that area.
> Therefore, while I do not like the idea of having any such rule,

one has to have some balance and see that the local people are not deprived of employment.[17]

Spokesmen for the central government justified their advocacy of preferential policies in several ways. But the dominant viewpoint in the central government was that expressed by Mrs. Gandhi. Noting on the one hand that national integration and productivity required a mobile labor force to which domicile restrictions would be inimical, she conceded on the other the need for preferential policies, stating: "And I do stand by this: that where there is any big industry or project it should be seen that those local people who cannot travel around seeking employment elsewhere should be given full opportunity. Otherwise tension will be created."[18]

Parliament, the body entrusted by constitutional prerogative to enact residential requirements, has exercised in fact little control over policymaking. The only action which parliament has taken under article 16(3) giving it alone the right to set residence requirements was to legislate the Public Employment (Requirement as to Residence) Act of 1957 as well as several other subsequent measures that were related specifically to the state of Andhra Pradesh. Following the recommendation of the States Reorganization Commission, the 1957 Public Employment Act aimed, according to the minister of state in the Home Ministry, to abolish all existing residence requirements in the states and to enact exceptions only in the case of the special instances of Andhra Pradesh, Manipur, Tripura and Himachal Pradesh. For these four territories, the 1957 act gave the central government the right to issue directives setting residence requirements in the subordinate services.[19]

The central government's influence over preferential policies regarding domicile requirements has resided, then, less with parliament than with the prime minister's office and with the cabinet. But the central government's working policy, based on the National Integration Committee recommendations cited earlier, focused primarily on the recruitment to lower-level jobs through the employment exchanges; even this policy neither explicitly recommended nor barred the practice of extending preferences in jobs and university admissions to local residents. The formulation, therefore, of residence requirements remained largely with the states.

State policies have in several instances gone well beyond the parameters outlined by central government policy. While some states, such as West Bengal (under particular ministries), have declined to endorse policies of localism, government spokesmen in other states, such as Maharashtra, Tamil Nadu, and Karnataka, have issued directives or exhortations to employers to prefer local persons not only in low-skilled positions but at all levels of employment. Examples follow of the kinds of preferential policies pursued by some of the state governments.

Maharashtra

In a circular dated September 25, 1973, the director of industries of the Maharashtra state government called on the public and private sectors to employ local persons in all categories of jobs. The circular urged that in all future recruitment, sixty percent of top managerial jobs and ninety percent of subordinate staff be drawn from among an applicant pool of local persons. The personnel or recruitment officer, the circular stated, should be Marathi speaking. The term "local" was initially defined as referring to people domiciled in Maharashtra for fifteen years or those whose mother tongue was Marathi. Later, in response to central government and other pressures, the Maharashtrian government redefined the term, removing all reference to mother tongue and defining "local persons" only by residential qualifications. Employers were asked to report periodically to the state government regarding progress in recruitment.[20]

West Bengal

In 1972, when the Congress government came to power in West Bengal, it made several declarations that in lower-level jobs, preference should be given to local persons. Nothing was done to implement such a policy until October 1972, when the state employment committee met to discuss the question for the first time. Labor Minister G. D. Nag noted that government policy was to give preference to local persons, defined as those whose mother tongue was Bengali or who had been domiciled in West Bengal for ten to fifteen years. When this issue came up before the state cabinet, there was considerable reluctance to take any active measure. The chief minister at the time, Siddhartha Sankar Ray, was known to oppose the pursuit of any policy of localism. While the government has been said to have urged employers privately to hire local persons, the West Bengal government has been more reticent than its Maharashtrian counterpart on this issue.[21]

Tamil Nadu

The Tamil Nadu government circulated a directive after the Maharashtrian model in August 1974, urging employers to hire local persons to not less than eighty percent of the jobs in technical, nontechnical, supervisory, and nonsupervisory categories. Like the Maharashtrian directive, the circular also stated that personnel or recruitment officers should be local persons. The Tamil Nadu government maintained, however, that its appeal to employers was more liberal than its Maharashtrian counterpart in that the official definition of local persons was strictly a residential one and made no reference to mother tongue. "Local persons," the directive said, should be interpreted to apply to those residing in Tamil Nadu for fifteen years or more.[22]

Meghalaya

The distinctive feature of the Meghalaya government's policy is that it has been formulated not only through administrative fiat but also through legislative action. The legislature in 1974 passed a residence permit bill which required that those who seek to stay in Meghalaya longer than four months secure a special permit. The bill further specified that only those who had lived continuously in Meghalaya for twelve years or more and who had made Meghalaya their fixed and permanent home would be considered true locals.[23]

Andhra Pradesh

The Telangana case in Andhra Pradesh is different from those mentioned above in two ways. First, it involves a controversy between people of two regions of the same state. Second, the preferential treatment of local persons in Telangana has roots in the history of the region which are absent in the cases described above. Prior to independence and the incorporation of Telangana (formerly the princely state of Hyderabad) within the Indian Union, the Nizam of Hyderabad had made a practice of offering special privileges in the state services to *mulkis* (those local to the Telangana region).

Preferential policies were extended to *mulkis* after independence through a parliamentary act, the Andhra Pradesh Public Employment (Requirement as to Residence) Rules, passed in 1959. This legislation followed by two years the law mentioned above, which had been passed pursuant to article 16(3) of the constitution, permitting parliament to set residential requirements. The 1959 act, renewed in 1964 and placed before parliament again in 1968, made provision for the preferential hiring in jobs and university admission of Telangana residents. In 1969, the Supreme Court declared such provisions, and the original residential requirement act in particular, *ultra vires* the constitution, ruling that the constitution does not allow such discrimination by one region against another region of the same state.

The Supreme Court's rejection of the *mulki* provisions was followed by the central government's appointment of the Wanchoo committee, which underscored the correctness of the Supreme Court's ruling, observed that regional preferences within a state could be legitimized only by a constitutional amendment, which the committee advised against, and recommended the decentralization of recruitment. "There is no constitutional bar to such a procedure for recruitment to local offices to fill class III and class IV posts for there is no impediment to anyone competing for such appointment," the committee suggested. "But in actual practice the experience has been that the recruitment being made for local offices by the heads of those offices and the vacancies in each case being small, the persons who compete for such posts are by and large local people."[24] Subsequently, the *mulki* rules were revived by a Supreme Court decision (A.I.R. 1973 SC 930). The thirty-second constitutional amendment, however, which became effective in the spring of 1974, abolished the *mulki* rules but made way for a series of presidential orders which "regionalized," by zone and district, university admissions and employment. The recommendations of the Wanchoo committee proved prescient; preferential policies in Andhra Pradesh are now formulated largely through the decentralization of recruitment.

Policies of preferential treatment in educational admissions and employment have, thus, varied from direct legislative enactments (Meghalaya) and explicit administrative orders (Maharashtra) to a more indirect expression of localism (West Bengal). The policy of most state governments goes well beyond the recommendations of the national government. Departing from the central government's policy as represented by the 1968 National Integration Committee recommendations, many state governments have requested not simply that recruitment be done through the local employment exchanges but rather that domicile or residence requirements be made mandatory for employment. Many of the state governments, moreover, have directed employers to hire local persons not only in lower-grade jobs but at all levels of employment.

Domicile requirements also exist in higher education and appear to have become increasingly more restrictive. As in the United States, preference in admissions and in the tuition levied are often accorded state residents. A 1968 report submitted to parliament documented the existence of preferences for state residents in engineering colleges by showing the limited number of places "reserved" for out-of-state students:

> 1. Andhra Pradesh—The State Government has agreed to admit some students from other States on reciprocal basis and this arrangement continued since 1966–67.
> 2. Mysore—Only 10 per cent seats will be filled by students from other States apart from seats arranged on reciprocal basis.
> 3. Madhya Pradesh—There is no domicile restriction but students should have qualified from institutions situated in M.P., or should have spent three years of study in such institutions.
> 4. Assam—Reservation of seats in engineering institutes exist only for Union Territories and J. & K. [Jammu and Kashmir].
> 5. Punjab—No domicile restrictions for admission to engineering courses.
> 6. Madras—10 per cent reservation on reciprocal basis.
> 7. Kerala—Reservation only on reciprocal basis and that no more than 5 per cent.
> 8. Uttar Pradesh—Admissions to technical institutions are made purely on merit and no domicile restrictions exist except in the Regional School of Printing, Allahabad.

9. Gujarat—5 seats in each college can be reserved on recipro-
cal basis.

10. Maharashtra—63 seats are reserved in various institutions
for students from other States and Union Territories. The Government considers this adequate reservation for ex-State students.

11. Orissa—7 per cent seats in the University college are reserved for students from other States.

12. West Bengal—No candidate of Indian nationality is denied
admission on grounds of domicile.

13. Bihar—15 per cent seats in engineering colleges will be open
for admission of students from other States.

14. Rajasthan—The Jodhpur University admits 50 per cent
students from outside the State. The Birla Institute is an all-
India Institute. The third one is a Regional Engineering College
where 50 per cent students are admitted from outside the State.

15. Jammu & Kashmir—There is only one Regional Engineering College.

16. Haryana—There is only one Regional Engineering College.
(In Regional Engineering Colleges reservation of ex-State students already exists.)[25]

There are also domicile requirements in the selection of medical school
applicants. In Maharashtra state medical schools in Bombay, for example,
a rule was adopted in 1969 which required that in addition to passing the
qualifying examination from the local university, an applicant must produce
evidence of having completed secondary education in the state.[26] Medical
school admissions procedures elsewhere indicate that although a domicile requirement of five years was once usual, states are now moving to set domicile
qualifications at ten or fifteen years.

The central government has not abdicated responsibility for preferential
policies. But it has allowed the states wide latitude in setting policies. Where
a situation has threatened national stability (such as the Telangana separatist
movement and the protests since 1979 in Assam which have paralyzed the
shipment of Assam-refined oil to the rest of India), the central government
has entered into direct negotiations to work out compromise policies. But in
less crisis-filled situations, it has played a low-keyed role, rarely taking public
issue with a state's decision to extend preferences to its own residents. Here,
too, there are exceptions: it did successfully, for instance, pressure the Maharashtra government in 1973 to alter its definition of local persons from an
ethnic to a residential one. But, generally, the state directives and exhortations
by state ministers have been left "uncorrected" by central intercessions.

To what extent have the courts stepped in where the central government
has declined to tread? Have the courts ruled on the constitutionality of policies of localism?

Preferential Treatment and the Courts

In confronting state preferential policies, the courts have faced a complex set of constitutional issues. Most constitutional provisions would appear to bar residence qualifications. Article 14 provides generally for equality before the law. Article 15 sets out more specifically the grounds on which discrimination is prohibited, including among them place of birth, but not residence. Articles 16(1) and (2) bar discrimination in state employment on grounds of either birthplace or residence. Articles 19(1,d) and (3) guarantee to all citizens the right to move freely, reside, and settle anywhere in India. Only article 16(3) would suggest an opening for the preferential treatment of local persons by allowing parliament (not the states) the right to set residential requirements in state services.

Because of this apparent opposition between constitutional provisions and policies of preferential treatment, it seems likely that the courts would seek to counter the states' adoption of preferential policies. The courts, however, have not played this role. In the area of employment, they have ruled on only a very limited number of cases and have not formulated any identifiable doctrine. In the area of educational admissions, courts have rejected state preferences in some areas and upheld increasingly restrictive policies in others.

Very few cases challenging sons of the soil policies have involved matters of employment. Among the few that have reached the courts, there are a number that seek the abolition of language requirements favoring local persons. An early case in Orissa involved both a language and a residence requirement. A governor's resolution stipulated that applicants to the Orissa administrative service must be permanent residents of the state. Permanent residence could be established if the applicant or one of the applicant's parents could provide evidence of having lived in the state for twelve years and of a certain standard of fluency in Oriya. Interestingly, the court upheld the requirement until such time as parliament were to make a law under article (16)3.[27] Later, in 1969, the Orissa high court upheld a policy which made knowledge of Oriya mandatory for appointment to the position of district judge.[28]

As described earlier in the chapter, parliament did pass a law in 1957 under which such rulings as the Orissa government's resolution would have been held unacceptable. Nevertheless, domicile rules like those enunciated in the governor's resolution have been replicated in orders issued by a number of state governments in the late 1960s and early '70s. Challenges to these executive orders, however, have not yet been brought before the courts. Although there have been a number of cases, related to the *mulki* rules in Andhra Pradesh, which have held as unconstitutional any discrimination in public employment against people of regions of the same state, curiously, the constitutionality of state-wide domicile rules in employment has not been tested in the courts.[29]

In contrast to the paucity of job-related cases, there has been a large amount of litigation related to sons of the soil policies in educational admissions. Here, the trend in court decisions since independence has been to uphold increasingly restrictive residential requirements.

The articles of the constitution bearing on educational admissions include article 29(2), which bars discrimination in admissions on grounds of religion, race, caste, and language. No mention is made in this article, however, of either birthplace or residence. Residence or domicile restrictions in educational admissions are usually challenged, therefore, under the more general strictures of articles 14 or 15. The latter bars discrimination on grounds of birthplace but not residence. Residential classifications in university admissions can be challenged only under article 14 and must be justified on grounds of "reasonableness"—one must demonstrate that the residential restrictions have a reasonable nexus to the object of classification.

Reservations for specified classes of people are very common in admissions policies of Indian universities. In medical and technical institutions particularly, an elaborate system setting aside a proportion of seats for specified groups has become commonplace. The groups to whom reservations are most usually extended are scheduled castes, tribes, and other backward classes, but there is a range of other classes, including women, athletes, children of people who served in national causes, and Colombo Plan scholars. A fairly typical arrangement is that of the Punjab Medical College, which reserves fifty percent of the seats by the following categories:[31]

20%	Scheduled castes/tribes
2%	Backward classes
10%	Backward areas
2%	Sportsmen
6%	Central government nominees (including those from Jammu and Kashmir)
1%	Women
2%	Children of political sufferers of the freedom struggle, with Punjab domicile
5%	Candidates from border areas of Punjab
2%	Children of defense personnel who have lost their lives or been disabled during National Emergency and released from service, and children of personnel of the Border Security Forces killed/disabled during enemy action.

In most medical and technical colleges, preference is given to persons domiciled and/or residing in the state. The courts have consistently barred reservations based on place of birth but have sustained domicile and residential requirements, which are defined in terms of an individual's intention to make the state the locality of future residence and/or ability to provide evidence of previous residence (five to fifteen years) within the state.

In an early landmark case, *D. P. Joshi* v. *State of Madhya Bharat* (1955), a tuition differential for state and out-of-state residents was upheld. (The actual term used is "capitation" fee.) The challenged ruling governed the admissions fees requirement of the medical college at Indore. It stipulated that for all students who had bona fide residence and original domicile in Madhya Bharat, no special admissions fee would be required. Bona fide residents, the rules allowed, included citizens of India whose original domicile was not in Madhya Bharat but who had acquired a domicile in the state and had resided there for not less than five years. Justice Ayyar, writing for the majority of the court, noted that residence and place of birth were "two distinct conceptions with different connotations both in law and in fact." While article 15(1) prohibited discrimination based on place of birth, it did not prohibit discrimination based on place of residence. Justice Jagannadhadas, dissenting, argued that the phrases "bona fide residence" and "original domicile in Madhya Bharat" could have meant only place of birth and were thus in contravention of article 15(1).[32]

The five-year requirement necessary for the establishment of domicile under the Madhya Bharat rules appeared at the time quite restrictive. This requirement, however, has since been followed by far more exacting requirements of ten and fifteen years.[33] In an essay on interstate preferences and discrimination written in 1956, Lawrence Ebb observes that such a five-year rule made the acquisition of state domicile equivalent to the five-year naturalization period required to attain national citizenship.[34] In his opinion, if there were constitutional doubt as to the propriety of a state's use of the national five-year naturalization period in formulating its local residence rule, there would be serious doubt as to constitutionality of a longer residence requirement.

Since the mid-1950s, however, several cases have been decided which sustained residential requirements of ten and fifteen years. State courts as well as the Supreme Court of India have taken a position which, while barring discrimination on grounds of place of birth,[35] nevertheless upholds lengthy residential requirements.

In 1971, for instance, the Supreme Court handed down a decision which sustained rule 3 of the rules for selection of candidates for admission to the state medical colleges of Mysore, framed by the state on July 4, 1970. The rule stated that "no person who is not a citizen of India and who is not domiciled and resident in the state of Mysore for not less than ten years at any time prior to the date of the application for a seat shall be eligible to apply." The court held that a domicile requirement (met by demonstrating the intention to reside in the state) and, in addition, the ten-year residential rule were not in contravention of article 14. In a brief decision, Justice Dua, delivering the judgment of the court, conceded the likelihood of some cases of hardship under the impugned rule but noted that "cases of hardship are likely to arise in the working of almost any rule which may be framed for selecting a limited number of candidates for admission out of a long list."[36]

A later case challenged the applicability of the same rule to private colleges in Karnataka. In this case, *Arun Narayan* v. *State of Karnataka,* decided in the Karnataka high court in 1976, Justice Chandrashekhar concluded in a forceful decision that "the right to move freely throughout the territory of India...and to reside and settle in any part of India...do not by themselves ensure that every citizen of India will have all the advantages and privileges in every state available to citizens domiciled or residing therein and that no kind of preference is permissible to citizens who are domiciled in or residents of that state."[37] Alluding to a possible distinction between essential and non-essential claims, the justice argued that residential or domicile requirements infringing on rights to the protection of life, property, water facilities, and other basic needs would not be reasonable. But other preferential policies applied in granting agricultural lands, house sites, or university admission would not necessarily be in violation of an individual's constitutional rights.

The court's position on the susceptibility of private educational institutions to constitutional guarantees prohibiting discrimination is not yet clearly evolved. In the 1976 Karnataka case mentioned above, the court held that it would be too technical to dismiss the petition solely on grounds that the respondent university was a private institution. Since the university "feels obliged to obey the direction of the government," the opinion stated, "the petitioner is entitled to ask for a writ restraining the State of Karnataka from enforcing its ruling on the respondent university."[38]

The Karnataka ruling made no mention of the deliberations of an earlier case in Andhra Pradesh which had reached quite different conclusions.[39] This 1972 decision concerned a private medical college which required fifteen years' domicile in the state of Andhra Pradesh. The Andhra court held that, because the medical college was private, article 14 was not applicable. (Although the college received a grant-in-aid from the government and was attached to a government hospital, and although membership of its executive committee included ministers and other officers of the government, it was still considered a private institution.) The court, however, went on to observe that even if article 14 could be invoked, the admissions rule requiring *fifteen* years' domicile was reasonable and in consonance with article 14.

The Andhra decision stands out because of its strict view of the immunity of private institutions, because of the exacting *fifteen*-year residential requirement that it supports, and because the residential requirement pertains to domicile within one *region* of the state rather than within the state as a whole.

There has been judicial disagreement over the legitimacy of domicile regulations that distinguish between persons from different regions of the same state. Most of the decisions upholding within-state reservations in university admissions have been decided by the Andhra Pradesh courts. Three cases that

34

came before the Andhra bench (in 1959, 1962, and 1972) all held preferential treatment of students from the Telangana region to be consonant with article 14 of the constitution.[40]

Outside of Andhra Pradesh, however, the courts have tended to strike down classifications that distinguish between students from different regions of the same state. In *State of Kerala* v. *R. Jacob Mathew* (1964) and *P. Rajendran* v. *State of Madras* (1963), the court declared unconstitutional university procedures admitting students on the basis of the district in which they resided. Two other cases involving admissions procedures that apportioned places according to region and territorial units were also held to be in contravention of articles 14 and 15.[41]

Although the courts have rejected most selection procedures which require residence in a particular district or area of a state, they have allowed admissions procedures which favor the university's own students—students who have attended the constituent colleges of the local university. In *Sidappa* v. *State of Mysore* and *Chanchala* v. *State of Mysore,* such a requirement was held not to be violative of article 14.[42] In delivering his opinion, Justice M. Shelat noted that the preferential treatment of a university's own students "does not have the disadvantage of districtwise or unitwise selection as any student may pass the qualifying examination in any of the three universities irrespective of the place of his birth or residence."[43]

Although the legal distinction Shelat makes between residential and intra-university preferences is a sharp one, the de facto result of an admissions policy favoring the university's own students may not be greatly different from reservations drawn up by district or region. Under both schemes, university enrollment would probably be composed largely of those from the immediate region. Since the qualifying examination to some medical colleges can include P.U.C. (preuniversity course) or even S.S.C. (secondary school certificate) results, a student wishing to qualify for a medical school outside his or her area of residence may have to leave home and enroll in a secondary or preuniversity course at a young age (sixteen to eighteen years). Thus, even university admissions procedures which merely require that a student qualify in the university's own examinations pose a barrier to enrollment outside a student's area of residence.

A related issue which has proved controversial in the courts is whether the presumed backwardness of a territorial unit can be considered in granting preferential admission. In northern India, several cases have reached the courts which question the practice of extending preferences to persons from rural areas or from designated backward regions of a given state. In the Uttar Pradesh medical colleges, for instance, the admissions process has set aside a number of places for candidates from rural and hill areas and from the Uttrakhand area, an impoverished region of the state. In 1973, in *Subhash Chandra* v. *State of U.P.,* the Uttar Pradesh high court (Allahabad bench) upheld the practice.[44] Curiously, the very same year, the same high court (Lucknow bench) in another case struck down the reservation for candidates from rural and hill areas, arguing that there was insufficient justification to consider those areas backward.[45] The decision, however, did not denounce the principle of territorial restrictions. Justice D.S. Mathur, writing for the court, observed that "from the limited viewpoint of admission in medical colleges, classification based on areas may not be proper; but another object which can be kept in mind is that the services of qualified doctors be available to all the residents of the country."[46] A territorial classification aimed at achieving such an objective, Mathur commented, would not be unreasonable. A later case, also argued before the Supreme Court, *State of Uttar Pradesh* v. *P. Tandon,* partially overruled the Chandra case, declaring that reservations of seats for candidates from rural areas was unconstitutional while that for the hill and Uttrakhand areas was valid.[47] Chief Justice A. N. Ray, in his opinion, declared the reservation for rural areas invalid, since "this reservation appears to be made for the majority population of the State. Eighty percent of the population of the State cannot be a homogeneous class."[48] Ray went on to argue, however, that the state had presented sufficient evidence to demonstrate that the people living in the hill and Uttrakhand areas constituted a socially and educationally backward class of citizens.

The Judiciary's Rationale

Judicial arguments over the legitimacy of domicile restrictions revolve around issues of efficiency, equity, and state interest. In reaching a ruling, the courts have dealt with three questions:

1. Are domicile practices in admissions procedures consistent with the selection of the most meritorious student body?
2. Will domicile rules advance the interests of the state?
3. Can domicile rules be justified by a region's claim of backwardness?

It is frequently on the basis of the first question that domicile rules are struck down. A number of decisions have held that domicile rules have no reasonable relation to the object of the admissions rules, namely, to admit the most qualified student. A representative instance of this reasoning is found in *Periakaruppan* v. *State of Tamil Nadu.*[49] Striking down a unit admissions policy, Justice K. S. Hedge of the Supreme Court observed:

> Before a classification can be justified it must be based on objective criteria and further it must have a reasonable nexus with the object intended to be achieved. The object intended to be achieved in the present case is to select the best candidate for being admitted to medical colleges. That object cannot be satisfactorily achieved by the method adopted.[50]

In *D. N. Chanchala* v. *State of Mysore,* also decided in 1971, a university-based admission procedure was upheld by the same reasoning. Writing the decision for the Supreme Court, Justice Shelat noted that although a university-based admissions process might mean that a candidate with lower marks from the university in question could be preferred over a candidate with higher marks from another university, this would not necessarily mean, given the possible difference of standards, that a less meritorious student was chosen over a more capable one.[51]

The preeminent importance ascribed in these decisions to standards of achievement and merit has been modified on numerous occasions by the claims either of state interest or of equity. The legitimacy of claims of the state was recognized explicitly in one of the early (1955) landmark decisions, *Joshi* v. *Madhya Bharat.* Upholding a tuition differential for in-state and out-of-state students, the Supreme Court decision noted: "We are in this petition concerned with a Medical College and it is well known that it requires considerable finance to maintain such an institution. If the State has to spend money on it, is it unreasonable that it should so order the educational system that the advantage of it would to some extent at least enure for the benefit of the State?"[52]

Upholding a ten-year domicile rule on similar grounds, the Supreme Court in a 1971 decision explained that an important objective of admissions rules was to select candidates who will serve the people of the state, at the same time paying attention to recruiting qualified students: "The objective of framing the impugned rule seems to be to attempt to impart medical education to the best talent available out of the class of persons who are likely so far as it can reasonably be foreseen to serve as doctors, the inhabitants of the State of Mysore."[53] The decision goes on to note that while it is not possible to say with certainty that those admitted to the medical colleges would necessarily stay in Mysore state to practice, and while they have a fundamental right as citizens to settle anywhere in India, the desire of the state to formulate admissions rules which will advance the medical interests of people of the state must be deemed acceptable.

Such "service" justifications for within-state residential distinctions have usually been rejected. In the 1975 Tandon case mentioned earlier, the Allahabad high court struck down the preferential treatment in admission of students from rural areas that the state justified on "service" grounds:

> Medical graduates hailing from rural areas may also be disinclined to return to the villages for medical practice on account of poor facilities and they will also try to build their career in the urban centers where they hope to have a better job satisfaction. The assertion on behalf of the State of U.P. that the reservation of seats for candidates of these areas was with a view to feed the dispensaries of these areas appear to be pretentious and cannot be a justifiable ground for making reservations.[54]

The court has thus tried to reconcile the objectives of merit and state interest. It has also struggled with the still further conflicting claims of equity. Former Supreme Court Justice M. Hidayatullah has alluded to the role that residential preferences may play in reducing uneven levels of development. Noting that discrimination on grounds of residence may be justified, the former chief justice remarked: "Sometimes local sentiments may have to be respected or sometimes an inroad from more advanced states into less developed states may have to be prevented."[55]

Most decisions that uphold on grounds of equity the preferential treatment of persons from backward areas involve within-state rather than statewide restrictions. In *Uttar Pradesh* v. *Tandon,* for instance, the Supreme Court allowed the reservation in medical admission for people of the hill and Uttrakhand areas of the state on the grounds that those areas were socially and educationally backward. Similarly, the Andhra high court in a 1972 case held that preferential treatment of Telangana students in medical admissions was justified since

> Kakatiya Medical College was started for the spread of medical education mainly for Telangana region, which is educationally backward in the State. If in view of this object, provision is made to cater to the educational needs mainly of that particular region, as it badly requires such assistance, it cannot be said that the object to be achieved has no relation to the classification made by giving larger representation to the Andhra region. The increase in the Telangana quota is consistent with and promotes and advances the object underlying the establishment of the institution.[56]

The recognition in domicile cases of the claims of backwardness has raised two questions: (1) what constitutes backwardness? and (2) how can standards of achievement be upheld while recognizing the special needs of backward groups? Judicial discussion on the first question has revolved around whether the inadequacy of medical facilities in a given region constitutes sufficient evidence of backwardness and, if not, what other evidence must be provided. Although there has been little discussion in domicile cases of the second issue, the court has clearly stated that merit cannot yield entirely to the claims of backwardness. The case of *Kumar* v. *Uttar Pradesh,* decided in 1973, involved, among other issues, a ruling which set aside a number of seats for scheduled caste candidates and for candidates from the rural areas and hill and Uttrakhand divisions. The ruling relaxed for scheduled castes the level of minimum marks below which a candidate could not be considered, from 33 percent in the aggregate to 30 percent. For candidates from the Uttrakhand division, the admission procedure set *no* minimum percentage for candidates,[57] but this total absence of standards was rejected as unacceptable by the court.

The courts have, thus, sought to protect merit-based admissions by generally ruling against the practice of conferring preferences on people of one region of a state over persons from another region of the same state where there is no element of backwardness. The Andhra courts that have upheld preferential treatment for the Telangana region are, however, exceptions.

Even the court rulings sustaining medical college favoritism for students passing from their own preparatory courses have in some ways also detracted from an admissions system blind to the regional origins of its students. These decisions, taken together with the decisions approving increasingly stringent statewide domicile requirements, show the emerging pattern of a judiciary which has gone along with rather than resisted the increasing localism of state university policies.

With the trend toward the formulation of preferential policies through executive orders, there remains a small but potentially important unresolved issue: whether executive orders are legally binding. In a 1961 case in Madhya Pradesh, the court ruled that administrative directives could not be questioned under the equality clause of the constitution. The bench questioned the sensible ruling of an earlier Andhra Pradesh judgement:

> The government pleader [states] that the rules are only administrative directions given by the Government and that noncompliance with the rules does not confer on the petitioner any right to compel the respondents to proceed in strict conformity with the rules. The contention of the Government is a double-edged weapon and it cuts both ways...The Government, therefore, cannot rely upon the scheme embodied in the rules to sustain the selections and ignore it to defeat the claims of the petitioner.[58]

But the Madhya Pradesh court took exception to the Andhra bench reasoning and noted:

> It is obvious and is also not disputed that "Medical Colleges in Madhya Pradesh Rules for Admissions 1960" are merely executive or administrative instructions in a field which is not covered by any statute. If they had been statutory rules, we would not have hesitated to strike down such of those rules as offend against the provisions of Art. 14 or quash any discriminatory action taken.[59]

If administrative orders (the chief vehicle through which preferential policies in sons of the soil issues have been executed) are held neither legally binding nor an admissible subject of litigation, the court may abdicate even the small role it now plays in setting boundaries on the localism of state policies.

Under the emergency declared in June 1975, sons of the soil demands subsided, and the call for central government clarification of preferential policies

39

was muted. With the end of the emergency, however, and the return of a more open political system the debate over preferential policies resumed.

In summary, the following observations can be made with regard to the judicial position of domicile reservations:

1. No explicit doctrine has developed through decisions either of the high courts or of the Supreme Court. Rather, the rulings have been made on a case by case basis.

2. The courts, nevertheless, appear increasingly inclined to accept policies of localism, as is evidenced by: (1) the high courts' acceptance of domicile requirements of ten and fifteen years as stipulations for university admissions, and (b) the courts' acceptance of procedures extending preferences to the universities' own graduates (a policy with results similar to those rulings struck down by the courts which would have extended preference to persons from particular regions within a state).

3. The courts' role in this area may be shaped as much by their silence as by their decisions. Although the courts have dealt extensively with residence qualifications for university admissions, they have held aloof with respect to preferences in employment, leaving unexamined the state orders of the late 1960s and early 1970s. If cases challenging such orders were to reach the court it is not clear how they would be resolved. If the logic pursued by the courts in their consideration of university preferences were applied to preferences in jobs, the courts would probably attempt to evaluate whether residence requirements serve or impair the objective of enhancing job performance. Evidence on this would be hard to come by. Some state governments have argued that employing local personnel upgrades the work force because local people have lower rates of absenteeism and higher stakes in their job. Others have argued the inverse—that such preferences exclude a pool of highly talented migrant labor. Preferential treatment in jobs might, alternatively, be considered from the perspective of equity: do they advance the claims of disadvantaged groups? Here again, the courts would have to deal with a complex issue, for while residence requirements may favor ethnic groups who on the average are less economically advanced than other groups, any individual beneficiaries of such policies may not be disadvantaged at all. If the courts pursue a more active role in the review of residence requirements, these would be some of the considerations taken into account.

Domicile Restrictions: Who Makes Policy?

The formulation of policies favoring local persons over outsiders has fallen in large part to the states. For it is logically to the state governments that ethnic majorities have looked in their attempt to redress their sense of economic disadvantage vis-à-vis minority ethnic communities within their own states. Although the intended beneficiaries of protectionist policies advanced by the states are the majority ethnic groups within the states, policies of localism are indirectly targeted. On their face these laws and directives extend preferences to state residents rather than to particular ethnic groups. Thus the policies adopted by the states

1. prescribe proficiency tests in the regional language as prerequisites for recruitment to the public services;
2. set domicile tests requiring a period of residence in the state or region;
3. restrict nonresidents from acquiring property;
4. channel recruitment through local government employment exchanges where the practice is often to give preference to local persons in registration and placement;
5. devolve on local bodies responsibility for recruitment; and
6. set educational or other requirements such as previous degree or certification from local educational institutions as prerequisites for admission to a higher level of education.

While ethnically neutral on their face, these policies often result in the disproportionate recruitment of one ethnic group over another.

The central government has generally allowed, if not encouraged, the state governments to pursue protectionist policies. By endorsing the use of local employment exchanges, and, at least in the case of one state (Andhra Pradesh), by endorsing a scheme of regionalization, the central government has given limited assent to policies of localism. Not that it has welcomed such developments. Indeed, numerous spokesmen have emphasized the importance of upholding constitutional guarantees of the freedom of movement and noted the link between a mobile labor force and the recruitment of skilled personnel. Yet the center has rarely interceded to pressure the state governments to modify state protectionist policies.

The courts, for their part, have played a limited role. They are unlike the American judicial system where, as one observer has remarked (not necessarily approvingly), the court has "led in defining policy on divisive social issues," so that the "nation awaited the court's decision in *Bakke*."[60] In the case of domicile restrictions, the courts, as we have seen, have scarcely addressed preferences in employment, limiting their rulings to instances of residence requirements in university admissions.

Neither the central government nor the courts are uncritical of sons of the soil claims. And yet, as much by their inaction as by any active assent, they have lent their support to these policies. The explanation for this anomaly is intimated by Indira Gandhi's remark that a "balance" must be sought—a balance that will protect the mobility of citizens and guard against the political disruption which such mobility engenders. In the hands of the central government, the states, and the courts lies the responsibility of resolving the conflict between perceptions of disadvantage on the part of particular ethnic groups and the danger that inattention to such grievances may breed instability, on the one hand, and constitutional guarantees of the rights of the individual to move freely and to seek employment based on individual merit alone, on the other.

When the Public Employment (Requirement as to Residence) Act was being debated in parliament in 1957, an M.P. from the state of Tripura spoke in support of the bill which permitted protectionist policies to be extended to his state. Considering the relative backwardness and low levels of literacy in Tripura, he argued, persons from his region would fare poorly in any competitive recruitment for jobs in the state. Protective policies, he concluded, were thereby justified. Somewhat later in the debate, an M.P. from Punjab noted that claims of backwardness know no limit: "For instance a complaint has now come from Tripura." And in a remark that proved prescient, he added, "This is bound to come from other places also."[61] The succeeding chapters turn to the experiences of Maharashta, Andra Pradesh, and Assam.

Four
Preferential Policies in Bombay

The "Modernity" of Preferential Claims

The sons of the soil issue in India first attracted national attention with events in Bombay. In 1966 an organization was formed in the city around the objective of securing preferences in employment for the local population. Within a short time of its founding, the organization, known as Shiv Sena (army of Shivaji),[1] became an active force in electoral politics. In 1967 it lent its support to a Congress party candidate in the parliamentary elections, and one year later Shiv Sena contested the municipal elections, winning 42 out of the city's 140 seats.

Bombay was not the first place that sons of the soil demands had been voiced. But the highly organized nature of the Bombay movement and the very fact that it was situated in a leading commercial metropolis assured the events in Bombay quick national visibility. Had Bombay been a backwater town, it is possible that an organization such as Shiv Sena might have been overlooked. But because it is India's second most populous city and because of its industrial and commercial importance, Bombay receives considerable national attention. For over a century it has been a center of textile manufacturing. As distinct from Calcutta where foreign investment has played a great role, the industrial and commercial development of Bombay has been financed largely by Indian capital. In the last decades it has become a leading producer of chemical and engineering products. Its port, railway lines, and air connections see the heaviest traffic of any city on the western coast of India. The headquarters of some of India's biggest industrial establishments are situated in and around Bombay, as are numerous educational and scientific research establishments, including the Bhabha Atomic Research Centre and nuclear reactor facilities.

It might seem paradoxical that a sons of the soil movement should arise on the cement pavements and tile office floors of Bombay. Such nativist movements are often, by conventional wisdom, associated with remote, traditional regions and not with the frontiers of industrial development; yet the Bombay experiences suggest that demands for preferential treatment may be understood not as artifacts of tradition but, equally plausibly, as coterminous with modernization.[2]

43

In other respects, Bombay might seem an anomalous site for a nativist movement. The city prides itself on being "cosmopolitan," a term which refers in local usage to the rich ethnic heterogeneity of the population. The growth of commerce and industry has drawn migrants from every region of India. In 1961, nineteen percent of the city's population identified Gujarati as their mother tongue; eight percent were north Indian, or Hindi-speaking; slightly more than eight percent were of south Indian origin, speaking one of the four south Indian languages; Maharashtrians, those whose mother tongue is Marathi, the language of the state in which Bombay is located, were as of the 1961 census slightly under forty-three percent of the city's population.[3]

Out of this diversity has emerged an identity which often transcends linguistic and cultural background. Particularly for those of middle and upper-class origins, the terms "Bombayite" or "Bombay-wala" denote the existence of this interethnic identity. Although their particular ethnic backgrounds may be evidenced in the celebration of holiday rituals, the language spoken among family members, and often the choice of a marriage partner, other aspects of their day-to-day existence give little clue as to their ethnic origins. Their co-workers and friends may be drawn from a wide cross-section of ethnic groups; the language spoken at work and among friends is likely to be English. Dress and even eating habits are no longer so revealing of ethnic origin. The city's English-language publications (for instance, the recently published glossy magazine *Bombay,* which covers city events) appeal to a readership of diverse ethnic backgrounds. Bombay's convent and private schools, two of its prestigious colleges (Elphinstone and St. Xavier's), and its élite social clubs, are likewise composed of people of varied ethnic background who nevertheless share an identification with the city of Bombay.

For other, primarily lower-income sectors of Bombay's population, "Bombayite" is not a very meaningful self-definition. For these Bombay residents, there is another side to the cosmopolitanism of the city. For this sector, the diversity of the city's population implies (rightly or wrongly) the competition for jobs. At the origins of Shiv Sena's genesis, indeed, is the perception among sections of the Marathi-speaking community that jobs, particularly those in the modern sector of Bombay's economy, are less accessible owing to competition from the non-Maharashtrian population. South Indians, particularly, are singled out, for it is they, according to Bombay lore, who are especially successful at securing coveted office jobs in Bombay's secondary and tertiary sectors. Many young Maharashtrians whose fathers are laborers and who are the first in their families to get a secondary education set their sights on clerical and office work. It is thus south Indians rather than the more numerous Gujaratis (who are by reputation shopkeepers, traders, and industrial entrepreneurs) or north Indians (who are associated with industrial and manual labor in the textile mills and milk trade) that are thought to compete with

Maharashtrians for the valued posts. This competition for white collar jobs is at the root of Shiv Sena. In Calcutta, where the local Bengali population dominates white collar jobs, there has not been a nativist movement similar in organization or visibility to Shiv Sena. Resentment against outsiders in Calcutta is directed against the wealthy Marwari community. But perhaps because the large number of middle-class jobs are not the objects of interethnic competition, nativist sentiment is not so likely to feed the kind of city-wide organization in Calcutta that Shiv Sena became in Bombay.

This chapter gives less attention, however, to the causes of nativism than to its consequences.[4] Focusing on the Bombay case, the discussion that follows addresses a set of policy questions: how has the government reacted to claims for preferential treatment, and how have these policies affected employment patterns?

The Shiv Sena

Government policies can be best understood against the backdrop of Shiv Sena demands. The Sena's demands evolved as the party was able to politicize the resentment many Maharashtrians felt at having to compete for employment with those they regarded as "outsiders." A series of exposés published in the Marathi weekly, *Marmik,* now the Sena party organ, provided an effective catalyst. From the surnames on *Marmik*'s weekly lists of the top officers in Bombay's large business establishments, it was readily apparent that only small numbers of Maharashtrians held managerial positions. *Marmik*'s editor, Bal Thackeray, now the Sena party leader, amplified these lists with editorials and cartoons protesting the encroachment of "outsiders" in the Bombay job market. One of the party publications laid out the party demands explicitly: "In order to rescue Maharashtrians from the rut of poverty and consequent frustration on all fronts of life, 80 percent [of all] jobs, skilled or otherwise, must be reserved in governmental, semi-governmental, private and public undertakings. Existing concerns should be persuaded to meet this demand and licenses to new undertakings should be issued only on this condition."[5] The Sena's demands were not notable for their consistency. At times Thackeray called for the reservation for local persons of eighty percent of jobs in semiskilled and unskilled positions. At other times, as was evident from the *Marmik* managerial rosters, the Sena's concerns embraced skilled and executive jobs as well. The Sena vacillated not only on the question of which jobs should include quotas of local persons but also on the definition of the category "local persons." The Sena leadership alternately suggested that local should refer to those who lived in Maharashtra for a given period of years; those who identified with the "joys and sorrows" of Maharashtra; or those whose mother tongue was Marathi. The party's actions and numerous observations by the party leadership have made clear, however, that the Sena's real objectives lay in the extension of preferences in all job categories, in both the public and the private sectors, to those who are Maharashtrian by the definition of mother tongue.

Shiv Sena waged its campaign in the columns of *Marmik,* in the offices of the city corporation, in the headquarters of businesses, on the office and union floor, and on the streets. Shiv Sena leaders led *morchas* or public processions to many of Bombay's most visible company headquarters (Glaxo, the Fertilizer Corporation of India, the State Bank of India, etc.). In one instance recounted by a Shiv Sena party worker, a prominent Sena leader called on an executive of Indian Oil. Delivering Shiv Sena's ultimatum that more Maharashtrians must be hired, the Sena leader threatened: "You are sitting inside the office but your oil tanks are outside."[6] In the procession to Glaxo, according to another account, Thackeray and a small group of party activists were ushered into the office of the manager, where they demanded to know why so few employees were Maharashtrian. The manager insisted that most employees *were* Maharashtrian and proceeded to produce company records showing that most of the company employees had been born in Bombay. The Sena leaders retorted that Shiv Sena wanted to know how many employees were true Maharashtrians (Maharashtrian by mother tongue). "We made it clear what we meant."[7]

In other, less-publicized ways, Shiv Sena pressure has made itself felt. Small groups of workers have approached the management of individual firms; Shiv Sena municipal councilors have telephoned and visited with executives and personnel officers and government personnel.

Notwithstanding the *Marmik* columns, processions, and all the other pressures brought to bear on employers by Shiv Sena leaders, the party's demands would have carried little clout without the backing of the state government. The Sena was fully cognizant of this, stating in its party manifesto that the fulfillment of the party demands would require "the warm support and cooperation of the Government of Maharashtra."[8] Unlike in Andhra, Assam, or other localities where sons of the soil movements had arisen, in Bombay many employment opportunities are located in the private sector. The efficacy of Shiv Sena demands thus depended on whether the state government would attempt to influence private sector employment policies and whether, even if such efforts were made, government pressure would prove effective.

Preferential Treatment and Maharashtra Government Policy

The Maharashtra state government was initially quite cautious in responding to the Sena's claims. In 1968 it circulated a directive to large businesses and government offices in Bombay, urging employers to hire local labor.[9] The government argued that local employees were more stable and that, with presumed lower absenteeism, profits would be enhanced. The directive further reminded employers of their obligation to comply with the Notifications as to Vacancies Act, which stipulated that employers must notify the public employment exchange of job openings (thus permitting the public exchange to send local applicants upon notification of a job vacancy). The directive was more suggestive than threatening. It spoke only of the desirability of hiring those who were residents of Bombay. No mention was made of *Maharashtrian* claims. The reminder of the Notifications as to Vacancies Act would not have alarmed employers since the act simply required them to *notify* the employment exchange without obligating them to *hire* applicants sent from the exchange. For the next years, state government policy operated within the guidelines suggested by the National Integration Council that met in Kashmir in 1968. Accordingly, employers were advised that preferences were to be extended to local persons (those resident in Maharashtra for fifteen years) in class III and class IV (semi- and unskilled) government jobs.

In 1973 the Maharashtrian government's position on the employment issue had become more resolute. In a directive to government and business establishments, the commissioner of industries exhorted employers to set aside a quota in *managerial* as well as in subsidiary jobs. The directive also shifted the definition of local persons to include not only those who were locally domiciled but also native Marathi speakers. This marked an intensification in the state government's interest in the nativist cause. When quotas were limited to blue collar and lower-salaried white collar jobs, the government's policy called for little change, for Maharashtrians already predominated in lower-class jobs although they did not comprise the eighty percent called for in the earlier directives. Since the older preferences had been applied to local persons as defined by residence rather than language, many firms had been able to make a strong case that their employment rolls already complied with government stipulations.

The 1973 directive marked a sharp departure from the early policy. The *Times of India* reacted indignantly. In an editorial entitled "Parochialism," the *Times* conceded that it was understandable that the Maharashtra government was anxious to provide additional jobs to the people of the state who did not always have a fair deal. Nevertheless, the editorial exclaimed, the recent policy was "going towards the other extreme."[10]

The state's directive of September 1973 urging employers to hire personnel officers whose mother tongue was Marathi was in fact legally justifiable on the grounds that the Factory Act of 1948 required labor officers to speak the language of the majority of their workers. But the directive nevertheless aroused considerable anxiety. In March 1974, questions were raised in the national parliament.[11] Communications were sent from the central government to the government of Maharashtra, and in the next month the state redefined the term "local person."[12] The redefinition dropped the reference to mother tongue, retaining only the criterion of domicile in Maharashtra. Despite this retraction, the Maharashtra government's policy, in its inclusion of upper-level

47

as well as semi- and unskilled jobs, went beyond the central government policy of advocating preferences for only lower-salaried jobs and thus remains as one of the stronger state government policies endorsing local preferences.

The efficacy of the Maharashtrian government's policy depended not only on its pronouncements but also on the degree to which the government was willing to enforce them by the use of incentives and sanctions. Even with the measure of frankness contained in the government's 1973 request, resolutions and appeals would clearly not be effective unless followed up by considerable pressure. Resistance among employers against hiring from local labor pools was attributable to several factors. The attraction of recruiting from "outside," according to some industrialists, lies in the traditional specialized skills of particular migrant groups (e.g., Kamathis in construction, "Bhaiyas" in special areas of textiles such as carding). Recruiting migrant workers is also considered desirable when employers are confronted by a troublesome labor situation, since bringing in outside groups weakens the cohesiveness of labor and its susceptibility to organization. Resistance to hiring local labor is, further, in some cases specific to the Maharashtrian worker, who according to prevailing belief is less diligent and less eager than "outside" workers.

Given such perceptions, the disinclination among employers to accede to government appeals is strong and is overcome only by forceful application of governmental pressure. State government personnel observe that the government has made only appeals and that there is no question of coercion. The sanctions that can be and are applied to unreceptive businessmen represent strong encouragement, however, if not mandatory directives.

In interviews with a large number of industrialists it was eminently clear that government pressures have been intense enough to exact vigorous efforts on the part of companies to follow governmental policy. As one businessman who asked not to be cited by name remarked in a typical comment, "Now at the very least, when all things are equal, we hire the Maharashtrians."

Pressure from government takes many forms. All sizable businesses are required to submit a statement showing the linguistic and geographic origins of persons at different levels in the company. This information is usually collected by the company (particularly in the case of white collar workers) at the time of an employee's application. Officially the government's directive encourages employers to hire local persons, those resident in Bombay for fifteen years; but the form that businesses must submit to the government also calls for information on the *linguistic* composition of company employment rolls. Sometimes company officials are lax in reporting; the personnel officer from one company claimed to have submitted a form to the government stating that by the company's definition (length of residence), all its workers were Maharashtrian. But on the whole, most business managements attempted to avoid offending governmental sensibilities.

The costs incurred by irritating state government personnel are considerable, and are particularly high when licenses, permits, or ministerial favors are required. A business intending expansion needs governmental permission. For a water or electricity connection, particularly if it is to be expedited, government approval is required. The state government may likewise choose to enforce to the letter the health or safety regulations, thereby penalizing the company for minor infractions.

Such penalties are not often invoked. One manager recounted his inability to secure government permission for plans for a hotel because he could not show that the majority of the laborers were to be Maharashtrian. More commonly, it is the anticipation of such sanctions that accounts for their effectiveness. Almost all businessmen interviewed mentioned at least one encounter with the government over the issue of recruitment in which such pressure was informally applied. The following responses are representative:

—The government cannot enforce anything. But it is in our own interest to comply with them as far as possible. The government can create problems for us otherwise. Indirectly we are affected. We may have a licensing problem; or say we want to run a third shift; it's worthwhile keeping the government away.

Manager, pharmaceutical company

—Sometimes the government is insistent. For example, when we apply for additional spindles or machines. Once when we applied for power, Government required information from us on the numbers of local persons we employ. But since we were within the rules there was no problem.

Labor and welfare officer, textile mill

—Some years back, the government called attention to the fact that labor officers in the company are not Maharashtrian. We told the government that there were no vacancies. Did they want us to sack the officers at their responsibility? We agreed that future vacancies would be filled with Maharashtrians. This is necessary as it may be a question of our needing facilities, water power, etc.

Manager, rayon factory

—The government applies pressure indirectly, when applying for licenses, power, etc. They don't call them Maharashtrians, but rather "local people." I had to go there personally; it wasn't enough to send by mail, to make a statement that we would employ 80 percent locals; but they have no check as such.

Personnel officer, cigarette/cigar factory[13]

There are exceptions to this pattern. One instance, reported by an officer formerly with Hindustan Lever, involved a call from a minister of the state government who warned the company that it was not employing sufficient numbers of Maharashtrians. The minister then hastily added that he intended to communicate this to the manager publicly, that his constituency demanded this, but that privately he felt that it was the company's own affair whom they hired. Yet this is the exception, and, generally, as the above comments illustrate, government pressure is sufficiently strong to be taken seriously.

Municipal Government Policy

The activist policies pursued by the state government are not replicated at the municipal level. Most of the municipal policies relating to Maharashtrian interests do not concern issues of preferential employment. One measure adopted by the municipal body, for instance, called for the alteration of street and road signs from Hindi and English to Marathi. In another instance, the municipal corporation reaffirmed an earlier resolution providing for the compulsory teaching of Marathi as a second language in Bombay schools. This measure had been adopted years earlier, and almost all but the Gujarati medium schools had introduced Marathi. Even had the measure been a new one, its acceptance would not have materially affected the employment position of Maharashtrians in Bombay. Language policy, particularly the language of instruction in schools, can of course influence the employment opportunities of different ethnic groups. Some Maharashtrians claim that a much earlier policy in the 1950s, to extend the scope of Marathi medium instruction, proved to be a handicap to Maharashtrians in their later competition for modern sector jobs where fluency in English was an advantage. But since Shiv Sena's emergence, the corporation has not adopted any school language policies that would give particular advantage or disadvantage to Maharashtrian job seekers.

Other legislation adopted by the municipal corporation at first appeared designed to enhance Maharashtrians' career opportunities. With the support of the Sena, the corporation issued a regulation requiring that seventy-five percent of all seats in the three city-run medical schools be reserved for those who had passed their school matriculation in Bombay city. This law made the earlier requirement of having to pass the college interscience examination at a Bombay college more restrictive. But as the Sena legislators soon realized, the regulation did not work to the benefit of Maharashtrian applicants, but rather discriminated both against migrants from out of state *and* against migrants from elsewhere in Maharashtra itself. As one Sena corporator wryly commented: "It is ironic. Our legislation has probably kept out more Maharashtrians from medical school than ever before."[14]

Legislation concerning employment is clearly of greater direct importance than legislation concerning education to the future status of Maharashtrians in Bombay. Yet in this area the municipal corporation has been mostly silent. One resolution concerning jobs for local persons in the municipal body was proposed by a Shiv Sena corporator. It read: "In view of the fact that the government of Maharashtra has issued directions that 90 percent of posts in state government in Bombay as well as government offices in mofussil (outlying areas) be given to local residents, the same should be done for all posts

50

under municipal administration at all levels."[15] The resolution referred only to "local people" and not to Maharashtrians and contained no stipulation about enforcement procedures. Yet the measure lacked sufficient support in the corporation to assure its adoption.

The difference in responsiveness to Maharashtrian claims for preferential treatment on the part of the state and municipal governments has two explanations. The first is the politics of numbers. At the state level, Maharashtrians are in a clear majority. In both the state assembly and the bureaucracies, Maharashtrians predominate. At the municipal level in both the corporation and the municipal agencies, Maharashtrians do not exercise the same level of political control. In 1961, only 43.5 percent of the municipal corporators reported Marathi as their mother tongue. In 1968 (in part owing to the Shiv Sena victories), that number rose to 56 percent.[16] The fact that Maharashtrians are an ethnic majority within the state, if not the city, is a crucial explanation of the hearing that Shiv Sena claims received at the hands of the Maharashtra state government.

A second explanation involves party alliances. At the time of the Sena's formation, the state government stood to profit in a number of ways by Shiv Sena activity. The state was able to use the Sena's threats of violence to exact consideration from the central government on interstate boundary disputes. The Sena *bandh* (shutdown) over the Maharashtra-Karnataka boundary dispute, in which the party was able to bring city life to a halt, provided the state Congress party with grounds for claiming that its own position in the state would be jeopardized unless the issue was resolved in the state's interest. In certain periods the Congress party, as indeed the business community, also saw in the Shiv Sena a potential ally—or agent—that could oppose the communist unions. Although the Congress hoped to contain the Shiv Sena, at least in the early years the Congress party in the state appears to have seen the party as a useful electoral ally.

Preferential Policies and the Employment Status of Maharashtrians

How has government policy affected the actual economic status of Maharashtrians in Bombay? Or, to begin with a prior question, how has the economic status of Maharashtrians changed?

Measurement of the economic progress of different groups in Bombay is made difficult by the paucity of published data. Recent census and city-wide surveys do not record the ethnic breakdown of occupational categories. Consequently it is possible to offer only suggestive observations about employment changes. These observations, based on three studies of public and private employment in the city, point to a clear pattern of rising occupational status among middle-class Maharashtrians.

The first study was conducted in 1970 by a group of Bombay students who interviewed 125 managers from 25 Bombay companies. As table 4.1 illus-

51

trates, the percentage of Maharashtrian managers hired by these companies has grown steadily over the past two decades, largely at the expense of south Indian and Sindhi personnel.

Table 4.1   Recruitment of Managers in 25 Bombay Companies

Mother Tongue of Manager	Hired before 1950		Hired in 1950–60		Hired after 1960	
Marathi	0	(0%)	5	(12%)	10	(21%)
Gujarati	9	(56%)	14	(34%0	21	(44%)
South Indian	4	(25%)	12	(29%)	6	(12%)
North Indian	2	(13%)	5	(12%)	9	(19%)
Sindhi	1	(6%)	5	(12%)	2	(4%)

The percentage of Maharashtrian managers is very low; particularly when cast against the percentage (43 %) of Bombay's population in 1961 that was Marathi speaking. It is nevertheless striking that the growth in the number of Maharashtrians recruited to the twenty-five companies far exceeds that of any other ethnic group.

The second study, an analysis of Bombay telephone directories,[17] reveals a pattern of change in the status of the Maharashtrian middle and upper classes consistent with that indicated by the manager survey. The findings are reported in table 4.2.

The results are unambiguous: the percentage of Maharashtrians in high-level and middle-level positions in both the private and the public sectors has risen continuously, beginning before Shiv Sena's emergence and continuing in the years following.

The third study, a survey of 126 clerical workers in 12 private and government organizations, reveals a similar pattern. Of those hired during or before 1971, Maharashtrians are 45.6 percent. Of those hired after 1971, Maharashtrians are 61.7 percent.[18]

Perceptions of progress among Maharashtrians appear to bear out the changes suggested by the above data. By 1970, only four years after Shiv Sena's founding and two years after the party's election to the municipal council, sentiment was widespread among Maharashtrians that their status in Bombay was improving. As was perhaps to be expected, this feeling pervaded Shiv Sena offices and party meetings. But it also seemed to be a sentiment echoed by the ordinary voter, Shiv Sena supporter and nonsupporter alike.

Exuberance among young workers pervades Shiv Sena offices. In the tones of the true believer, young Sainiks relate stories of Maharashtrian success. The tales share a common theme. Whether it is the Bank of Baroda, Voltas, Glaxo, or any other of the numerous well-known Bombay firms, Maharashtrians, the account begins, had no opportunities. One young Sainik with typical enthu-

Table 4.2   Maharashtrians in Higher-Level Positions in Bombay Establishments

	1962	1967	1973
Central government			
(11 establishments sampled)			
Total employment	398	677	672
Percent Maharashtrian	19%	25%	29%
State and municipal government			
(7 establishments sampled)			
Total employment	70	102	114
Percent Maharashtrian	64%	75%	82%
Private sector			
(15 establishments sampled)			
Total employment	55	68	73
Percent Maharashtrian	7%	12%	16%

SOURCE: Bombay telephone directories, 1962, 1967, 1973. The central government establishments included in this analysis were Air India, Atomic Energy Department, Indian Oil, Indian Airlines, Directorate General of Shipping, New India Assurance, Posts and Telegraphs, Western Railway, Bombay Telephones, Reserve Bank of India, Life Insurance Corporation. The state and municipal offices included the State Directorate of Employment; the Industries and Labor Departments; Western Railway Police; Finance Department Transport Undertaking (B.E.S.T.). The private firms included Podar Mills, Shree Ram Mills, Shree Niwas Cotton, India United Mills, Phillips, Mafatlal, Larsen and Toubro, Bajaj, Burman Shell, Caltex, Glaxo, CIBA, Forbes, Forbes and Campbell, Indian Express, Crompton, Greaves and Co.

siasm told the story of a friend employed at CIBA. The friend had been called, along with other Maharashtrian workers, to speak with one of the managers after threats from Shiv Sena leaders. The manager requested their help in recruiting Maharashtrians and shortly thereafter more were hired.

One factor that may contribute to such perceptions is the obvious upward mobility of key Sena leaders. In 1970, for instance, Manohar Joshi, a prominent Sena figure who by his own account was raised in povery, planned a European vacation—his first trip outside India. While such meteoric improvements in life-style are hardly unique to Shiv Sena political leaders, they still help to reinforce the idea among Sena party followers that the lot of Maharashtrians is improving.

A distinct exception to such optimism is found within the Communist party. Most Communist party leaders and workers are strongly convinced that Shiv Sainiks are strikebreakers, "bourgeois lackeys," and that they are offering the Maharashtrians mere tokenism with the intent of dividing the working class by rewarding a selected few.

The ordinary Bombay voter seems to agree much more closely with the Shiv Sainiks than with the Communists. In a survey of over 450 Bombay voters conducted in 1971, six years after Sena's founding, 51.5 percent of the population said that they felt that more Maharashtrians were getting jobs than ever before, 19 percent felt that more Maharashtrians were not getting jobs, 25 percent replied that they were unsure, and 4.5 percent declined to respond.[19]

In answering another question, 14 percent claimed that they personally knew of people who had found jobs through Shiv Sena. While Shiv Sena supporters who felt that prospects for Maharashtrians had improved outnumbered those who did not by four to one, the ratio among Congress party supporters was two to one. The figures are a compelling indication that among Maharashtrians in Bombay, including those who do not support Shiv Sena, there has been a sense of improving job possibilities.

The manager survey, telephone book analysis, office survey, and voter interviews are not so comprehensive as census data. But it is striking that each accords with the conventional Bombay wisdom, which sees Maharashtrian job opportunities as distinctly improving.

Preferential Treatment as an Instrument of Public Policy

To what extent can the improvement in the job status of Maharashtrians be traced to governmental policy? The chronology of events is revealing. The improvements in Maharashtrian status noted in the managerial, telephone directory, and clerical surveys demonstrated that Maharashtrian job mobility began well before the Sena's founding in 1966. Since the surveys draw on pre-1973 data, they also indicate that marked advancement of Maharashtrians occurred prior to the stringent policy measures adopted by the state government in that year.

Might it be argued, then, that government policy and Shiv Sena pressure have been largely irrelevant to the enhancement of job opportunities among middle-class Maharashtrians? Might other factors such as the expanding educational system and the growing supply of educated Maharashtrians, or simply Bombay's growing economy, account for Maharashtrian improvements in recent years?

The underrepresentation of any social group in white collar positions is sometimes attributed to a scarcity of supply. Such an explanation in the Bombay case would presume an earlier shortage, and in more recent years a growing pool, of educated Maharashtrians. There *has* been an enormous growth in school enrollments in Maharashtra. Secondary enrollment rose from slightly under 2 million in 1950 to 6.5 million in 1965.[20] Between 1963 and 1970, enrollment in primary schools rose by thirty-one percent, in secondary schools by sixty percent.[21] At the University of Bombay alone, enrollment has risen nearly three hundred percent, from 24,000 in the early 1950s to almost 90,000 in 1971.[22] Not all of the growth is Marathi-speaking students, and there is in fact some indication that the *proportions* of Maharashtrians in higher education may have declined relative to other linguistic groups. The newer constituent colleges built since the 1960s in Bombay seem to cater more to the Gujarati than to other ethnic groups; in one prestigious Bombay college (El- phinstone), Maharashtrian enrollment fluctuated from approximately thirty- eight percent in 1956 to twenty-one percent in 1965 and thirty percent in 1975.[23] But even as the percentages of Maharashtrians may have declined, the number of Maharashtrians receiving B.A. degrees grew with the rapid expansion in college enrollment throughout the 1960s. Thus it is by no means clear that there has been a shortage of educated Maharashtrians, although it is patent that their numbers have rapidly grown.

It is a widely accepted maxim that job opportunities for previously under- represented groups are greatly enhanced in periods of general economic growth. If it could be shown that Maharashtrian occupational status improved marked- ly in a period of general recession, it might be possible to identify government pressure as a critical force explaining the change in Maharashtrian status. But such a disjunction between policy and economic forces has not occurred. In- stead, employment appears to have increased throughout the 1960s and early '70s except for a single brief slump in 1967–68.[24] Although employment in certain industries, most notably textiles, has declined, it appears that white collar job opportunities in other sectors have been expanding.

In addition to expanding job opportunities and the growing numbers of educated Maharashtrians, one other factor has favored job mobility among Maharashtrians. In 1960 the multilingual state of Bombay was divided into two states, Gujarat and Maharashtra. As with linguistic reorganizations else- where in India, the separation has encouraged the transition to greater use of the regional language. This development has probably resulted in less of a disadvantage facing Maharashtrians in job recruitment than was earlier the case.

Any explanation of the growing proportion of Maharashtrians in middle- class jobs must incorporate a combination of factors. The establishment of a separate Maharashtrian state in 1960 and the accompanying linguistic changes, the expanding economy, and the growing numbers of educated Maharashtrians have all favored the upward mobility of middle-class Maharashtrians. Given these other contributing circumstances, it is virtually impossible to identify the extent to which governmental policy is itself responsible for Maharashtrian advancement.

The Shiv Sena still remains active in Bombay municipal politics although the party's strength on the corporation has declined with each successive civic election since 1968. Sena candidates contested but have never won parliamen- tary seats, and only in a few cases have Sena leaders secured seats in the state legislature.

The party is still associated with Maharashtrian ethnic claims, but in its fifteen-year history it has also allied itself with other causes: it has described itself as virulently anticommunist, "patriotic" (a term which the Sena applies to everything from blood donation drives, to campaigns to prohibit movie patrons from leaving a theater before the national anthem is played, to anti-Muslim agitation). The party has also undertaken civic and social welfare causes (housing repair, connection of utility lines, anti-price-rise campaigns, etc.).

But the original source of Shiv Sena's success—its articulation of Maharashtrian demands for preferential employment—is still at the center of the party's political endurance. What then can be learned from the Sena's nativist claims? First, the emergence of a nativist party in the modern industrial center of Bombay challenges the assumption that preferential claims are the product of a tradition-bound society or even of the more tradition-bound communities within that society. Although Shiv Sena used tradition to mobilize a constituency (e.g., its appeals to Maharashtrian history and the heroic deeds of the Maratha ruler Shivaji Maharaj), the party's concerns are eminently modern: jobs in the offices and factories of Bombay's industrial and commercial sectors.

An even more important lesson to be gleaned from the Shiv Sena experience is the political basis of the decision to employ preferential policies. Maharashtrians have been a demographic majority in political control of Maharashtra state since the region was given a separate political existence in 1960. At the same time, Maharashtrians as a community have never been in the front ranks of Bombay's commercial or industrial enterprises, although the numbers of educated, aspiring, middle-class Maharashtrians have grown markedly with the postindependence expansion of schools and colleges. These economic, social, and political realities constitute a likely basis for the emergence of a movement seeking the preferential allocation of valued resources.

The Maharashtra government has proved responsive to preferential claims; it has not however adopted extremist measures. Whether because of constitutional proscriptions or other reasons, the state government has never attempted to bar migrants from entering the city; nor has it legislated direct ethnic quotas in employment or admissions. Rather, it has pursued a more indirect route by issuing circulars that exhort but do not compel employers to hire from a local—rather than specifically Maharashtrian—labor pool. The government has not openly espoused hiring Maharashtrians and has never made the sanctions attached to nonlocal hiring explicit. Although it has pursued a policy responsive to nativist claims, it has proceeded more by indirection than by explication.

Maharashtrians have made employment gains in the city's economy, gains which are probably due to a number of factors including but not limited to government policy. As suggested by the employment data cited earlier, Maharashtrians were moving into higher-level jobs before Shiv Sena's formation and before state preferential policies had been instituted. These gains were likely to have been a result of increased educational opportunities and a generally expanding economy as well as of the enhanced position Maharashtrians enjoyed in the aftermath of Maharashtrian statehood in 1960. What role the protectionist policies played in the late 1960s and early '70s is difficult to assess. What is clear is that in a modernizing society, an ethnic population with an aspiring middle class, strength of numbers, and access to political power will seek ways of securing for itself further economic opportunities. Pressure for the adoption of preferential policies is a predictable development that requires a governmental response. The history of Shiv Sena provides an instance of the political logic of such preferential policies.

Five

Protectionism and Separatism
in Andhra Pradesh

The case of protectionist policies in Andhra Pradesh represents one of the earliest and most enduring attempts by a state government in India to influence the patterns of internal migration and employment. The policy of intervention began in 1868 when the traditional ruler of Hyderabad state initiated steps to ensure that local people (*mulkis*) would be given preferences in employment in the administrative services, and it continues, in a more complex form, to the present day.

The state of Andhra, consisting of the Telugu-speaking region of the former princely state of Madras, was merged with the Telugu-speaking region of Hyderabad state in central India in 1956 to form a unified state known as Andhra Pradesh, the first state to be created on the basis of language in independent India. But by 1969 there was unprecedented agitation in both regions demanding that they be reconstituted as separate states. While there were a number of issues involved in the movement for separation, perhaps the most critical was the controversy over what were referred to as the "*mulki* rules," a set of government policies concerning rights of government employment for "local" people as against migrants from outside the Telugu-speaking area of the former Hyderabad state, an area known as Telangana. This chapter surveys these *mulki* rules from the time of their inception in the mid-nineteenth century to their abolition by a constitutional amendment in 1974.

Following an account of the origin and development of the *mulki* rules under the Nizams, the traditional rulers of Hyderabad, we shall turn to examine the controversies over the place of the *mulki* rules in the formation of the new state of Andhra Pradesh and over their implementation after the state was formed. We shall pay particular attention to university admissions, the sale of agricultural land, and domicile restrictions affecting the respective rights of *mulkis* and migrants. We conclude with an examination of the role of the central government in trying to resolve the conflict and preserve the unified state.

The Genesis of the Mulki Rules
The largest and most populous of India's native states, Hyderabad was founded in 1724 by Asaf Jah, appointed *subedar* (governor) of the Deccan in 1713 by

the Moghul emperor. Asaf Jah declared his independence of the empire but retained his title of *Nizam-ul-Mulk*. Henceforth, his descendants would be known as Nizams of Hyderabad, and their subjects as *mulkis* (*mulk* meaning country; hence, *mulki,* a native of the state, a "son of the soil"). Non-*mulkis* were *ghair-mulkis.*

Hyderabad was divided roughly into Marathi-speaking Marathwada and Telugu-speaking Telangana, the former including some Kannada-speaking districts as well. Although it was ruled by a Muslim, eighty-nine percent of Hyderabad's 1901 population were Hindu and only ten percent were Muslim and Urdu speaking, the latter mostly in urban areas. The percentage of Muslims was generally higher in the Marathwada than in the Telangana districts (excluding Hyderabad city).[1]

The three decades of Salar Jung's prime ministership in the nineteenth century (during the reigns of the fourth, fifth, and sixth Nizams) were the formative period of Hyderabad's history. Described as "one of the best Indian administrators and statesmen"[2] of the century, Salar Jung found the state's administration in chaos.[3] Fiscal disaster threatened the state; *jagirs* (traditional grants of revenue from a tract of land as a means of compensating government officials) had been farmed out to moneylenders. Salar Jung established a government treasury and salaried state employees. In the course of his reforms he recruited talented *ghair-mulkis* from the United Provinces, Bengal, Bombay, and Madras. Capable *mulkis,* it appears, considered government service beneath their dignity, and in consequence did not at first compete for administrative positions.[4] A large number of Muslims from north India were appointed to senior posts. Subsequently, the friends and relations of the appointees migrated into the city and were provided with employment by one means or another. With the ascendancy of the north Indians the earlier influence of the Madrasis (from British-ruled Madras province) and Parsees began to wane.[6]

Under these circumstances *mulkis* (particularly Muslim *mulkis*) became restive and then openly hostile toward the *ghair-mulkis.*[7] The issue for these early *mulki* aspirants was favoritism in the appointment of Hyderabad's administrators, but there was as yet no major debate on the relative qualifications of *mulkis* and *ghair-mulkis.*

Although under Salar Jung's reforms, *ghair-mulkis* had been brought into government service, Salar Jung was nevertheless cautious and viewed both his *ghair-mulki* administrators and the British residency officials as political and cultural threats. He avoided the use of *ghair-mulkis* in his personal affairs and in the royal palace, declaring that for all their talents, *ghair-mulkis* could not possibly match the devotion of those who had served the state for generations.[8] In 1868 orders were issued for the first time instructing all departments of Hyderabad's administration to recruit only *mulkis.*[9] Fourteen years later, it was further specified that without prior permission of the government, persons who were not either subjects or residents of the Nizam's dominions could not

59

be appointed to any post. The principles of merit and seniority in appointments and promotions of Hyderabad government officers were also laid down at this time.[10] Additional clarifications were periodically issued as to who might be considered "subjects" or "residents" for purposes of government employment. The foundation of the *mulki* rules was thus laid during the administration of Salar Jung, and a policy initiated of promoting the interests of natives against those of migrants in government employment.

Salar Jung also advocated educating and training *mulkis* for the efficient administration of the state. He proposed to send persons of good birth and education, to be selected by a Hyderabadi committee of nobles and high state officials, to British India for training in the administration of the revenue, judicial, and other departments.[11] His death occurred in 1883, before his intentions could be realized, and by 1891 instructions had been issued concerning the conditions and procedures for the appointment, where necessary, of *ghair-mulkis*. The *mulki* policy begun by Salar Jung was largely subverted by competing interests in the intervening years.

Mulki Rules under the Sixth and Seventh Nizams

Salar Jung I was succeeded by his son, Salar Jung II, who was English-educated and favorably disposed toward both the *ghair-mulki* officials and the British residency.[12] The *ghair-mulki* Muslims pressured the government for a change in the official language from Persian to Urdu.[13] Mir Mahboob Ali Khan, the sixth Nizam, who was never proficient in Persian, yielded to these pressures, and on February 21, 1884, he ordered the change in the language of administration from Persian to Urdu. By the summer of 1886 the change had been completed both in the court and in all departments of the administration.

In 1884 the council of state, presided over by the Nizam, issued rules for the recruitment and training of *mulkis* for the various grades of service and departments in the state administration. In 1885 and 1886, at the Nizam's request, Salar Jung II prepared lists of different categories of Hyderabad government employees that included their birthplace.[14] Table 5.1 summarizes the contents of the first civil list, submitted in March 1886.

It may be noted that the total monthly salary drawn by officers from Bombay and Hindustan (i.e., north India) is large in relation to their numbers, suggesting that they generally held very senior positions. After studying the list, the Nizam concluded that the proportion of *ghair-mulkis* to *mulkis* was excessive and requested further information concerning their ratio in the lower services.

The Nizam's limited intervention in the *mulki* employment questions chiefly affected urban-based Muslim *mulkis*. The switch in the language of government from Persian to Urdu, the language of the Muslim masses, doubtlessly improved their employment opportunities in the capital, where most government jobs were located. It did not help the majority Hindus.

Table 5.1   Birthplace of Officers of the Hyderabad Government in 1886

Birthplace	Number	%	Total Monthly Salary
Natives	246	52	75,867
Hindustan	97	20	44,173
Madras	66	14	20,602
Bombay	36	8	24,194
Other countries	7	1	1,310
(Details not mentioned)	24	5	12,570
Total	476	100	178,716

NOTE: The amounts shown here are in the Hali Sicca, later known as Osmani Sicca, the currency in the Nizam's dominions, Rs. 116 of which were equivalent to Rs. 100 in British India. The Nizam had his own currency, postal, and railway systems.

The growing *mulki-ghair-mulki* controversy was reflected in the press of the time. Thus, the *Hyderabad Record*[15] vigorously supported the cause of the *mulki* against that of the *ghair-mulki,* criticizing the prime minister for failing to keep the earlier promises to appoint *mulkis* only. The state, it was said, was controlled by a clique of north Indians, with the result that local Muslims and all Hindus were excluded from positions of honor and authority.

Similarly the *Mohammedan,* which defined Hindustanis as "men whose predecessors were invited by Salar Jung II," observed in 1901:

> One of the evil results of [the Hindustani Muslims' presence] is race hatred. The Hindu is held at arm's length where once he was an associate, nay a compatriot. The evil does not stop here. Between Mulki Muhammedans and the ghair-Mulki Muhammedans, a gulf rolls because of the arrogance of the Northern men who would have none interfere between them and their nobility—no rival near the throne. Everything as a consequence is at sixes and sevens.[16]

The subdued but growing antagonism between Hindu and Muslim *mulkis* over the inferior status of the former in the state was thus subordinated to and blamed on the *mulki-ghair-mulki* rivalry.

The *ghair-mulkis* in turn scoffed at the *mulkis.* In the *Hindu* in 1899, one writer queried: "Where is to be found the *mulki* intelligence to be entrusted with administrative responsibilities in Hyderabad?"[17]

By a *firman* (royal decree), on September 22, 1918, Osman Ali Khan, the seventh and the last of the Nizams, constituted Osmania University "to free the existing organization of education in the dominions to an appreciable extent from the control of outside universities and to organize higher education within the state with reference to local needs and conditions."[18] In contrast to universities existing in India at that time, which used English, Osmania designated Urdu, the official language of the state and the language of the Muslim minority, as the medium of instruction and of examination in all courses, including medicine and engineering. (English was a compulsory language.)[19]

Although the 1920s witnessed a large increase in the educated population of Hyderabad state, the literacy rate was still very low compared with other native states: among males aged five years and over, it was less than 9 percent, while the corresponding figures for the states of Mysore, Cochin, Travancore, and Baroda were 17 percent, 46 percent, 41 percent, and 33 percent, respectively.[20] Further, census data for 1911 and 1931 (see table 5.2) show that though more and more Hindus were getting the benefits of education, they still lagged behind Muslims. This was particularly true for Hindus in the Telangana districts, who were woefully backward in literacy in comparison with Muslims. The continued dominance of the Muslims in the Hyderabad administrative services until 1948[21] was due in part to their higher literacy rates, particularly in Urdu and in English.

Although the 1941 *Census of Hyderabad* observed that the people (referring to the Hindu majority) were not prepared to make the best use of education, at least one critic claimed to the contrary that *mulkis* in politically active Telugu, Marathi, and Kannada linguistic groups in the state were pressing continually for a greater number of schools, for instruction in their mother tongues, and for the abolition of Islam-oriented curricula.[22] The government not only ignored these demands but in the 1920s decreed that all educational institutions having more than fifteen students required permission of the Nizam's government to operate. Permission was denied frequently, and schools violating the provisions were closed down by the police.[23]

As a consequence of the educational policy of the Hyderabad government, many ambitious young Hindus went to colleges in British India. When they

Table 5.2   Literacy by Religion in Hyderabad State in 1911 and 1931

Religion	1911	1931
Hindus:		
Total Population	11,626,146	9,699,615
% Literate	2.29	4.03
% Literate in English	0.08	0.40
% Literate in Urdu	n.a.	0.81
Muslims:		
Total Population	1,380,990	1,534,666
% Literate	5.88	10.35
% Literate in English	0.51	1.26
% Literate in Urdu	n.a.	6.84

SOURCES: *Census of India,* 1911, vol. 19, Hyderabad, table 8, pp. 64–65; *Census of India,* 1931, vol. 23, Hyderabad, pt. 2, table 13, pp. 188–189. Those literate include 13,559 Hindu and 17,577 Muslim women.

returned to join the professions and the more modern section of the state administration, they brought with them new political connections. Eventually these linkages put them in touch with the growing movements of linguistic nationalism in Andhra and Maharashtra.[21]

The Growth of Political Consciousness

The 1920s saw the growth of political consciousness in Telangana and subsequently in the Marathwada and Karnataka areas.[25] Telangana *mulkis*, in particular, gradually became aware of their disadvantaged condition in the state. The *Star*, an English language weekly from Allahabad in north India, in a series of articles in 1931 and 1932 vividly described problems faced by the Telugu-speaking people in securing employment in government service. Out of eighty-two who passed the Hyderabad civil service examination and were appointed between 1913 and 1934, it was said, not one was from Telangana.[26]

In British India, the Indian national Congress movement had been in the forefront of the demand for Indianization of government services since its foundation in 1885. In the Telugu-speaking districts of Madras province, the cultural-linguistic Andhra organization, the Andhra Mahasabha, had since the 1920s demanded formation of a linguistic Andhra province, in part because Telugu-speaking people had not been adequately represented in the Madras province government.

By contrast, in Telangana, because the *mulkis* were not a homogeneous group either by language, religion, or class structure, virtually no *mulki* agitation occurred for the Hyderabadization of the state's administrative services.[27] Nor did they try to mobilize nonurban, non-middle-class Hyderabadis. The Nizam's rule was autocratic. Political liberties were curtailed to the extent that no public meeting could be held even to mourn the deaths of Pandit Motilal Nehru and Dr. Ansari, key figures in the national Congress movement. Nor could the Hyderabad Political Conferences be held within state boundaries.[28] Under these circumstances the Andhra Mahasabha limited its role in Hyderabad to urging that Telugu-speaking officers be included among appointees to key posts in the state. Agitation could not be considered.

During the 1930s, when constitutional reforms were being discussed in British India, the relationship between native states such as Hyderabad and the proposed Indian Federation became a matter of interest to all *mulkis*. In January 1930 the Hyderabad Association was started to maintain the political status of Hyderabad state, promote patriotism, and strive for reforms—including the establishment of responsible government in the state. Muslim opposition to the last goal provoked the nascent political activity of Hindu *mulkis* against Muslim *mulkis*.

The Nizam's Subjects' League was organized in 1935 in Hyderabad to promote goodwill and cooperation between the various classes and communities of the Nizam's subjects, safeguard the constitutional rights and privileges of citizenship in Hyderabad, and seek establishment of a constitutional form of government. Its membership, which consisted primarily of some prominent liberal *mulki* Muslims of Hyderabad city and a few of their personal Hindu friends, put forward the case of the *mulkis* without directly addressing the relative status differences among communities (Hindu and Muslim, urban and rural). The organization attempted to unite all Hyderabadis behind the demand that all economic resources—jobs, contracts, licenses, and agencies— should be in the hands of *mulkis*. The Nizam's government opposed the most important of their demands, namely, the granting of equal civil liberties and rights to all Hyderabadis, gradual achievement of responsible government, and an independent and supreme judiciary.[29]

The Ghair-Mulki Presence in Hyderabad: An Assessment of Census Data

The immigrants into Hyderabad state from adjacent Bombay, Central Provinces, Berar, and Madras were distributed generally in those districts bordering the respective provinces. Immigrants from Uttar Pradesh, Ajmer, Marwar, the Punjab, and Rajputana were concentrated in the city of Hyderabad, as shown by the censuses of 1911 and 1931.[30]

While the number of immigrants from these provinces fell between 1911 and 1931, the proportion living in Hyderabad city and the ratio of females to males among them increased. It was these immigrants, located mainly in the administrative capital of Hyderabad, who aroused *mulki* ire. Comparing immigrants from Uttar Pradesh and Punjab to those from Madras, Bombay, Mysore, the Central Provinces, and Berar (all contiguous to Hyderabad state), Syed Abid Hasan remarked: "But the immigrants from U.P. and the Punjab are mostly those who come here to seek employment, thereby depriving educated *Mulkis* of an important means of earning a livelihood. Immigrants from Rajputana and Marwar come here as money lenders and trade on the poverty of the local people." He also observed that north Indians formed a clique to keep others out of the administration; they regarded themselves as the state's rulers and displayed, in his view, an unpardonable superiority complex galling to the *mulkis*.[31]

A major irritant was the de facto disregard for the *mulki* rules by outsiders on the grounds that they were better educated and qualified. Administrative posts were restricted on these grounds to persons of the "urban classes" only.[32] This experience sensitized *mulkis* to the various excuses for *ghair-mulki* favoritism—a recurrent and increasingly volatile issue in the region.

More Stringent Mulki Rules

In 1937 a special committee was appointed by the Nizam under the chairmanship of Dewan Bahadur Aravamudu Iyegar to study conditions in the state and make proposals for political reforms.[33] It received a number of memoranda which demanded the introduction of fundamental rights of citizenship. Some memoranda accused the "non-*mulki*" of spreading the "venum of communalism," demanded the discontinuance of the practice of employing *ghair-mulkis,* be they Europeans or non-Europeans, and urged the formation of a public service commission.

These demands may appear somewhat misdirected, in view of the decrease in migration from northern India by 1931 and the existence of *mulki* rules for about seventy years. Resentment against the north Indian *ghair-mulkis,* however, was accentuated by the large number of positions they occupied; their attitudes toward the *mulkis*; the increasing number of matriculates, graduates, and postgraduates within the dominions after the establishment of Osmania University; and the growing unemployment during the depression of the 1930s. They had, it was felt, deprived the *mulki* of his bread and butter.

In addition, a large number of exemptions to the domicile requirement of the *mulki* rules may have been granted by the government in appointments in education (including to Osmania University), agriculture, and other departments. Further, the natives of the state visualized a *mulki* as one whose forefathers for generations had lived in the state and served it loyally, while the legal definition of *mulki* in the civil service regulations was more limited. One may note in this connection the opinion of Nizamat Jung on the *mulki* rules prevailing in the 1930s:

> This benevolent (*mulki*) rule enacts that a man who has lived in the Hyderabad state for 12 years or who has served the government for 12 years (however long ago) shall be a *mulki* in perpetuity:...A son or grandson of the first favoured person (*mulki*) may, even after the lapse of a century, come from some far off country to claim this birthright. There is a romance in the idea. I do not believe there is any other state in the world that can compete with ours in such a thoughtless generosity. It is possible that the framers of our law may not have known the essential condition of domicile, namely, the absence of intention to revert to the land of birth, or they may have regarded it as unduly obstructive to the spirit of adventure.[34]

The Nizam's special committee recommended that:

> Consistently with the sovereign rights of the Ruler, it is essential for the internal and external security of the State that the people should have an effective association with the government. In order that such association of the people might be secured and their needs and desires properly ascertained it is necessary that public services should be manned by persons who have a lasting attachment to the State [i.e., the sons of the soil]. An independent and impartial agency should be established to raise the standard of efficiency and the morale of the public services.[35]

65

As a consequence of these recommendations, reforms announced on July 19, 1939, by the government proposed that the then-existing *mulki* rules should be made more stringent and suggested certain procedures for recruitment. These proposals were approved by the Nizam.[36]

The period was one of declining governmental authority in Hyderabad state. The rise of the Communist movement in the villages of Telangana after 1945 diverted the government's energies to law and order concerns and its own doubtful survival. Hindu *mulkis* leaned increasingly toward the Congress national movement.

Other political issues outside Hyderabad, such as the formation of Pakistan and the future of the native states, also shaped Hyderabadi politics. Many middle class *mulki* Muslims were becoming active in Ittehad-ul-Muslimin, a cultural-religious organization founded in 1926 in Hyderabad with the object of uniting the Muslims in the state in support of the Nizam. Soon the *ghair-mulki* administrators and advocates educated at Aligarh, who were sensitive to the Hindu (majority) domination in the nationalist politics of north India, transformed the Ittehad into a political body to convert untouchables and build a Muslim majority in the state. Bahadur Yar Jung, the founder of Ittehad, claimed that the sovereignty of the state rested not with the Muslim ruler alone, but with the entire Muslim community.

In turn both Hindu *mulkis* and *ghair-mulkis* were establishing close ties with the Arya Samaj, a Hindu reform movement. The growing debate over the future role of different communities in the state thus overshadowed the *mulki* issue, which remained unresolved.

The Police Action

The paramountcy of British power lapsed in India on August 15, 1947. The Nizam did not accede to the Indian Union but signed a standstill agreement in November 1947. As the Razakars (militant Muslim volunteers) created a state of terror, a vast number of Hindus fled Hyderabad to neighboring areas. The government of India intervened through the police action of September 13, 1948. Within a week the Nizam's forces surrendered and Hyderabad joined the Indian Union.

Steps were soon initiated to reduce the role of Urdu and the predominance of Muslims in the administration of Hyderabad. The Hyderabad army had been composed entirely of Muslims. Between 1946 and September 1948 about fifty thousand Muslims were said to have been recruited in the police, military, and excise departments. The share of Hyderabadis in these appointments had been meager.[37] In the wake of the police action many Muslims were thrown out of employment.

But, Hindu *mulkis* who had been excluded from government employment under the old regime and had entertained great hopes for the new were disillusioned when *ghair-mulkis* were appointed instead.[38] Although the change

WEST PAKISTAN

Delhi

BERAR

HYDERABAD

Hyderabad

EAST
PAKISTAN

MYSORE

TAMIL NADU
(MADRAS)

KERALA
(TRAVANCORE)

Scale

km   250   500

mi   100 200 300

Map 1.   India at Independence, 1947

to English as the language of instruction at Osmania University and as the official language of government was welcomed by Hindu *mulkis,* it was an obstacle to *mulkis*—Hindu and Muslim alike—who had already been trained in Urdu. Seventeen thousand out of twenty-two thousand villages in Hyderabad were without primary schools, and over sixty percent of teachers were untrained; as the government set about initiating instruction in the regional languages (Telugu, Marathi, and Kannada), displacing Urdu in the schools, knowledge of the vernacular languages became an additional necessary qualification which justified recruitment of *ghair-mulkis* to Hyderabad.

The issue of qualifications for service in the state's administration was dramatized when seven to eight thousand *ghair-mulki* policemen were recruited. Agricultural assistants, too, were brought in from outside the state. Once again, the *mulki* rules became a focus of urban *mulkis'* attention. The Muslim élite which had dominated the state's administration before the police action was gradually being displaced by *ghair-mulkis.* The Telugu-speaking *ghair-mulkis* succeeded the north Indian *ghair-mulkis* as targets of *mulki* discontent.

Mulki Rules from 1949 to 1955

According to the *mulki* rules, embodied in article 39 of the Hyderabad civil service regulations (1949), no person could be appointed without the specific sanction of the Nizam if he were not a *mulki.* The regulations state that a person shall be called a *mulki* if (a) by birth he is a subject of Hyderabad state; (b) by residence in Hyderabad state he has been entitled to be a *mulki;* or (c) his father had completed fifteen years of service and was in the government service at the time of his birth.

A person was defined as a subject of Hyderabad state by birth if at the time of his birth his father was a *mulki.* A permanent resident in Hyderabad state for at least fifteen years, who had abandoned the idea of returning to the place of his previous residence and had obtained an affidavit to that effect on a prescribed form attested by a magistrate was a *mulki* by residence. Wives of *mulkis* were also considered *mulki.*

Hyderabad became a "Part B State" in January 1950 with the Nizam as titular head, designated as Raj Pramukh. A circular in June 1950 directed that the conditions of birth and descent prescribed in the *mulki* rules should not be insisted upon for purposes of recruitment to government service. The residence qualification of fifteen years would continue to be applied until a uniform policy in regard to residential qualifications was established by the government of Hyderabad in consultation with the central government. Further, exemptions from the *mulki* rules, which were previously granted by the order of the Nizam, would now be granted only by the government.

The Hyderabad general recruitment rules, framed in November 1955 by the Raj Pramukh, superseded all previous rules and orders. They provided that no person would be eligible for appointment to state or subordinate services unless he (a) was an Indian national, and (b) possessed a domicile (i.e., *mulki*) certificate issued by a competent authority as evidence of his residence in Hyderabad state for a period of fifteen years or more.

The *ghair-mulkis* employed by Hyderabad state by 1952 can be classified into three categories: (a) admitted *ghair mulkis* employed on a permanent basis because of the unavailability of qualified persons in Hyderabad state; (b) *ghair mulkis* appointed on a temporary basis; and (c) *ghair mulkis* with bogus *mulki* certificates.

For persons in the first category, exemptions from *mulki* rules were obtained in most cases at the time of appointment, and the government could not discharge them from service. Persons appointed to temporary posts, unless their services were necessary, were to be replaced by qualified *mulkids*. Action could be taken by the government against those in the third category if there was proof of deception. Nepotism, corruption, and appointments on the basis of bogus *mulki* certificates had been prevalent before the police action;[40] now these matters could be openly raised in public with a view to altering practices in favor of *mulkis*.

The growing opposition to employment of *ghair-mulkis* was evident in the innumerable questions asked by persons of diverse political views in the Hyderabad state legislative assembly soon after its inauguration. The strong *mulki* sentiment was also reflected in July 1952, when the assembly discussed a resolution aimed at a government takeover of Osmania University. A section of the legislators opposed it because the admissions and appointments, until then more or less limited to the Hyderabadis, would be thrown open to all Indians. K. V. Narayana Reddy, a former lecturer in economics at the university and member of the state legislative assembly from the Telangana region, threatened to lead a *satyagraha* (peaceful resistance) in the event of such a takeover.[41] The government dropped the proposal in view of the strong opposition.

Another instance of the growing *mulki* opposition was the agitation in Telangana in 1952. It began with a strike in Warangal as a consequence of a dispute over an alleged transfer of *mulki* teachers by an official said to be *ghair-mulki,* who had also taken disciplinary action against some of them. The issue became politicized and soon led to agitation in which assaults were organized on Telugu-speaking *ghair-mulkis.* The agitation lasted from July until mid-September.

Mulki Reservations and the Demand for a Telugu Linguistic State

A movement had begun in Madras presidency in 1913 which, while retaining as its ultimate goal the formation of a Telugu linguistic state comprising all the contiguous Telugu-speaking areas, in Hyderabad and Madras states, aimed more immediately at carving out an Andhra state consisting of Telugu areas of Madras state. In 1953 the state of Andhra was formed of Rayalaseema and the Circars (coastal Andhra).

HYDERABAD

O Hyderabad

O Kurnool

ANDHRA

MYSORE

Bangalore O   O Madras

TAMIL NADU
(MADRAS)

KERALA
(TRAVANCORE)

km   100
Scale |——+——|
mi   100

Map 2.   South India, 1947–56

Meanwhile, popular, chiefly middle class pressures throughout the country led the central government to appoint the States Reorganization Commission in 1953 to examine the question of the reorganization of all the states of the Indian union on linguistic-cultural lines. Thus, within less than five years of the police action, and within two years after the establishment of its democratic government, the future of Hyderabad as a state came to be seriously reconsidered.

The consensus among Hyderabad politicians was that the state should be divided and the Marathi and Kannada linguistic areas merged, respectively, with the neighboring states of Bombay and Mysore. Public opinion in Telangana, however, on whether their region should be merged with Andhra remained split. On one hand, though accents differed, the Telugu dialects spoken in Telangana and in Andhra were mutually intelligible, and there had been social contact between the two populations even before 1947. Moreover, they took pride in the same literary and cultural heritage, and after 1950 both regions were exposed to the same political influences. On the other hand, the influence of the Urdu language and Muslim rule was evident in the language, dress, and manners of the urban Telanganites, whereas in Andhra the English language and British rule dominated. Furthermore, Telangana politicians who had come into their own only three years previously were uneasy at the possibility that if they united with Andhra they might be pushed into positions of minor importance. Though comprising fifty percent of the area and population of Hyderabad state, Telangana had occupied a politically subordinate place under the Nizam, but as a result of demands beginning in 1950 Telangana politicians became chief minister of the state, president of the Hyderabad State Congress, and mayor of Hyderabad.[42]

The urban middle class and aspiring entrants into it thus had their doubts about a united Andhra state. They were especially apprehensive about the effect on the middle classes of Telangana of large-scale in-migration of Andhra cultivators, students, lawyers, and unemployed youth in the event of a merger. The aggressive, mobile people of the Circars were a particular worry.

Their apprehensions relating to the economy and employment were well understood by the States Reorganization Commission, which in its report in 1955 recommended: "It will be in the interest of Andhra as well as Telangana, if, for the present, the Telangana area is constituted into a separate state, which may be known as the Hyderabad State with provision for its unification with Andhra after the general elections likely to be held in or about 1961, if by a two-thirds majority the legislature of the residuary Hyderabad State expresses itself in favour of such unification."[43] The central leadership, though initially reported to be divided on the question of the formation of one Telugu state, ultimately adopted this solution and suggested discussions between the Andhra and Hyderabad leaders concerning the various safeguards necessary to protect the interests of Telangana people in an eventual united state. The result was the "gentlemen's agreement" of February 1956.[44]

71

The gentlemen's agreement outlined measures to be adopted to protect the interests of the different sections of Telangana. Its politicians were assured of a fixed percentage of seats in the ministry, including representation for a Telangana Muslim, and of specified important portfolios. The interests of students were to be safeguarded by giving preferences to them in educational facilities in the Telangana region. Existing service personnel were to be protected from retrenchment following integration. Most important, in view of subsequent *mulki* efforts and aspirations, employment prospects were to be assured in Telangana people by laying down domicile rules for employment in Telangana. The *mulki* rules, in short, were to be perpetuated.

The sale of agricultural land was to be regulated to protect agriculturists from severe competition. Surpluses in Telangana revenues were to be utilized in Telangana and efforts were to be made for its economic development. A regional council was to be established to watch over all these matters. The position of the Urdu language in administration was to be protected, and a knowledge of Telugu was not to be required at the time of initial recruitment. Telangana Congress party members were assured of a separate Congress committee until 1962.

To preserve the identity of Telangana, the Telangana representatives desired at first that the united state be known as "Andhra-Telangana." Later they agreed to the name of "Andhra Pradesh" ("Andhra State"). The new state was inaugurated on November 1, 1956.

The first step in the implementation of the gentlemen's agreement was the incorporation of a new article 371 in the Indian constitution (seventh amendment, 1956), by which the president was empowered to constitute regional committees of the state assembly. *Thus a special responsibility for overseeing the implementation of the gentlemen's agreement was placed in the central government.* Accordingly, the president issued the Andhra Pradesh Regional Committee Order (1958), establishing a regional committee consisting of the members of the assembly representing Telangana constituencies, to have jurisdiction over the following scheduled matters: local self-government, public health and sanitation, local hospitals and dispensaries, primary and secondary education, regulation of admissions to the educational institutions in the Telangana region, agriculture, sale of agricultural land, cooperative societies, prohibition of the consumption (except for medicinal purposes) of intoxicating liquors and of drugs which are injurious to health, and development and economic planning within the framework of general development plans and policies formulated by the state legislature.[45]

The regional committee discussed and reported on all non-money bills affecting the Telangana region. Differences of opinion between the regional committee and the legislature on the contents of bills were to be referred to the governor of the state, whose decision in such cases was final. The regional committee also considered and passed resolutions recommending legislation

72

Map 3. Andhra Pradesh, 1956–

73

or executive actions which did not involve any financial commitment apart from expenditures of a routine and incidental character. The Council of Ministers was normally required to give effect to such recommendations. In case the ministry felt that the regional committee was not competent to make a particular recommendation or that it was inexpedient, the matter was referred to the governor; his decision would be final and binding on the Council. Thus the regional committee was an essential organ in the lawmaking process, as far as scheduled matters relating to Telangana were concerned, and its recommendations, intended to safeguard the interests of Telangana, could not easily be ignored by the executive or the legislature.

By and large, the gentlemen's agreement has been implemented.[46] We will discuss in detail here those items which have had an impact on the educational and employment markets in Telangana and on the sale of agricultural land.

Restrictions on University Admissions

Outside competition for admission to Osmania University did not pose a problem until 1949, when Urdu ceased to be the medium of instruction and examination. Until then, students from neighboring Andhra had attended distant universities such as Nagpur, Saugar, and Banaras for postgraduate studies and higher technical and professional courses when the number of seats in Andhra University was inadequate in relation to demand.

As regulation of admissions to educational institutions in the Telangana region was within the purview of the Andhra Pradesh Regional Committee, the committee was quite active in formulating and amending the rules so as to reserve to residents of Telangana the bulk of the seats in all government institutions—professional colleges, arts and science colleges, polytechnics, and Osmania University. These institutions were statutorily required to implement the recommendation of the regional committee. The high court of Andhra Pradesh held in the case of *Ramakrishna* v. *Osmania University* that such reservations did not offend the principles embodied in article 15 of the constitution.[47]

Private collegiate and professional institutions did not come under these regulations, and the regional committee did not seek to regulate admissions to secondary schools.

The Sale of Agricultural Land

The 1951 census of Hyderabad revealed that of all immigrants into Hyderabad state, those from Madras were most likely to take up agricultural occupations, principally as owner cultivators but to a lesser extent as tenant cultivators and agricultural laborers. Their presence had had a beneficial effect on agriculture.[48] The Nizamsagar canal system in the Nizamabad district had attracted the first wave of immigrants in search of fresh opportunities in paddy cultivation in the 1920s.

S. Kesava Iyengar, referring to the land transfers in Hyderabad state during 1949-51, observed:

> In the Nizamabad district land transfers are on the increase in recent years on account of the influence of enterprising cultivators from the Andhra districts of Madras, who have been purchasing dry lands and developing them into paying wet lands under the Nizamsagar canal system. The average yield of paddy for the area is between 900 and 1000 pounds per acre whereas the peasants from Bezwada and Rajahmundry (by using the transplantation system) take out 3,000 pounds per acre. Especially in canal areas, land values have tended to increase steeply on account of enterprising immigrants from urban areas and from the Andhra districts of Madras.[49]

The villages where *raiyats* (farmers) from the Circars settled were and are spoken of as Andhra colonies by the local people. Strong fears had been expressed before the formation of Andhra Pradesh that the *raiyats* from Andhra might buy up all the lands in Telangana that would be irrigated when the Nagarjunasagar and Ramapadasagar projects were completed.[50]

In accordance with a resolution of the regional committee in 1959, the Revenue Department prepared the Andhra Pradesh Agricultural Lands (Restriction of Sale) Bill. The central government, to whom it was sent for approval, wanted it to be modified to avoid the criticism that its provisions were parochial in character and conflicted with the accepted notion of common citizenship. After the regional committee was informed of these views, no further action was taken.

Domicile Rules

The States Reorganization Commission strongly recommended that domicile rules in force in several states, not only Hyderabad, should be replaced by appropriate parliamentary legislation, since they not only were inconsistent with articles 16 and 19 of the constitution, but went against the conception of Indian citizenship. Yet by virtue of section 119 of the States Reorganization Act and the Andhra Pradesh (Adaptation of Laws) Order (1957), the *mulki* rules, preserved by article 35(b) of the constitution, continued in operation in the Hyderabad area of Andhra Pradesh.

In 1957 parliament passed the Public Employment (Requirement as to Residence) Act. The central government subsequently promulgated the Andhra Pradesh Public Employment (Requirement as to Residence) Rules (1959). The rules provided that a person would not be eligible for appointment to a post within the Telangana area, under the state government or under a local authority (other than a cantonment board), unless (1) he had been continuously residing within the area for not less than fifteen years immediately preceding the prescribed date, and (2) he produced, before the appointing authority concerned, if so required, a certificate of eligibility granted under these rules. Covered by the rules were all nongazetted posts which carried a salary of three hundred rupees or less. For posts in the secretariat departments and offices of heads of state government departments situated in the cities of Hyderabad and Secunderabad, the requirement of residence applied only to the second vacancy in every bloc of three vacancies filled by direct recruitment.

In response to the demand for jobs for the "sons of the soil" in public sector undertakings, the central government, by the Employment Exchanges (Compulsory Notifications as to Vacancies) Act (1959), required public sector undertakings to notify local employment exchanges of all vacancies carrying a basic salary of less than Rs. 500. It was hoped that this would give local people priority in such employment.

The Telangana and Andhra Agitations

Although the implementation of the gentlemen's agreement proceeded reasonably well, there was considerable agitation in Telangana in 1969 for stricter implementation of the Telangana safeguards. This was followed later by a backlash in the Andhra region in 1973 in favor of scrapping the *mulki* rules. In turn, each of these conflicts gave rise to demands for reconstitution of each region into a separate state.

The agitators in both places were mainly state government employees (especially nongazetted, junior-level officers) and students. Each region had its own union of government employees bidding for state government attention and favor. And in each place attempts were made to mobilize villagers and farmers around broader regional concerns.

The major factors giving rise to the agitation were: (1) the rapid growth of educational facilities in both regions; (2) unprecedented migration into the Hyderabad city/district from the coastal districts; (3) dwindling employment opportunities in the state as a whole, and the projected 1969 expiry date of the Public Employment (Requirement as to Residence) Act.

Education. The increase in the educational facilities in the Telangana region at the high school and college levels during the decade 1956–57 to 1966–67 was far higher than in the Andhra region. The rise in capacity among institutions of technical education was similarly high (see table 5.3), thus leading to a rapid increase in the supply of educated youths seeking nonmanual employment.

Migration. After the formation of Andhra Pradesh, immigration from the Andhra region in general and the Circars in particular into Hyderabad city/district increased at an unprecedented rate. Many of these immigrants belonged to the middle classes.

76

Table 5.3   Education in the Telangana and Andhra Regions

	Telangana		Andhra	
	1956–57	1966–67	1956–57	1966–67
1. (a) High/higher secondary				
multipurpose schools	105	1,055	627	1,600
(b) Students	82,100	440,200	299,600	620,000
2. (a) Colleges (including				
professional schools)	30	80	68	108
(b) Students	12,300	37,700	39,400	59,100
3. Technical institutions				
(a) Students in degree colleges	215	677	336	953
(b) Students in polytechnics	370	1,410	490	2,093

SOURCE: Planning and Panchayati Raj Department, Government of Andhra Pradesh, *Regional Development in A.P.* (Hyderabad, 1969).

There had been migration from districts in the Madras state[51] to the Telangana region and Hyderabad city even before the formation of Andhra Pradesh, but the steep rise in the percentage of females and in the number in districts adjacent to Madras state at the 1951 census reflects a rise in long-term family migration (see table 5.4).

Following the formation of Andhra Pradesh the rate of migration into Hyderabad city increased sharply.[52] Of the migrants into Hyderabad city between 1951 and 1961, ten percent were from Hyderabad district and thirty-five percent were from other districts of Telangana. Those from the Circars and from the Rayalaseema districts numbered 30,865 and 14,398, respectively, constituting fifteen percent and seven percent of the migrant population. Immigrants from other states constituted thirty-two percent. The occupational

Table 5.4   Migrants from Madras State (Percent Female in Parentheses)

Year	Total		Residing in Districts Adjacent to Madras State		Residing in Other Districts	
1901	55,369	(49)	33,637	(52)	21,732	(45)
1911	67,821	(49)	46,932	(51)	20,899	(44)
1921	84,143	(38)	33,988	(48)	50,155	(31)
1931	132,954	(23)	50,391	(25)	82,527	(21)
1941	142,323	(36)	52,796	(37)	89,527	(35)
1951	129,455	(50)	83,563	(53)	45,892	(47)

SOURCE: *Census of India, 1951*, vol. 9, Hyderabad, pt. 1-A, p. 72.

Table 5.5   Migrant Workers to Metropolitan Hyderabad, 1951–61 (Percentage)

Region of Origin	Craftsmen, Factory Workers, and Laborers	Clerical and Related Workers	Administrative, Executive, and Managerial Workers	All Categories
Telangana	61%	31%	22%	45%
Circars	9	31	13	15
Rayalaseema	4	10	4	6
Total Andhra Pradesh	74	72	39	66
Other Indian states	24	27	58	32
Other countries	2	1	3	2
Total	100%	100%	100%	100%

SOURCE: Manzoor Alam and Waheeduddin Khan, *Metropolitan Hyderabad and Its Region: A Strategy for Development* (Bombay: Asia Publishing House, 1972), p. 22.

distribution of the migrants from the Circars was also significant. Among migrants into Hyderabad district holding clerical and allied jobs, those from the Circars topped the list, a sizable section of them being the gazetted and non-gazetted officers of the government of Andhra who, with the shifting of the capital from Kurnool to Hyderabad, naturally migrated to Hyderabad with their families. Immigrants from other districts within the Telangana region, other Indian states, the Rayalaseema region, and other countries came next. Among immigrant administrative, executive, and general workers, those from the Circars were again numerous (see table 5.5).

In the absence of published census data on migration to Hyderabad city from different districts of Andhra Pradesh in 1961 and 1971, data for Hyderabad district may be used to understand the pattern of migration from the Andhra region. The pace of migration from the Circars into Hyderabad district increased between 1961 and 1971. In both census years the largest numbers of immigrants were from the neighboring districts of Mahboobnagar, Medak, and Nalgonda (table 5.6). Migration from all other districts in Telangana, except Nizamabad and Adilabad, also increased. However, what is most significant for a proper understanding of the relations between Andhra and Telangana regions is the increase in the number of migrants into Hyderabad from the four Circar districts of East Godavari, West Godavari, Krisha, and Guntar, from 39,348 in 1961, to 70,757 in 1971. From Ongole and Nellore districts immigrants numbered 4,653 in 1961 and 10,070 in 1971.

The reasons for this large migration are not hard to find. Besides the tendency for capitals of state governments in India to attract migrants from the different districts of the state, for Andhras the formation of Andhra Pradesh was the realization of a long-cherished dream. As the government was stable and there were no threats to the integrity of the state, a steady and increasing stream of migrants flowed into the capital.

Table 5.6 Migrants to Hyderabad District from Other Districts of Andhra Pradesh in 1961 and 1971

Region and District	1961 Census	1971 Census	Difference between 1961 and 1971
Circars:			
Srikakulam	1,563	2,050	+ 487
Visakhapatnam	3,256	4,755	+ 1,499
Total	4,819	6,805	
East Godavari	8,420	16,145	+ 7,725
West Godavari	7,687	12,630	+ 4,943
Krishna	12,564	22,841	+10,277
Guntur	10,677	19,141	+ 8,464
Total	39,348	70,757	
Ongole*		4,170	+ 4,170
Nellore	4,653	5,900	+ 1,247
Total	4,653	10,070	
Rayalaseema:			
Chittoor	2,186	3,340	+ 1,154
Cuddapah	2,751	3,495	+ 744
Anantapur	2,771	3,400	+ 629
Kurnool	8,770	8,180	− 590
Total	16,478	18,415	
Telangana:			
Mahboobnagar	53,794	61,505	+ 7,711
Medak	51,044	57,767	+ 6,723
Nalgonda	36,322	47,676	+11,354
Total	141,160	166,948	
Nizamabad	9,795	7,895	− 1,900
Karimnagar	17,403	18,486	+ 1,083
Warangal	13,541	18,920	+ 5,379
Khamman	3,929	5,395	+ 1,466
Adilabad	4,293	2,545	− 1,748
Total	48,961	53,241	

*Ongole district, formed in 1970 out of some areas of Guntur, Nellore and Kurnool districts, was later renamed Prakasam district in honor of Tanguturi Prakasam, the first chief minister of Andhra.

SOURCES: 1961 data are from *Census of India, 1961, vol. 2, Andhra Pradesh*, pt 1-A(i), p. 437. Data relating to the 1971 census have been obtained through the courtesy of the census office in Hyderabad.

The rules relating to admissions to educational institutions and employment in the Telangana region were at best only a marginal constraint to migration from the Circars. In part this might have been because admissions to high schools and private colleges were not restricted.

Employment. Vacancies listed in the employment exchanges provide some indication of employment opportunities in the state. This number rose only from 1,678 in 1956 to 3,263 in 1961, although the number of registered job seekers in the corresponding years were 10,852 and 16,237, respectively. In 1962, owing to an expansion of the categories of persons eligible for registration, registrations rose to 308,298; for that year, 35,841 vacancies were listed. The number of persons placed in employment increased from 26,077 in 1962 to 41,176 in 1965, but afterward decreased (table 5.7).

1965 was the last year of the third five-year plan. The three annual plans that followed saw a slackening in the tempo of development, which was reflected in diminishing new employment. Combined with the tremendous rate of increase in educational facilities, this led to a growth of over four hundred percent in the numbers of matriculates registered with the exchange between 1962 and 1972, from 30,000 to 128,000.[53] Meanwhile, the total number of persons employed by the state government, particularly in the nongazetted services, remained more or less constant between 1960-61 and 1965-66, and it was only about 300,000 by 1970-71.[54]

The increasing migration of middle class families from the Circars districts into the capital intensified pressures on the employment market. Competition for jobs in the state in general, and in Hyderabad city in particular, became acute after 1965-66, when the suspension of the third five-year plan (the "plan holiday") brought the tempo of development to a standstill. In addition to job competition, a feeling that the state administration and government were

Table 5.7   Applicants Placed in Employment under Different Categories in Andhra Pradesh through Employment Exchanges

	1962	1965	1970	1973
Central government	3,636	4,246	1,855	3,152
State government	16,886	23,863	16,040	13,156
Quasi-government	5,921	10,255	6,610	9,704
Total public sector	25,443	38,364	24,505	26,012
Private sector	634	2,812	1,549	740
Total	26,077	41,176	26,054	26,752
Total registrations by end of year	308,298	251,031	312,210	317,030
Total vacancies notified during year	35,841	52,210	35,690	35,860

SOURCES: Bureau of Economics and Statistics, Government of Andhra Pradesh, *Economic and Statistical Bulletin,* 16, (1972), pp. 118-20; 1973, pp. 34-35.

dominated by people from the Andhra region who behaved condescendingly gave rise to bitterness among different sections of the Telangana population. Latent tensions between regions became intense.

The government of Andhra Pradesh reviewed the operation of the domiciliary rules in 1968 and found that in regard to certain categories of posts, to which recruitment was by competitive examination, the proportion of successful candidates able to meet residency qualifications would be low if the examination was to be a combined one open to all. Therefore it recommended to the government of India that the 1957 Public Employment Act and the 1959 employment rules should be extended for a further period of five years. In 1968 the National Integration Council, constituted by the government, also became concerned about job preference demands by local residents.

Telangana Grievances

Telangana *mulkis* stated their grievances, alleging that (1) Telangana's development was neglected as a consequence of nonutilization of the Telangana surpluses; (2) there were injustices in the integration of the service cadres of Andhra and Hyderabad; and (3) there were violations of safeguards relating to employment in Telangana.

Surpluses. Surpluses of receipts over expenditures on different items were allocated between the Andhra and Telangana regions in specified ratios, according to a set of principles agreed to in 1959. Periodic efforts were made to ascertain and utilize these surpluses for the development of Telangana in accord with the regional committee's recommendations. For the period of the third five-year plan, for example, they were estimated to be Rs. 305 million. Telangana legislators suspected this to be an underestimate. An officer deputed by the comptroller and auditor general in 1969, at the request of the state government, calculated the surpluses from November 1956 through March 1968 to be Rs. 382 million. Stating that certain items of expenditure should not be included and suggesting its own methods, the regional committee estimated the surpluses for that period at Rs. 1,071 million. Telangana's élites and politicians alleged that these surpluses were being diverted to the Andhra region, to the detriment of Telangana's development. Finally, a committee appointed by the central government decided on the principles for allocating receipts and expenditure and determined the surplus for the same period to be Rs. 283 million.[55]

Integration of Cadres. Owing to differences not only in the scales of pay, but also in the rules of the Andhra and Hyderabad governments regarding such conditions of service as promotion, increments, probation, seniority, and confirmation, some anomalies disadvantageous to Telangana service arose in certain departments in the preparation of integrated lists of seniority. These disadvantages were proclaimed by the Telangana employees to be deliberate attempts by the Andhra officers to subordinate *mulkis* in the state government services.[56]

Violations of Safeguards. The Telangana employees often alleged that the Public Employment (Requirement as to Residence) Act of 1957 was not being implemented in good faith by the state government. But it should be noted that by and large the residential requirement for appointment to state government posts in the Telangana area was actually applied, with few exceptions. The figures of appointment from March 21, 1959, to the end of September 1968 show that 92, 552 posts which required the residence qualification under the rules of 1959 were filled. Of these 88,164 were filled by persons with the requisite residential qualification, and only 799 by persons without the domicile qualifications, for whom exceptions were made by the government. The remaining 3,589 posts were apparently filled by persons who were not qualified in accordance with the residential qualification and in whose case no exception was made by the state government.[57]

In July 1968 the state government directed that no relaxation should thereafter be made to these rules. Yielding to persistent demands by the Telangana nongazetted officers union, the government further extended the domicile rule to cover appointments to the state electricity board in the Telangana area.

This was the opening of the Pandora's box of regionalism. Considering such cases, the high court of Andhra Pradesh held on January 3, 1969, that autonomous bodies such as the state electricity board did not come under the purview of the domicile rules. Student agitation in Telangana for the strict implementation of the safeguards followed, which nongazetted officers soon joined. Certain factional leaders within the Congress party, opposed to the chief minister, encouraged it. The opposition parties then jumped into the fray. From this point on, the demand for one or two thousand jobs per year per district became transformed into a violent mass struggle for a separate Telangana state.

The chief minister discussed the situation with leaders of various parties and arrived at an accord on January 19, 1969.[58] Following their agreement the state government appealed against the January 3 court judgment.[59] An order was issued under the 1959 employment rules relieving all nonresidents appointed on or after November 1, 1956, of their posts as of February 28. In deference to the wishes of the state government, a bill was passed by parliament in March 1969 extending the operation of the Public Employment Act by five more years, and including a provision bringing into its purview statutory and other corporations financed by the government. By then, however, the situation had undergone a drastic change, due to several related court judgments.

Justice Chinnapa Reddy held, on February 3, 1969, that "requirement as to residence within the state" in article 16(3) could mean only within the state, not in a particular region of the state. Hence, section 3 of the 1957 Public Employment Act and the rules based upon it were void and not enforceable. As the judgment threatened to intensify the agitation in Telangana and thus affect the integrity of the state, the state government immediately filed an appeal. On February 20, 1969, a division bench of the high court set aside the judgment of Chinnapa Reddy and validated the act and the rules. However, six weeks later, in hearing a similar case (*A. V. S. Narasimha Rao v. State of Andhra Pradesh*), the Supreme Court of India declared section 3 of the 1957 act and the rules made under it unconstitutional as they related to Telangana.[60] The decision intensified the agitation.

Central Intervention

Telangana politicians were unanimous in blaming the state government for neglecting the development of Telangana and for failing to utilize the Telangana revenue surpluses set aside under terms of the gentlemen's agreement. They argued that Telangana could not develop so long as it was part of Andhra Pradesh and demanded the creation of a separate Telangana state.

The central government was not inclined to consider the demand, since if the demands for a separate Telangana state were to be conceded on account of its underdevelopment, similar demands from other parts of the country could not easily be rejected. There were backward areas in many states that were as undeveloped as the Telangana region—for example, the Rayalaseema area in Andhra Pradesh itself and the eastern districts of Uttar Pradesh. Further, Vidarbha in Maharashtra had already been pleading for separate statehood. The central government hoped to contain the agitation by trying to remedy regional grievances.

The immediate problem was to see that the safeguards given to Telangana with respect to employment were implemented. For a decade the central government had only cursorily exercised its special responsibility, implicit under article 371, for safeguarding the interests of Telangana; now it became directly concerned. Prime Minster Indira Gandhi herself began to take keen personal interest in these affairs.

In accord with Mrs. Gandhi's statement in parliament on April 11, 1969, a jurists' committee was appointed to enquire into the possibility of providing appropriate constitutional safeguards to encourage public employment of people belonging to the Telangana region.[61] The committee advised that recruitment be decentralized to the regional and district level to enable local people to get jobs. The state government had already, in March 1969, withdrawn certain posts from the purview of the Andhra Pradesh Public Service Commission and entrusted recruitment for these posts to the district collectors. On the suggestion of the jurists' committee,[62] the regional committee order was also amended in March 1970 to include inter alia the following:

1. methods of recruitment and the principles to be followed in making appointments to subordinate services and posts under the state government in the Telangana region (that is, those for which openings are not posted in the official gazette), not including any service of *tahsildars* (i.e., *taluk* administrative officers);

2. provisions securing adequate employment opportunities to the people of the Telangana region in the state government, quasi-government institutions, statutory authorities, and corporate bodies in the Telangana region.

The Mulki Rules Revived

The high court of Andhra Pradesh ruled in 1970[63] that in view of the judgment of the Supreme Court of March 28, 1969, the *mulki* rules repealed by the 1957 Public Employment Act stood revived and continued to be in force as if that act had not been enacted at all. This momentous decision revived the hopes of Telangana employees and strengthened the hand of government in the implementation of safeguards pertaining to services. The chief minister told the state assembly on December 18, 1970, that the government would abide by the judgment and that it was considering proposals for regionalization of the service cadres, as suggested by the jurists' committee.[64]

In the midterm elections to parliament held in March 1971, the Telangana Praja Samiti, which was formed during the agitation and was led by Dr. Chenna Reddy, a former Congress party member, ran on the sole plank of a separate Telangana state. The party won ten of the fourteen seats in Telangana, obtaining forty-eight percent of the votes. The Congress party (Mrs. Gandhi's party) trailed well behind with thirty-seven percent of the votes. As a result of the initiative taken by the central Congress leaders, the Telangana Praja Samiti merged with the Congress party in September 1971, under an agreement that the *mulki* rules would continue in the Telangana region. For the first time, a Telangana Congressman, P.V. Narasimha Rao, became the chief minister in place of Brahmananda Reddy, who resigned.

On the eve of the 1972 elections to the Andhra Pradesh legislative assembly, Indira Gandhi assured the Telangana people that due protection, including a constitutional amendment, would be offered by the government for the continuance of safeguards. But the following day, the full bench of the state high court affirmed that the *mulki* rules had been validly repealed.[65] The government immediately appealed to the Supreme Court. The election manifesto of the Andhra Pradesh Congress Committee promised further steps, "administrative, statutory and otherwise," depending on the final judgment of the Su-

Table 5.8   Employment in the Public and Private Sectors in Andhra Pradesh, March 1972 (Figures in Thousands)

	Central Govt.	State Govt.	Quasi- Govt.	Local Govt.	Private Sector		Total
					Larger Establish- ments	Smaller Estab- lishments	
Andhra Pradesh	152	242	159	203	250	61	1,067
India	2,841	4,282	2,171	1,915	6,036	733	17,978

SOURCE: Government of India, *Statistical Abstract India 1972* (1973), p. 328.

preme Court, to safeguard the interests of the Telangana region in public employment.

The Supreme Court, overriding the high court, decided on October 3, 1972, that the *mulki* rules *were* valid and in force.[66] The implications of the judgment were far-reaching, as the *mulki* rules stipulated that all superior as well as inferior posts could be occupied by *mulkis* only. Thus all government appointments made until then that were in contravention of the *mulki* rules would be null and void, nor could anyone from the Andhra region aspire to any job in the capital of the state since it was located in the Telangana region. There was intense jubilation in Telangana, and extreme discontent in the Andhra region.

The Andhra Grievance: Employment in Hyderabad City

In Andhra Pradesh as in other states, the state government is the largest employer, followed by local governments and quasi-government institutions. The central government employs less than each of these (table 5.8).

The bulk of industrial investment since the formation of the state had been in Hyderabad city. Investment by the central government from 1956 to 1969 amounted to Rs. 844 million in Telangana, most of it in and around the twin cities of Hyderabad and Secunderabad, while investments in the Andhra area totaled only Rs. 417 million. Private sector investments during the second and third plan periods were also largely in Hyderabad city and its surroundings,[67] and after 1969 a number of central government institutions were established there. Thus, compared with other towns in the state, Hyderabad afforded exceptional employment opportunities.

With the change in the language of instruction from English to Telugu, the possibility of getting employment outside the state was almost ruled out for educated people of the Andhra region.[68] Opportunities for employment had already been poor in the state, and the decision of the Supreme Court barred any prospect of government employment in the capital. In view of these factors and the already growing unemployment, intense agitation was begun by

85

students in the Andhra districts for scrapping the *mulki* rules. They were soon supported by the nongazetted (lower) officers.

The Five-Point Program: Mulki Rules Reviewed

The prime minister announced her five-point program on November 27, 1972. According to it, the Public Employment Act was to be extended to include civil assistant surgeons and junior engineers, with the proviso that the safeguards were to be in force only until December 1977 in the twin cities and until December 1980 in the rest of the Telangana region. Regionalization of various service cadres up to the first or second gazetted level was also proposed. A composite police force for the twin cities was contemplated.[69] To give effect to the program, the Mulki Rules Act passed by parliament in December 1972 provided for a number of amendments to the *mulki* rules.[70]

But feeling persisted among Andhras that in view of the Mulki Rules Act they had become second-class citizens in Hyderabad, their own capital. Opposition leaders and leaders of factions within the Congress party opposed to the chief minister, P. V. Narasimha Rao, made use of this opportunity to organize a popular movement in the Andhra districts. The inclusion in the act of junior engineers and assistant civil surgeons, among whom there was large-scale unemployment, inspired gazetted (senior) officers also to join the movement.[71] Lawyers boycotted the courts. The administration ceased to function. Soon the agitation snowballed into a demand for constituting the Andhra districts into a separate state and involved almost all sections of the population. (No active steps were taken, however, to build a coalition with the sections of Telangana which had unsuccessfully agitated in 1969 for a separate Telangana state.) In view of the mounting pressures, president's rule was imposed in January 1973. By May 1973 the agitation had ended.

A new dimension was added to the political crisis by a judgment of the high court on February 16, 1973.[72] The court noted that the definition of *mulki* appearing in *mulki* rules 1(b) and 3 did not apply to all persons born in the former state of Hyderabad, but only to those who had come from outside the Telangana area of the Nizam's dominion, had resided in Hyderabad state for at least fifteen years, and did not intend to return to their previous residence.

Since this new definition disadvantaged most permanent residents in Telangana, parleys soon began between leaders of different political parties in both Andhra and Telangana. A scheme known as the Six-Point Formula, presented by K. C. Pant, minister of state for Home Affairs, to the Congress M.P.'s belonging to both the regions, gained their approval in September 1973. It outlined a strategy for development, a method of recruitment, and a policy for admissions to educational institutions in different regions of the state. It also proposed a machinery for redress of grievances among government employees.

The Constitutional Amendment: The Regionalization of Employment
President's rule was revoked in December 1973. Vengal Rao, who was born in the Andhra region but had been a prominent politician in the adjacent Khamman district of Telangana, became chief minister. The first step in giving effect to the Six-Point Formula was the Constitution (Thirty-Second Amendment) Act passed by parliament; it became operative on May 3, 1974. Under the act the regional committee was abolished, and the *mulki* rules ceased to operate.

A presidential order in June 1974 defined local candidates and local areas in Andhra Pradesh for purposes of admission to educational institutions. This divided the state into three local areas,[73] and specified that eighty-five percent of the "available seats" in every course of study in government educational institutions or universities were to be reserved for local candidates from the area in which the institution was situated.

Parliament enacted the University of Hyderabad Act in early 1974. Under it, admissions to the different faculties of the university would be open to all, but local students would have preferential treatment. Master's-degree-level courses in about a dozen science subjects were started during 1975–76.

By another presidential order the administrative tribunal envisaged under the Six-Point Formula was constituted in May 1975 to deal with grievances with respect to government appointments, seniority, promotion, and other allied matters.

The president issued still another order in October 1975 providing for organization of local cadres and regulation of direct recruitment to public employment. The order established that each part of the state for which a local cadre had been organized with respect to any category of posts was a separate unit for purposes of recruitment, appointment, discharge, seniority, promotion, transfer, and other such matters. The state was divided into seven zones, two in Telangana, one covering the four Rayalaseema districts, and three dividing the remaining eight districts. Posts belonging to each of the fifty specified gazetted categories in each department and zone were organized into separate cadres. Each zone was regarded as a local area for direct recruitment to any nongazetted category of services above that of lower-division clerk. Also included were the categories of *taluk* administrative officers (*tahsildars*) and junior engineers. The districts were local areas for direct recruitment to posts in any local cadre under the state government, and posts in any department in the district equivalent to or lower than the category of lower-division clerk. Of local cadre posts to be filled by direct recruitment at any time, eighty percent of lower-division clerks, seventy percent of other nongazetted categories, and sixty percent of *tahsildars* and junior engineers were reserved for local candidates; sixty percent of the posts of civil assistant surgeons under the state government to be filled by direct recruitment at any time were also reserved for local candidates.

Posts in the secretariat, offices of heads of departments, special offices of establishments, state-level offices or institutions, major development projects, and police officers of Hyderabad city were not covered by the order.

Organization of local cadres and regulation of direct recruitment in this way had the effect of diluting the regional identity of employees from the Andhra and Telangana regions. The application of the principle underlying the *mulki* rules—reserving jobs for "sons of the soil"—to the *zone* and the *district* may prove beneficial to job seekers from backward areas. The main forces creating agitation in the past, students and nongazetted employees, have been appeased and divided, so it may be difficult for politicians to stir up antagonism in the future.

Until its abolition by the Constitution (Thirty-Second Amendment) Act, the regional committee for Telangana, by considering itself a protector of the interests of Telangana people, had in a way preserved the political identity of Telangana. Now it does not exist. To take care of the development needs of the different regions of the state, the government has created planning and development boards for Telangana, Rayalaseema and the Circars. Thus, the political identity of the three historical areas is preserved for purposes of economic development except in matters relating to employment. By separating the issue of employment for local people from the issue of regional development, the central government hopes to dissipate the demands for separation and maintain a single state.

Conclusion

The central feature of the Telangana claim for "safeguards" was the argument that only through such explicit policies could people of the region be assured of government employment in competition with people from more "advanced" regions. An argument once used to support the claims of backward classes, scheduled castes, scheduled tribes, and other minorities was now used on behalf of the majorities.

The claim by the majority community was, in reality, merely the claim of sections of the middle classes: the university students, the lower-level (nongazetted) civil servants, the lawyers and professional people, but these interests succeeded in arousing the emotions of the entire Telangana region by linking their claims to employment with the broader issue of regional underdevelopment. The triumph of the Telangana Praja Samiti, a party committed to the claims of the *mulkis*, in the parliamentary elections of 1971 against the Congress party (headed nationally by the then-popular Prime Minister Indira Gandhi) stands as testimony to the success of the middle class in building a broader constituency to support its demands.

As a consequence of a series of complicated (and at times bizarre) court decisions, the Telangana political leadership concluded that the only way they could be assured of closing public employment in the Telangana region to outsiders was through creating a separate Telangana state. The central government endeavored to find a formula that would keep the state intact, for it feared that the bifurcation of Andhra would stimulate demands for the breakup of other states. The Six-Point Formula, which ended the *mulki* rules for Telangana, created regional development councils for the state, and, most critically, prevented the state from falling apart. It should be noted, however, that while in a technical sense the *mulki* rules were terminated, in fact the principles which underlay them were simply extended to all areas of the state. Henceforth, admission into educational institutions and employment in state and local governments would be under a system of preferences based upon *place of birth*. Where an individual is born or has resided over a fifteen-year period would determine his opportunities for obtaining admission into an educational institution or a position in the state or local government. In short, a policy initially intended to benefit the aspiring middle classes of the Telangana region of the state was extended to the middle classes in each of the regions of the state. The spatial mobility of Andhra's middle classes was slowed, and the policies of localism were institutionalized.

Six
Seeking Ethnic Equality in Assam

Since the middle of the nineteenth century ethnic groups in India's northeastern state of Assam have viewed the state government as an instrument by which to extend, consolidate, or transform their position in the economy and social system of the region. For a large part of the nineteenth and early twentieth centuries it was the Bengalis, particularly Bengali Hindus, who sought to use their dominance within the government administration to consolidate their position in the educational system, in the professions, and within the state administration itself. In the 1930s and '40s it was the Bengali Muslims who won control over the state government, and then attempted to use their position to facilitate further the migration of Bengali Muslims from East Bengal, to strengthen their position in the land system, and to press for the incorporation of Assam into the proposed Muslim majority state of Pakistan. And since 1947 it has been the Assamese, particularly the emerging Assamese Hindu middle class, that has sought to use their control over the state government to assert the paramountcy of Assamese cultural identity and to seek economic and social equality in relation to the Bengali middle class. In these struggles ethnic coalitions have been made and unmade, state and even international boundaries have been moved, and the central government has been called upon by various groups within Assam for either support or protection.

The clash between the Assamese and the Bengalis—sometimes with Bengali Hindus and most recently with Bengali Muslims—has had two overlapping dimensions. One, which Assam shares with Andhra Pradesh and with the city of Bombay, is the familiar phenomenon in which the local middle class competes with migrants for similar jobs in the modern sector and natives and migrants each see themselves as belonging to different ethnic groups. The other dimension, which the Assamese share with some of the tribal people in India, is the fear of a massive migration influx which would overwhelm the local population numerically, politically, and culturally. The former dimension is sufficient to explain the advocacy of preferential policies by the Assamese middle class, but it is the latter development which helps to explain the persistence, intensity, centrality, and extensiveness of popular involvement in Assam's nativist-migrant conflict.

90

The most recent eruption of this conflict was in late 1979 on the eve of India's parliamentary elections. The All-Assam Student Union (AASU), which claims to represent a large section of the state's 1.3 million school and college students, its major literary association, and several regional parties, demanded that the electoral rolls prepared by the election commission be screened to eliminate the names of those who had entered India illegally and who, therefore, were not entitled to vote. The election commission agreed in principle, but a conflict arose over how to decide who was a citizen—whether it was sufficient to scrutinize only new names on the electoral rolls or whether it was necessary to reassess the status of those who had been entered since 1971 or 1967 or even, as the Assamese demanded, 1951. It soon became clear that what was at issue was the status not only of illegal migrants who had crossed the borders from Bangladesh after the Indo-Pakistan war of 1972, but also of Bengalis who had fled East Pakistan after partition in 1947, and who were entitled to citizenship,[1] and even of Bengalis who had migrated to Assam from West Bengal. India being a country in which few people have birth certificates, school certificates, or other documents to prove their citizenship, this scrutiny of electoral rolls created anxieties among all Bengalis in the state. These anxieties were intensified as the movement increasingly took an anti-Bengali turn, and anti-India slogans were raised ("Get out Indian Dogs from Assam," and "Assam for the Assamese").[2]

Faced with a civil disobedience movement that demanded that elections not be held in the state until the electoral rolls were reviewed, the election commission decided not to hold elections in twelve of Assam's fourteen parliamentary constituencies. Assam thereby became the first state in postindependence India which failed to take part in national parliamentary elections.

The conflict widened in 1980 as the Assamese launched a movement to prevent Oil India, Ltd., a public sector corporation in Assam, from transporting oil out of the state. Civil disobedience paralyzed the economy and government of the state, houses were burned, and some Bengalis fled. The central government deployed more units of the central reserve police and the border security forces, and the Congress (I) in West Bengal adopted an economic blockade halting the movement of all goods from West Bengal into Assam. Moreover, the antiforeign movement spilled across the borders of Assam into the nearby states of Tripura and Manipur. In Tripura, indigenous tribals launched violent attacks against Bengali settlers who, by now, outnumber the locals and control the state government. And in neighboring Manipur, Manipuri students attacked Bengalis, Biharis, Punjabis, and especially the numerous and increasingly prosperous Nepali dairy and cattle farmers.[3]

The entire northeast was being ripped apart by the migrant issue, and fundamental questions were being raised about the rights of citizens. "My party demands that each person staying in Assam must have two certificates of citizenship, one for India and the other for Assam," said Girin Barua, president

91

of the Asom Jatiyotabadi Dal (Assam Nationalist Party). When told that dual citizenship was against the constitution, he replied, "Get the Constitution changed then."[4] To the Bengalis, the West Bengali government, and the central government, it appeared as if the Assamese were using the conflict over the electoral rolls as an opportunity to force non-Assamese citizens of India out of the state.

Why had the movement against migrants taken such an extreme form in Assam? The conflict over electoral rolls is simply the latest of many efforts by Assamese political groups and by the Assamese-dominated state government to reduce migration and to improve the occupational position of the Assamese in relation to migrants and their descendants. This chapter takes a retrospective look at a variety of policies adopted by the state government to expand employment and educational opportunities for the Assamese, correspondingly reduce the opportunities for migrants and their descendants, and reduce or halt the flow of migrants from other states of India as well as from neighboring Bangladesh. We shall consider why these policies have had only a limited impact—and on which Assamese—and then explore some of their indirect and unintended effects.

We shall begin by briefly describing the state of Assam, the factors that have changed its demographic composition, and the impact of these demographic forces on the politics of the state. We shall then turn to a description of the preferential policies adopted by the state government, and assess their political as well as economic and demographic consequences.

The Political Setting

Assam, a state in northeastern India with 79,000 square miles and (in 1979) 19.2 million people, is about the size of Austria with two and a half times as many people. In both area and population it is among the smaller Indian states; in population density (245 per square kilometer) it is slightly above the India average, but well below West Bengal (615 per square kilometer) or Bangladesh (608 per square kilometer).

Except for a brief moment in world history during the second world war, when Japanese forces occupied northern Burma and Assam became a supply center for Chinese nationalist forces in southern China, Assam has been a relatively obscure region in southern Asia. Even to most Indians Assam has been comparatively remote, linked to the rest of the subcontinent by a small corridor between Bangladesh and Tibet. Its one major trade connection with the world is its tea, a plentiful crop whose rich color makes it an attractive addition to a variety of blends. When Chinese troops moved from Tibet to the gates of the Assamese town of Tezpur, Prime Minister Nehru in a memorable (but erroneous) statement bade farewell to Assam; to most Indians, few of whom had ever met any Assamese, Assam was nearly as remote as the border regions of Ladakh which also fell under Chinese attack. Even the national anthem, which mentions most of the regions of India, neglects Assam—a sore point, incidentally, to many Assamese.

Though obscure to the world and to most of India, Assam is very much a part of the consciousness of large numbers of people in the neighboring Indian state of West Bengal and the neighboring country of Bangladesh. To many of the 140 million Bengalis, Assam has been a historic frontier region, a place where the landless could seek land and the middle class could find urban employment.

From 1826, when the British dislodged the Burmese invaders who had conquered Assam a few years earlier, to 1874, when it was made a separate province, Assam was part of the presidency of Bengal. During this half-century the British created tea plantations in the hill areas and linked the region by steamship on the Brahmaputra River to the expanding port at Calcutta. Unable to persuade Assamese cultivators, most of whom owned their own land, that they should work as tea pickers in the plantations, the British "imported" a labor force from the tribal region of southern Bihar. This migration was soon followed by an influx of Bengali Muslim cultivators, by educated Bengali Hindus seeking positions in the administrative services and in the professions, and by a variety of other migrant traders, merchants, bankers, and industrialists. In time these migrations changed the ethnic composition of the entire region and resulted in a political system in which questions of ethnicity and migration became central.

Assam was separated from Bengal in 1874 and placed under the administration of a chief commissioner; a decade later the area was given the status of a separate state responsible directly to the viceroy. But its independent status did not last for long. The changes in the political geography of the new state were to play a critical role in the patterns of migration into the entire northeast, and in the kinds of political cleavages which characterized the area.

In 1905 the British partitioned the sprawling, densely populated province of Bengal into a predominantly Bengali Muslim province in the east and a predominantly Bengali Hindu province in the west. Assam was incorporated into the eastern province. The partition of Bengal was deeply resented both by the Bengali Hindus and by the Assamese. In 1912 it was annulled, and Assam was reestablished as a separate chief commissioner's province that included two Bengali districts—a predominantly Hindu district, called Cachar, and a predominantly Muslim district, Sylhet. Assam also included the plains of the Brahmaputra valley, where the Assamese-speaking people were predominant, and the surrounding tribal areas—the Garo, Khasi, and Jaintia hills, the Naga Hills, and the Mizo Hills.

In the latter part of the nineteenth century Bengali Muslim peasants moved into the plains of Assam. But it was not until after 1901 that the major influx took place. By 1911 there were 118,000 migrants, almost all Bengali Muslims, forming twenty percent of the district of Goalpara alone. The 1911 census commissioner, alarmed by the massive influx, wrote that the migration was "likely to alter permanently the whole future of Assam and to destroy more surely than did the Burmese invaders of 1820 the whole structure of Assamese culture and civilization."[5]

Why the massive influx?

Bengal was one of the most densely populated agricultural regions of the subcontinent. A gradual growth in population on this rice and jute-producing delta, and a landlord system that contributed to tenancy and to the fragmentation of landholdings, resulted in the growth in the number of landless laborers and low-income tenants.

In contrast, nearby Assam had a relatively low population density, possibly because of the high mortality rate engendered by rampant malaria and the plague. One district officer, noting that in his district the indigenous population had decreased by thirty percent from 1891 to 1901, wrote that "not a single British district in the whole of the Indian Empire lost so large a proportion of its population as the unfortunate district of Nowgong."[6]

As the public health situation improved in Assam, and the agrarian situation worsened in Bengal, the migration of landless Muslims accelerated. Assam had considerable virgin lands, some in the easily flooded lowlands along the Brahmaputra valley that are similar to the deltaic areas of East Bengal, and also substantial forest tracts that were occupied, often illegally, by land-hungry peasant migrants.

Later on, political factors may have played a role in the migration. With the inclusion of Sylhet and Cachar districts in Assam in the reorganization of 1912, Assam had a large local Bengali Muslim population within its borders. As the Muslim population grew, Muslim political parties increased in political importance. A Muslim League government took power in 1937 and remained in office, except for a one-year interlude, until the close of the second world war. During this period there was an increasing influx of Bengali Muslim migrants into the state, which aroused fears among both Assamese and Bengali Hindus that all of the province might be incorporated into the proposed Muslim state of Pakistan.[7]

Bengali Hindus had been coming into the state ever since Assam had been incorporated into the presidency of Bengal. The British recruited their administrative staff from among the educated Bengali Hindus in the province. Bengali Hindus were among the first to join the administrative services. Later they entered the modern professions. By the beginning of the twentieth century, the doctors, lawyers, teachers, journalists, clerks, and railway and post office officials as well as officers of the state government in Assam were Bengali Hindu migrants.

Bengali, along with English, became the language of the state government. Bengali became the medium of instruction in the primary and secondary schools, and Bengalis became the teachers of the Assamese. Soon the Assamese perceived themselves as having two sets of alien rulers. Assamese nationalists fought back and by the 1880s managed to have Assamese adopted as the medium in the primary schools. As the number of educated Assamese increased in the twentieth century, they turned against the Bengali Hindus, resentful of their domination of the administrative services, fearful of what appeared to be their cultural imperialism, and angry at being treated by them as culturally inferior provincial cousins.

In 1947, when independence was achieved, the political geography of Assam was again changed. The Muslim majority district of Sylhet was transferred to the new country of Pakistan. But even without Sylhet, Assam remained one of the most diverse cultural regions in the Indian subcontinent. It included three groups of native peoples: the Assamese-speaking Hindu population residing primarily in the Brahmaputra valley; the hill tribes (Garo, Khasi, Naga, Mikir, and Mizo); and the indigenous plains tribals known as the Bodo or Kachari.

The migrant communities included tribal laborers from Bihar and Orissa working in the British-owned tea gardens; Bengali Muslims, mainly from East Bengal, who settled primarily on land along the Brahmaputra valley; Bengali Hindus, originally from East Bengal and especially Sylhet district, who settled in the towns throughout the Brahmaputra valley, where they held middle class jobs, and in the predominantly Bengali district of Cachar; the Marwaris, an entrepreneurial community from Rajasthan, who engaged in trade, commerce, and moneylending; Nepalis, who settled in the low-lying hills around the valley tending cattle; Biharis, who worked as seasonal migrants in construction projects and in the towns plying rickshaws; and a small but economically significant number of Punjabis working in the transport industry and in their own businesses.[8]

The Assamese are the largest single ethnic group in the state, 56.7 percent of the population in 1951, 62.4 percent in 1961, and 61 percent in 1971. (The Bengalis were 16.5%, 18.5%, and 19.7%, and the Hindi-speaking population 3.8%, 4.8%, and 5.4%.)[9] The facts of ethnic demography have had an important impact on state politics and policies. Despite the population influx, the proportion of Assamese-speakers increased in every decade from 1911 (when Assamese formed only 21.7% of the population) to 1961 (62.4%), mostly because the border changed, but partly because the tribal laborers from Bihar and Orissa and the Bengali Muslims reported Assamese as their mother tongue to the census enumerators. After independence the Assamese-speaking population was thus in a position to dominate electoral politics. But between 1961 and 1971 the proportion of Assamese declined for the first time, while the proportion of Bengali speakers continued to increase. This demographic shift, though small, was in a direction which aroused the anxieties of many Assamese.

Perhaps the most important demographic factor, however, was the ethnic composition of the urban centers. In 1961 (the last census for which language figures are available for urban areas), 913,000 people lived in the urban areas of the Brahmaputra valley. Of this population, thirty-eight percent was Bengali, thirty-three percent Assamese, and another thirteen percent spoke Hindi. In their own urban centers the Assamese were outnumbered by the Bengalis, while the surrounding countryside was predominantly Assamese. The towns of Assam had become centers of alien life.

How and why had this happened? Historically, the jobs available in the urban areas were less attractive to the Assamese than to migrants from neighboring states. A predominantly agricultural people with relatively few landless laborers and tenant farmers, the Assamese had less economic incentive to seek low-paying urban jobs than the rural people of other states.[10] According to the 1961 census, only 3.8 percent of the rural labor force in Assam were agricultural laborers, as compared with 18.9 percent for India as a whole. Even a decade later, when agricultural labor in India sharply increased to 30 percent, only 10 percent of the rural Assamese labor force were agricultural laborers. In contrast, 40.8 percent of the rural labor force in neighboring Bihar were agricultural laborers in 1971 (24.4% in 1961), and 33.8 percent in rural West Bengal (20.2% in 1961). Furthermore, the skilled positions in urban Assam had been taken by educated workers from urban West Bengal and from other parts of India. A large proportion of the clerical positions, technical staffs, and managerial personnel consisted of migrants, or were native-born descendants of earlier waves of Bengali Hindu migrants.

As the Assamese middle class grew after independence, the major policy goals of the Congress-controlled, Assamese-dominated government were how to expand the employment opportunities for the Assamese in general, and the Assamese middle classes in particular; how to halt (or at least slow) the flow of migrants into Assam's urban centers (and later into the rural areas as well), and, though less explicitly, how to diminish the position of the locally born Bengali Hindu population. The central political problem was how to build a coalition within the Assamese community and between the Assamese and other ethnic groups to make and implement policies in pursuit of these objectives.

Policies

The government of Assam had to deal with three groups of employers whose actions affected the job opportunities for the Assamese, the locally born non-Assamese, and the migrants: (1) the state administration of Assam itself, including the large educational sector; (2) the central government, which not only maintains its own administrative staff within the state, but also runs a number of public sector enterprises, including railroads, an oil refinery, fertilizer plants, coal mines, and banks; and (3) the organized private sector.

Actually, only a small proportion of the entire labor force in the state falls within these three sectors. According to the 1971 census, Assam had a total labor force of 4,240,000.[11] Of these workers, a total of 722,000 (in 1974) were employed in the "organized" sector of the economy.[12] The remainder were in agriculture, household industry, self-employed, or engaged in services and industrial activities involving fewer than ten workers.

In the organized sector, 459,000 worked for private firms, and 263,000 were in the public sector. Most private sector workers (404,000) were in tea plantations; the remainder were largely in veneer, plywood, and match factories, in the repairing and servicing of motor vehicles, and in cotton-spinning and weaving mills. In the public sector 31,000 were in central government services, 114,000 in the state or local government, and 43,000 in the central government railways. Another 75,000 persons were in public sector industries, including electric power, coal mining, oil refining, and banking.

The largest number of people working for state and local government was in education—about 70,000; the medical and health services employed another 11,000. Only 55,000 workers—8.0 percent of the labor force in the organized sector and a mere 1.3 percent of the total labor force in the entire state—were employed in the organized private sector. Nearly five times that number worked for the central government (including the public sector), and one and a half times that number were in educational services.

It is important to note, however, that while government policy was directed at affecting only a small portion of employment in the state, it was this, the organized sector that employed the bulk of the secondary school and college graduates, paid the highest wages, and provided the greatest security of tenure. This was also the sector dominated by the non-Assamese, especially by Bengali Hindus and Hindi speakers. It was, in short, the "modern" sector into which the expanding Assamese middle class aspired to enter.

Three sets of policies were adopted by the state and central governments to influence migration and employment:

1. education policies,
2. employment policies, and
3. migration policies.

Education Policies

In an ethnically divided society, there are invariably struggles over the control of the school system. What is at stake are some of the most central values in a society: social mobility for the young, employment opportunities for graduates as teachers, and, of course, control over an institution that shapes the fundamental cultural symbols of the society. By the middle of the nineteenth century the Bengalis had established for themselves a central place in the educational system. Because Bengali was the medium of instruction, the teachers were Bengali. Local colleges were affiliated with institutions in Calcutta, and Assamese who sought higher education often went to Calcutta for advanced studies—again in Bengali.

The struggle by Assamese nationalists to gain control over the educational system began at the end of the nineteenth century when they established Assamese as the medium of instruction for Assamese children in the primary and secondary schools. After independence the primary and secondary school system was substantially expanded, and whenever possible the government created Assamese language schools even in areas in which Bengali Muslims or tea plantation migrant laborers were numerous. Under central government law, state governments were required to provide schools in the mother tongue if requested by parents. In Assam, however, Bengali Muslims and migrant tribals were generally provided with Assamese schools. Bengali Hindus continued to insist that their schools be in Bengali. The Bengalis also opposed efforts to declare Assamese the exclusive official language of the state, a move they interpreted as a step by the Assamese to undermine the position of the Bengali schools whose graduates might find themselves handicapped when they sought jobs in the state government.

Throughout the 1960s there were bitter clashes over the question of language in the schools and the status of Assamese as the official language of the state. Perhaps the bitterest and most violent conflict took place in 1972 over whether Bengali could be used for examinations at Gauhati University—a decision that had obvious implications for primary and secondary school language policies. The academic council of Gauhati University, whose jurisdiction extended to colleges in the predominantly Bengali Cachar district as well as throughout the Brahmaputra valley, ruled that Assamese would be the exclusive medium of instruction in the colleges and university, but that students could retain the option of answering examination questions in Bengali. Demonstrations by the student union, teachers at Gauhati University, and the Assam Sahitya Sabha, the state's paramount literary association, led the council to reverse its decision on the question of a Bengali option. There was then an uproar in Cachar district where one of the colleges filed a petition in the Supreme Court arguing that the university's decision to restrict the medium of instruction to Assamese was a violation of a constitutional provision which assured protection for linguistic minorities. Large-scale arson and looting took place in several towns in the valley, and as the violence spread the central government called in the military to reestablish order. The chief minister announced that he would stand by the final decision of the academic council, and that he would not carry out a compromise proposal by the state assembly to create a separate Bengali university for Cachar district. While the assembly's compromise was interpreted by Assamese militants as an unacceptable step toward a multilingual state, the new announcement of the chief minister was greeted by the Bengali Hindus as a step toward forced Assamization. One Bengali letter writer to a Calcutta newspaper expressed his fear that "the recurring disturbances are aimed not at usurping the Bengali language but at driving out the entire Bengali population from Assam."[13]

The objectives of the policy itself thus became an issue. Some saw the Assamese as guided by a cultural nationalism, concerned with assuring that their own language, and hence they themselves, would be in a politically and culturally dominant role. Others saw the policy as directed at increasing the need for Assamese teachers in the colleges and secondary schools. And finally, some saw the policy as intended to "drive out" Bengalis or at least discourage potential Bengali migrants from entering the state. Most likely, among Assamese supporters of the chief minister there were individuals who held each of these views.

While data on the ethnic composition of schoolteachers and college faculty in Assam are not available—indeed, it is striking how scarce hard data are on the relationship between ethnicity and education, employment, or income in a state whose government is so explicitly concerned with improving the position of one ethnic community—it is generally agreed that there has been a substantial increase in the number and proportion of Assamese in the state's educational system at all levels.

Employment Policies

The pressure for a policy of giving preferences to local people both in public and in private employment had been mounting for many years, but it became more acute in the 1960s at a time of growing educated unemployment. In 1959 the Employment Exchanges (Compulsory Notification as to Vacancies) Act was passed by the national parliament requiring that all employers, both public and private, were required to inform local employment exchanges of newly available jobs. Employers were not, however, required to hire candidates submitted by the exchanges.

Two bodies pressed for a more active "hire-local" policy: the centrally appointed National Labour Commission, and the National Integration Council, which consists of state chief ministers and high officials of the central government.

The National Labour Commission recommended that both central and state governments actively pursue a policy of giving preferences to local people in their own employment and that they use their influence to urge private employers to do likewise.[14] The chairman of the National Labour Commission noted that the problem was less one of objectives than of implementation. He reported that the commission had received many complaints that instructions issued earlier by the central government to public sector undertakings to give preferences to local people were not properly observed. "In one public sector undertaking," he said, "not even a car driver was recruited locally." The tendency, he continued, "was that almost all the employees in a public sector undertaking were from the same region to which the top officials of the undertaking belonged."

99

The National Integration Council similarly recommended that the public sector give preferences to local people in order to "remove the discontent in the States arising from the inadequate share of the local people in employment opportunities in the public and private sectors."[15]

In August 1968, the deputy minister of the Ministry of Labour and Employment announced that "the public sector undertakings have been asked to fill vacancies carrying a monthly salary of less than Rs. 500 through the local employment exchanges. The recruitment to higher posts has, however, to be made on an all-India basis in order to attract the right type of talent. Local people, possessing the required qualifications will, of course, be eligible and shall be considered for all such posts."

The government further explained that gazetted posts within the government—the higher-salaried, more senior positions in the administrative services—would continue to be filled through the Union Public Service Commission, but that recruitment for the lesser, nongazetted positions would be through the local employment exchanges. The Labour Ministry also announced that the government had asked the All-India Organization of Employers to use their good offices to ensure that their constituents would implement the recommendations of the National Integration Council concerning the employment of local persons. State labor ministers were also instructed to persuade private sector employers to take similar actions.

One labor minister replied that in his state the private employers seldom made use of the employment exchange machinery, and he raised the issue of whether more pressure could not be put on private employers to hire locally through the exchanges. Some raised the question of whether the act could be amended so that employment through the exchanges would be compulsory.[16]

The central government was unwilling to amend the legislation. The National Labour Commission, which considered the proposal, expressed a reluctance to give up the notion that a citizen of India should be able to secure employment in any part of the country, even as it pressed employers to give preferences to local people. Article 16 of the Indian constitution provides that there shall be equality of opportunity for all citizens in matters relating to employment, and that no citizen shall on grounds only of religion, race, caste, sex, descent, *place of birth,* residence, or any of them be ineligible for or discriminated against in respect of any employment.

The commission noted too that although ordinarily industry preferred to employ local people, "certain regional groups have traditionally specialized in particular jobs." Dock workers in Bombay, for example, tend to be Telugus, and construction workers are often from Rajasthan. The commission reported that "because some groups have been identified as suited to particular types of work, employers have shown preference for them" and that, in any case, there were advantages in having a homogeneous labor force. While the commission concluded that there was a need nonetheless to shift employment to local people, they were evidently reluctant to press for a policy that would break up these traditional employment patterns.

The commission recommended that in the case of unskilled and semiskilled workers, clerks, and other nontechnical staff, preferences should be given to local people, but that as the skill requirements increased, recruits should be sought from a larger area than covered by a local employment exchange. Hence, middle-level technical and nontechnical posts (known as Class I junior scale in the central government) should be recruited on an all-India basis, even by the private sector. The same considerations seemed to the commission to be relevant for higher nontechnical posts (e.g., top general management, officials in finance, accounts, sales, purchase, personnel management) and for the higher technical posts where "the best qualified persons will have to be recruited, either by advertisement on an all-India basis or by personal contact."[17]

Finally, the commission members evidently recognized that whatever employment procedures were established for the private sector—such as the compulsory use of employment exchanges—would have to be applied to the public sector as well, and that such a change in policy was likely to be opposed by the nationally minded Union Public Service Commission.

Alternatively, the commission recommended that a variety of new employment procedures be adopted both by public and private sector firms to increase the possibility that qualified local persons would be given preference over equally qualified persons from other areas. It was proposed that each firm establish a special recruitment committee, with one member a nominee from the state government, and that there be regular reporting procedures by the firm to the state government.

In any case, government policy calling for the employment of local people in both private and public sector jobs provided no sanctions. There were no penalties against employers who failed to notify employment exchanges of vacancies, and there was no requirement that anyone had to hire through the exchanges for any level of job. Moreover, the directives of the central government were not always explicit about whether locality referred to city, district, or state, or whether "local" meant place of birth, length of residence, or ethnic origin. To the extent that the central government was explicit, however, "local" meant birthplace and residence, never ethnic origin, a definition at variance with the thinking of most state political leaders.

Nonetheless, it would be a mistake to conclude that the vagueness of the notion "local" and the absence of legal penalties indicate that the policies discussed here served only the symbolic purpose of assuaging the demands of local people for more employment. As far as the government of Assam was concerned, it was quite clear what was meant by "local," nor was the state government without any powers to enforce its policy objectives.

The explicit policy of both the central and the state governments was to slow the pace of migration into a state by giving preferential employment to local people. For the government of Assam there was another objective: to increase the ratio of employment between Assamese and local Bengalis. While none of the legislation or directives to employers explicitly distinguished between Assamese and locally born but ethnically non-Assamese, the government of Assam clearly did not intend to provide job preferences for Bengalis born in Assam. The actual intent of the policy was set forth by the employment review committee appointed by the Assamese state legislature to review the status of Assamese employment in the state: "In the absence of any clear-cut definition of the term 'local people,' the Committee has had to base its analysis on place of birth in Assam as being the yardstick of local people. This yardstick is palpably inadequate and misleading and a clear understanding should be there in government and all others concerned in the matter as to what is meant by the term 'local people'."[18] But the committee was evidently legally restrained from providing its own "clear-cut definition"of the term "local people."

There are many ways in which a determined state government can press employers—particularly in the private sector—to implement such a policy. Private firms need the support of the state government in their dealings with central government ministries over licenses for imports, exports, the purchase of rationed raw materials, and so on. There are also innumerable ways in which the state government can harass uncooperative employers, involving the enforcement of labor laws, the factory acts, and taxes. Finally, there is always the threat that young street gangs will burn, loot, and vandalize shops, warehouses, and factories owned by alien entrepreneurs who do not pay sufficient attention to local demands over hiring.

Migration Policies

An act of the Indian parliament passed in 1950 entitled the Immigrants (Expulsion from Assam) Act to remove "infiltrators" who had entered the country illegally after 1949, and a bill passed by the Assam legislature shortly after independence declaring squatter settlements illegal, were both important instruments for controlling the Bengali Muslim population. Bengali Muslims were fearful that these two acts might be used to force earlier migrants (many of whom held land illegally, and few of whom could prove that they had migrated before 1949) to leave the country. It is not surprising, therefore, that Bengali Muslims declared their mother tongue was Assamese,[19] accepted the establishment of primary and secondary schools in Assamese for their children, supported the government against the Bengali Hindus on the issue of an official language for the state and the university, and cast their votes for the Congress party.

In neighboring Tripura, a state dominated both politically and demographically by Bengali Hindus, the Immigration Act was enforced, resulting in a substantial return migration of Bengali Muslims to East Pakistan between 1961 and 1971, as reflected in an absolute decline in the Muslim population from 230,000 in 1961 to 103,000 in 1971. But in Assam, where the Bengali Muslims proved to be politically supportive of the Assamese Hindus, the Muslim population continued to grow between 1961 and 1971 more or less at the national rate. In contrast, the earlier 1961 census indicated that the Muslim population in Assam had increased by a quarter of a million more than could be accounted for through either natural population increase or migration of Muslims from other states. This "surplus" may be taken to reflect illegal migration from East Pakistan.

There was a very substantial influx of Bengalis, both Muslims and Hindus, into Assam after the civil war broke out between the Pakistanis and the Bangladeshis in March 1971. The overwhelming majority of the refugees reportedly returned after Bangladesh became an independent country, but some illegally remained. How many, and with what impact on the size of the electorate, were the issues.

From 1971 to 1977 the electorate for all of India increased by 17 percent; for Assam the increase was slightly greater, 18.4 percent. From 1977 to 1980 the electorate for India increased 10 percent, but the voters list increased by 15 percent in Assam, despite the exclusion according to newspaper reports of 5 to 6 percent of the voters on suspicion of their being aliens. In the two constituencies in which elections were held in 1980—Karimganj and Silchar—the electorate had increased by 20 percent over 1977, double the all-India figure. These increases gave credence to the assertion by Assamese that there was a substantial illegal migrant population in the state—not so many perhaps as some of the Assamese claimed, but enough to generate Assamese anxieties that they could be politically if not demographically overwhelmed.

Policy Effects

A central objective of government policies in education, employment, and migration was to increase the share of employment of the local Assamese-speaking population in the "modern" sectors of the economy, including administration. In assessing how effective these policies have been, we must distinguish between the outcomes that were sought, direct, and visible, and those that were unintended, often indirect, and even invisible to the policymaker and to the public. The former, to which we turn first, can be measured by changes in the composition of the labor force, while the latter require a broader look at a number of economic, social, and political changes in the region.

Direct, Intended, and Visible Effects

In 1968 the government of Assam established an employment review committee to conduct a survey of employment and report their findings to the Assam Legislative Assembly.[20] Over a period of forty-one months, from May 1969

103

to December 1972, the committee studied twenty-eight firms, both public and private, located in the Brahmaputra valley. A questionnaire was completed by each of these firms providing data on its labor force—their place of birth, mother tongue, occupation categories, wages, duration of service, and educational levels. Some of the data proved to be unusable for our purposes, partly because each company devised its own format on some categories, the standard job classification schema was not followed, and information on procedures for recruitment was only sporadically collected. Within these limitations, however, the survey provides us with an unusually rich source of information concerning the relationship between ethnicity and employment in one region of India, and makes it possible to examine how this relationship has been changing.

In one sense it may be premature to look at the impact of government policy on employment, for the central government did not issue detailed directives until 1968, and the survey was conducted within only a year or two after the policy was formally put into effect. However, the government of Assam has been pressing firms to give preferences to local people at least since the early 1960s. Moreover, labor turnover for many of the low-paying manual occupations is quite high, so that changes in the ethnic composition of the labor force are possible within a brief time period. One can, therefore, discern some trends by examining recent recruitment.

These twenty-eight firms employed 29,537 persons out of a total labor force in the organized sector of 722,000. Excluded from this latter figure are those employed in agriculture, the self-employed, all who worked in establishments in the private sector employing less than ten workers, and members of the defense forces.

The firms surveyed included banks, trading companies, transportation, extractive and manufacturing industries, and a research laboratory. Eighteen of the firms were privately owned; several were partially owned by the government of Assam; and ten were wholly in the public sector. Ten of the firms operated exclusively in Assam (e.g., Sarda Plywood Factory, Woodcraft Plywood Factory, Assam Oil Company, Assam Railways and Trading Company, Everest Cycles), while eighteen were branches or divisions of firms outside Assam (e.g., the banks, Indian Airlines, Fertilizer Corporation, Food Corporation, India Carbon, Indian Refineries, Oil India, Oil and Natural Gas Commission, Regional Research Laboratory). All were among the largest firms in Assam, all were highly visible, and most had a substantial white collar labor force.

Not included in the survey were tea plantations, central, state, and local government services, and education, which together employed nearly three-quarters of the labor force in the organized sector. The survey, therefore, really represents only the industrial sector in which about 183,000 persons were employed.

Assamese and Non-Assamese Employment. Approximately one-half of the employees in the survey (14,367 or 49%) were born in Assam. Nearly three-quarters of these (10,469 or 73%) reported Assamese as their mother tongue. In other words, slightly more than a third of the labor force in the survey (35%) were Assamese "sons of the soil."

The Bengalis constituted the second-largest ethnic group. Of all employees, 23 percent (6,713) were Bengali, with slightly less than half of these (46%) born in Assam. No other major linguistic minority had such a large proportion of its members born in the state.

Hindi speakers were a close third, with 21 percent (6,183) of all employees. But most of these (94%) were born outside the state. The remaining 21 percent of the labor force whose mother tongue was neither Assamese, Bengali, nor Hindi were almost entirely migrants. Of these, 43 percent spoke Nepali, 31 percent Telugu, 8 percent Punjabi, and 6 percent Malayam. Of this group, 93 percent came from outside the state.

It should be noted that the indigenous tribal population, though constituting six percent of the total population of the state, accounted for less than one percent of the employees in the firms surveyed.

Were there a typical firm that perfectly reflected the ethnic distribution of the labor force, it would look like this. For each one hundred workers, forty-nine would be born in Assam: thirty-five Assamese, eleven Bengalis, one Hindi speaker, one local tribal, one speaker of another regional language. Fifty-one would be migrants: twelve Bengalis, twenty Hindi speakers, eight Nepalis, six Telugu speakers, one Punjabi, one Malayalee, and three speakers of other regional languages.

These figures only partially reflect the ethnic distribution in urban areas. As noted earlier, in the Brahmaputra valley (where all the firms surveyed were located), the Assamese constituted 33 percent of the urban population, Bengalis 38 percent, and Hindi speakers 13 percent, while 16 percent spoke other languages. The Hindi speakers thus held a disproportionate share of jobs in industry, as did speakers of other minority languages. But it should be noted that these groups are primarily migrants, and that therefore a larger proportion of them are members of the labor force than of the locally born Bengalis and Assamese.[21] The "underrepresentation" of the Bengalis probably reflects the fact that many Bengalis work in government services, in the professions, or in smaller firms, and were not included in this survey. Nonetheless, it is interesting to note that the Assamese in the urban areas were proportionately represented in industrial employment.

Who Employs the Assamese? What kinds of jobs do the Assamese get? How does the pattern of employment for Assamese differ from that of the non-Assamese? And what kinds of firms hire few Assamese?

The public sector firms, with the notable exception of the banks (which were nationalized in 1969), tended to hire Assamese to a greater extent than did the private firms. The seven large public sector firms in the survey, employing nearly 12,000 persons, were 51 percent Assamese, 15 percent Bengali, and 17 percent Hindi. Of the 15,000 persons employed by the sixteen private firms, only 23 percent were Assamese, 23 percent were Bengali, and the largest share, 27 percent, were Hindi. Five banks, employing about 2,500 persons, were predominantly Bengali, with the Assamese forming about a fourth of the labor force. In short, public sector firms, banks excepted, hired Assamese at more than twice the rate of privately owned firms (table 6.1).

Two factors, surprisingly, seemed not to be significant determinants of the ethnicity of the labor force: the size of the firm and the location of its head office. There was a slightly higher proportion of migrants employed in the smaller firms than in the larger ones, but the differences were not great. There is no reason to believe, therefore, that larger firms are more easily affected by government pressures to hire Assamese. And when the head office was located outside of Assam, there was also no tendency for firms to hire more migrants, largely because most recruitment takes place locally.

To assess the reason for the differences between the public and private sector recruitment, let us take a look at the recruitment procedures and at the occupational characteristics of the firms that had a high proportion of Assamese and the firms that had a high proportion of migrants or local non-Assamese.

There were fifteen firms whose labor force was less than one-third Assamese.[22] One, Indian Airlines, was owned by the government, two were publicly owned banks, and the remainder were private, primarily low-technology industrial firms: five plywood and match factories, three textile mills, one bicycle factory, one small steel-processing factory, one carbon plant, one oil refinery, one railway shipper. A large part of the labor force in these factories were low-paid, unskilled, or semiskilled workers.

Keeping in mind the characteristics of the labor force of these firms, let us now examine their recruitment procedures. A number once used labor contractors to import unskilled laborers from other states. Even when labor contractors were no longer used, laborers were often recruited from among the friends and relatives of those who already worked in the factory. In either

Table 6.1 Mother Tongue of Employees in 28 Firms in Assam

Mother Tongue	Public Sector excl. Banks	Private Sector	Banks	Total
Assamese	6,073 (51.4%)	3,555 (23.3%)	845 (34.1%)	10,473 (35.4%)
Bengali	1,799 (15.2%)	3,548 (23.3%)	1,366 (55.1%)	6,713 (22.7%)
Hindi	1,998 (16.9%)	4,084 (26.8%)	101 (4.1%)	6,183 (21.0%)
Other	1,939 (16.5%)	4,062 (26.6%)	167 (6.7%)	6,168 (20.9%)
Total	11,809 (100.0%)	15,249 (100.0%)	2,479 (100.0%)	29,537 (100.0%)

NOTE: Table refers to mother tongue of employees, *not* to migrant status (place of birth) as in some later tables. Many Bengali speakers, for instance, are not migrants.

Table 6.2   Occupations of Employees in Assam by Place of Birth

Occupation	Assam-Born	Born outside Assam	Total
Managerial	652 (39.0%)	1,021 (61.0%)	1,673 (100.0%)
Clerical/Supervisory/Technical	2,810 (59.4%)	1,916 (40.6%)	4,726 (100.0%)
Total White Collar	3,462 (54.1%)	2,937 (45.9%)	6,399 (100.0%)
Skilled	5,750 (57.4%)	4,261 (42.6%)	10,011 (100.0%)
Unskilled	5,153 (39.3%)	7,971 (60.7%)	13,124 (100.0%)
Total Manual	10,903 (47.1%)	12,232 (52.9%)	23,135 (100.0%)
Total	14,365 (48.6%)	15,169 (51.4%)	29,534 (100.0%)

event the results were a well-established chain migration to Assam from the Hindi-speaking areas, particularly from nearby Bihar.

Some firms hired "at the gate." As labor was needed each day, especially when there was considerable absenteeism of migrant workers who had returned home, employers hired from among those who appeared at the gate in the morning. Wages for such workers are initially very low—often as little as Rs. 1.50 per day. Those who remain for three months or longer are then given higher wages. Since the initial wages, and even the wages after three or six months, are often below what Assamese earn in the countryside (but higher than agricultural laborers can earn in Bihar or U.P. when there is no employment at all), few Assamese seek such jobs.

Migrants held jobs at both ends of the occupational spectrum. In the twenty-eight firms surveyed, 79 percent of the jobs were manual, compared with 21 percent white collar. The majority of the manual jobs (53%) were held by migrants. In the white collar positions, only 39 percent of the managerial positions were held by persons born in Assam, and 59 percent of the subordinate clerical or technical positions (table 6.2). But a large proportion of these jobs were held by locally born Bengalis, not Assamese. Unfortunately, data on mother tongue were available for only eight of the twenty-eight firms. Among the *locally born,* in these eight firms, 44 percent of the managers, 48 percent of the clerical and technical workers, 59 percent of the skilled workers, and 44 percent of the unskilled workers were Assamese speakers. In short, even among the locally born, less than half were Assamese speakers (table 6.3).

For the higher-status managerial jobs, therefore, the Assamese compete primarily against migrants; for the clerical and technical positions, the Assamese lose out to locally born Bengalis and then secondarily to migrants; and in the low-skilled positions, the Assamese compete—to the extent that they are interested in these jobs—against migrants.

In what respect do these patterns differ in firms that hire a larger proportion of Assamese? We have already noted that public sector firms tend to hire few migrants and more Assamese than private firms: 51 percent of the workers in seven public sector firms were Assamese, as against only 23 percent in the

Table 6.3   Mother Tongue of Nonmigrant Employees in 8 Firms in Assam

Occupation	Assamese	Non-Assamese	Total
Managerial	80 (44.0%)	102 (56.0%)	182 (100.0%)
Clerical/supervisory/technical	653 (48.1%)	704 (51.9%)	1,357 (100.0%)
Total White Collar	733 (47.6%)	806 (52.4%)	1,539 (100.0%)
Skilled	322 (58.6%)	227 (41.4%)	549 (100.0%)
Unskilled	315 (43.6%)	407 (56.4%)	722 (100.0%)
Total Manual	637 (50.1%)	634 (49.9%)	1,271 (100.0%)
Total	1,370 (48.8%)	1,440 (51.2%)	2,810 (100.0%)

NOTE: 8 firms are Assam Hardboards; Assam Railroads and Trading Co., India Airlines; National Grindlays Bank; Punjab National Bank; State Bank of India; United Bank of India; United Commercial Bank. Note the high proportion of banks—this may bias the sample because the banks have a reputation for employing nonmigrant Bengalis.

sixteen private firms in the survey (see table 6.1). But the differences are not in the categories of managerial or clerical personnel. In these categories, in fact, public sector firms hired proportionately more migrants than did private firms: 69 percent of the managers and 53 percent of the clerical staff in the public firms were migrants, compared with 53 percent and 45 percent, respectively, in private firms (tables 6.4 and 6.5). In the public firms, senior jobs are advertised nationally and job interviews are ordinarily held outside of Assam. Many of the senior positions are held by men who have been transferred from other parts of the country by the same firm.

It is at the level of the employment of manual workers that local people do substantially better in the public sector firms. Migrants made up only 36 percent of the manual labor force in the public sector as against 67 percent in the private sector.[23]

Several of the public sector firms had made a special effort to seek locally qualified personnel for jobs in the lower clerical positions. One company, for

Table 6.4   Employees in Public Sector Firms in Assam by Occupation and Place of Birth

Occupation	Assam-Born	Born outside Assam	Total
Managerial	266 (31.1%)	590 (68.9%)	856 (100.0%)
Clerical/supervisory/technical	563 (46.8%)	640 (53.2%)	1,203 (100.0%)
Total White Collar	829 (40.3%)	1,230 (59.7%)	2,059 (100.0%)
Skilled	3,801 (65.9%)	1,966 (34.1%)	5,767 (100.0%)
Unskilled	2,420 (60.8%)	1,558 (39.2%)	3,978 (100.0%)
Total Manual	6,221 (63.8%)	3,524 (36.2%)	9,745 (100.0%)
Total	7,050 (59.7%)	4,754 (40.3%)	11,804 (100.0%)

NOTE: Banks are excluded here and in all subsequent tables on public sector employment.

Table 6.5   Employees in Private Sector Firms in Assam by Occupation and Place of Birth

Occupation	Assam-Born	Born outside Assam	Total
Managerial	216 (47.0%)	244 (53.0%)	460 (100.0%)
Clerical/supervisory/technical	1,128 (54.6%)	939 (45.4%)	2,067 (100.0%)
Total White Collar	1,344 (53.2%)	1,183 (46.8%)	2,527 (100.0%)
Skilled	1,508 (42.1%)	2,073 (57.9%)	3,581 (100.0%)
Unskilled	2,733 (29.9%)	6,413 (70.1%)	9,146 (100.0%)
Total Manual	4,241 (33.3%)	8,486 (66.7%)	12,727 (100.0%)
Total	5,585 (36.6%)	9,669 (63.4%)	15,254 (100.0%)

example, had a selection committee with a liaison officer from the government of Assam, seeking local people for such positions. At the more senior administrative and technical levels, the public sector firms all recruited nationally; that is, they hired personnel through national advertising and through the Union Public Service Commission, with interviews in Delhi, Calcutta, and Madras and almost never in Gauhati.

In considering why public sector firms have been more successful in hiring local people for the lower-paid, less-skilled jobs than have the private firms, a number of differences should be kept in mind: wages are generally higher in the public sector; there is no practice of initial low-wage apprenticeships; there is no daily wage labor recruitment at the gate; conditions of work are generally preferable; a higher proportion of the manual work force is engaged in jobs requiring some skills; and there is more security and less turnover. These factors may explain why Assamese are more likely to seek recruitment in the public than private sector firms.

Changing Patterns of Employment. What changes have taken place in the pattern of employment for various types of jobs, and to what extent can these changes be attributed to government policy?

There have been only modest increases in employment in the organized sector in Assam in recent years. The industrial slowdown that has affected the entire country since the late sixties has affected Assam as well. Private sector employment actually declined slightly between 1964 and 1969. Much of the new employment, especially in the private sector, represents replacements rather than expansion. There has been some increase in employment by the banks since they were nationalized, and some of the public sector firms are themselves relatively new and have recruited their labor force since 1960. It is interesting to note that the older firms (pre-1947) have a higher proportion of both unskilled (70%) and skilled (55%) workers who are migrants as compared with firms started in 1960 and after (46% unskilled and 39% skilled; see table 6.6).

Table 6.6 Employees in Assam by Occupation, Migrant Status, and Founding Date of Firm

Occupation	Pre-1947			1947–1959			Post-1959		
	Total Employees	Migrant Employees	% Migrants	Total Employees	Migrant Employees	% Migrants	Total Employees	Migrant Employees	% Migrants
Managerial	445	230	51.7	330	176	53.3	898	615	68.5
Clerical	1,736	653	37.6	1,523	471	30.9	1,467	792	54.0
Total White Collar	2,181	883	40.5	1,853	647	34.9	2,365	1,407	59.5
Skilled	2,146	1,175	54.8	754	301	39.9	7,111	2,785	39.2
Unskilled	6,995	4,915	70.3	1,242	816	65.7	4,887	2,240	45.8
Total Manual	9,141	6,090	66.6	1,996	1,117	56.0	11,998	5,025	41.9
Total	11,322	6,973	61.6	3,849	1,764	45.8	14,363	6,432	44.8

Comparisons of place of birth of employees recruited within the last four years of the survey compared with the remainder of the labor force reveal a number of trends:

1. There has been an overall decline in the proportion of migrant employment.

2. The decline has been primarily in manual jobs. Migrants make up 55 percent of recently employed unskilled workers as compared with 67 percent for those with more than four years of service (tables 6.7 and 6.8).

3. The proportion of migrants among white collar employees has not significantly changed, although there has been an increase in the proportion of migrants holding managerial positions.

4. The patterns are somewhat different between the public and the private sector firms. In the public sector there has actually been an increase in the employment of migrants for white collar positions, both managerial and clerical (75 percent and 65 percent, respectively, among recent appointments, as compared with 49 percent and 34 percent for those with four or more years of service; see tables 6.9 and 6.10). In contrast, in the private sector there has been an increase in the employment of local people for managerial positions, but not for clerical positions (tables 6.11 and 6.12). Among manual workers, there has been relatively little change in the public sector where local people have always been more numerous, but in the private sector 40 percent of the recently employed manual workers are locals, as against 29 percent for those employed for four or more years.

110

Table 6.7 Occupations of Recent Employees in Assam by Place of Birth

Occupation	Assam-Born	Born outside Assam	Total
Managerial	414 (35.6%)	750 (64.4%)	1,164 (100.0%)
Clerical/supervisory/technical	1,263 (59.2%)	872 (40.8%)	2,135 (100.0%)
Total White Collar	1,677 (50.8%)	1,622 (49.2%)	3,299 (100.0%)
Skilled	3,446 (61.5%)	2,156 (38.5%)	5,602 (100.0%)
Unskilled	3,039 (45.1%)	3,695 (54.9%)	6,734 (100.0%)
Total Manual	6,485 (52.6%)	5,851 (47.4%)	12,336 (100.0%)
Total	8,162 (52.2%)	7,473 (47.8%)	15,635 (100.0%)

NOTE: Recently employed refers to employees with 0–4 years length of service, save in the cases of Oil and Natural Gas Commission (0–5 years); Sarda Plywood Factory (0–3 years); Woodcraft-Mariani (–); Punjab National Bank (0–2 years).

Table 6.8 Occupations of Employees in Assam with More than 4 Years Service by Place of Birth

Occupation	Assam-Born	Born outside Assam	Total
Managerial	238 (46.7%)	271 (53.3%)	509 (100.0%)
Clerical/supervisory/technical	1,547 (59.7%)	1,044 (40.3%)	2,591 (100.0%)
Total White Collar	1,785 (57.6%)	1,315 (42.4%)	3,100 (100.0%)
Skilled	2,304 (52.3%)	2,105 (47.7%)	4,409 (100.0%)
Unskilled	2,114 (33.1%)	4,276 (66.9%)	6,390 (100.0%)
Total Manual	4,418 (40.9%)	6,381 (59.1%)	10,799 (100.0%)
Total	6,203 (44.6%)	7,696 (55.4%)	13,899 (100.0%)

NOTE: For cases listed in previous table, length of service is above the limits indicated.

Table 6.9 Recent Employees in Public Sector Firms in Assam by Occupation and Place of Birth

Occupation	Assam-Born	Born outside Assam	Total
Managerial	161 (24.7%)	491 (75.3%)	652 (100.0%)
Clerical/supervisory/technical	254 (34.6%)	479 (65.4%)	733 (100.0%)
Total White Collar	415 (30.0%)	970 (70.0%)	1,385 (100.0%)
Skilled	2,502 (68.4%)	1,155 (31.6%)	3,657 (100.0%)
Unskilled	1,620 (54.7%)	1,339 (45.3%)	2,959 (100.0%)
Total Manual	4,122 (62.3%)	2,494 (37.7%)	6,616 (100.0%)
Total	4,537 (56.7%)	3,464 (43.3%)	8,001 (100.0%)

111

Table 6.10   Employees in Public Sector Firms in Assam with More than 4 Years of Service by Occupation and Place of Birth

Occupation	Assam-Born	Born outside Assam	Total
Managerial	105 (51.5%)	99 (48.5%)	204 (100.0%)
Clerical/supervisory/technical	309 (65.7%)	161 (34.3%)	470 (100.0%)
Total White Collar	414 (61.4%)	260 (38.6%)	674 (100.0%)
Skilled	1,299 (61.6%)	811 (38.4%)	2,110 (100.0%)
Unskilled	800 (78.5%)	219 (21.5%)	1,019 (100.0%)
Total Manual	2,099 (67.1%)	1,030 (32.9%)	3,129 (100.0%)
Total	2,413 (77.1%)	1,290 (22.9%)	3,703 (100.0%)

Table 6.11   Recent Employees in Private Sector Firms in Assam by Occupation and Place of Birth

Occupation	Assam-Born	Born outside Assam	Total
Managerial	143 (51.8%)	133 (48.2%)	276 (100.0%)
Clerical/supervisory/technical	305 (56.9%)	231 (43.1%)	536 (100.0%)
Total White Collar	448 (55.2%)	364 (44.8%)	812 (100.0%)
Skilled	680 (42.3%)	928 (57.7%)	1,608 (100.0%)
Unskilled	1,481 (38.6%)	2,356 (61.4%)	3,837 (100.0%)
Total Manual	2,161 (39.7%)	3,284 (60.3%)	5,445 (100.0%)
Total	2,609 (41.7%)	3,648 (58.3%)	6,257 (100.0%)

Table 6.12   Employees in Private Sector Firms in Assam with More than 4 Years of Service by Occupation and Place of Birth

Occupation	Assam-Born	Born outside Assam	Total
Managerial	73 (39.7%)	111 (60.3%)	184 (100.0%)
Clerical/supervisory/technical	823 (53.8%)	708 (46.2%)	1,531 (100.0%)
Total White Collar	896 (52.2%)	819 (47.8%)	1,715 (100.0%)
Skilled	828 (42.0%)	1,145 (58.0%)	1,973 (100.0%)
Unskilled	1,252 (23.6%)	4,057 (76.4%)	5,309 (100.0%)
Total Manual	2,080 (28.6%)	5,202 (71.4%)	7,282 (100.0%)
Total	2,976 (33.1%)	6,021 (66.9%)	8,997 (100.0%)

There are three factors at work which encourage an increase in the employment of nonmigrants at both ends of the occupational spectrum apart from government policy. One is that there has been a substantial increase in the proportion of agricultural laborers in rural Assam, from 3.8 percent in 1961 to 10 percent in 1971, so that a larger number of rural Assamese are available for unskilled, low-wage occupations than previously. One test of this hypothesis is whether there is an increase in the movement of Assamese from the countryside to the city. In the past the rate of urbanization of the Assamese was considerably below that of the rest of the country. There is some preliminary evidence that this rate is changing, though we shall know better when detailed migration data are available.

A second factor is the increase in higher-paying, low-skilled jobs in the public sector that are attractive to rural Assamese. To the extent that wages in these positions have become competitive with wages in the rural sector, we can expect Assamese to move at a greater rate into the industrial labor force.

Third, at the clerical and managerial levels, there are now more educated Assamese available than ever before. Even without a system of preferences we should expect some changes in the composition of this section of the labor force.

Undoubtedly, government pressure on employers to hire more local people has made some difference. Public sector firms, most of which are newer than the private firms, do not use labor contractors and explicitly seek to hire local people. Private firms, responsive to pressures, have made a greater effort to hire local people, especially Assamese, for the more visible staff positions. But it is important to note that policy is supportive of trends that are in any event already at work. For a policymaker the politically most attractive policy is the one which requires individuals to do what they might do anyway, and which the electorate welcomes. One is reminded of the comment of the king in St. Exupéry's whimsical tale, *The Little Prince,* that he governs his happy kingdom by ordering his subjects to do what they want to do. But perhaps the analogy is too strong—in this instance, of course, nativist agitation and public policy combine to encourage employers to do what they can easily do, but which some employers might prefer not to do.

Indirect, Unintended, and Invisible Effects

Whenever policies are intended to single out a social or ethnic group for benefits, there are bound to be effects upon those who do not benefit from the policy as well. Employers are asked to hire some people whom they might not have otherwise hired. Local people who do not belong to the preferred ethnic group fear that they are being discriminated against, and members of the preferred ethnic group are likely to be angry with employers who do not satisfactorily adhere to the government's policies. There are many consequences of the policy that are not easily measurable or observable: the fears and anxieties of the minorities over their own employment and job promotions and the educational and employment prospects of their children; fears of violence; and, above all, a sense that their personal prospects are determined not by their individual behavior and educational attainments, but by the ethnic group to which they belong. Moreover, when the objective of government is to change the income and status of one ethnic group in relation to another, one of the central effects of policy is to reinforce ethnic group identities.

In the 1960s and early '70s, a number of major political and social changes took place in Assam that were reinforced by its preferential policies. That there was little change in the economy may also be partially related to these policies. Of course, most Assamese, including government policymakers, would probably deny any relationship at all between these policies and some of the trends described here, for the side effects of policies are not easily discernible. The relationships are even less discernible when the side effects are unwelcomed. Neither policymakers nor citizens readily perceive how policies intended to affect employment might indirectly, but nonetheless significantly, influence the patterns of investment, or citizen loyalties, or intergroup relations, or political coalitions, or have any of a number of other indirect and sometimes undesirable consequences. The "goods" of policy were visible; the "bads" were not.

Industrialists: Investment and Employment. In a society in which labor is not free to move from one locality to another, investors may consider the quality of the local labor force as an additional element in the determination of where to invest. Where capital is mobile, but labor is not, investors may be reluctant to invest in areas where there are excessive restrictions on the recruitment of manpower.

Whether these considerations did in fact slow the pace of investment in Assam is difficult to discern. The remoteness of the region from the large urban markets, the difficulties in transportation and communication, and the lack of infrastructures compared with some of the more-developed states are all factors which affect the rate of investment. Some Marwari businessmen with investments in Assam, especially those who have experienced violence at the hands of street mobs, have said that they are reluctant to expand their investments in the state and have instead invested elsewhere in the country. Assam has not apparently succeeded in attracting any major new private investment. None of India's major industrial investors has entered the state. And in the central government there are some officials with the power to influence public sector locational decisions who view with concern the intense nativist sentiment, or, as they put it, the "parochial" and "chauvinist" tendencies that have prevailed in Assam.

From 1961 to 1971 factory employment in Assam actually declined, from 80,000 to 77,000, while for India as a whole factory employment during this period increased from 3.9 million to 5 million. Indeed, Assam was the only state where factory employment went down.[24] From 1969 through 1972 only 20 industrial licenses were issued in the state, out of 1,772 issued in the country.[25]

There is no conclusive evidence that the attacks against Marwari shopkeepers, the clashes between the Assamese and the Bengali Hindus, or the protectionist labor policies of the government have actually slowed the rate of investment in the state. Even in the absence of these developments, there are few incentives for private investment in Assam. Nevertheless we can say that these developments are among the factors which investors consider as they make their locational decisions.

Indigenous Minorities: Political Loyalties and Separatism. Since independence there has been a growing disaffection of indigenous non-Assamese from the Assamese-dominated state government. When India became independent, Assam, as we noted earlier, included a number of districts outside the Brahmaputra valley in which non-Assamese predominated. The surrounding hill districts were populated by indigenous tribal peoples who were increasingly hostile to what they saw as a policy of Assamization on the part of the state government. The prescription of Assamese as an official language of administration, the movement toward the use of Assamese as the medium in the schools and colleges, and the system of employment preferences for Assamese all tended to strengthen sentiment within the tribal population for separation. Separation seemed feasible to the tribals since most of them live in homogeneous contiguous areas outside the valley. Moreover, since these regions border on neighboring countries—the Northeast Frontier (NEFA) region touches Tibet, the Garo and Khasi hills touch East Pakistan (now Bangladesh), the Mizo Hills border on both Burma and East Pakistan, and the Naga Hills are next to Burma—the central government feared that separatist sentiment could be converted (by enemy arms) into secessionist movements, as indeed it was among the Nagas.

Sentiment for political separation increased in direct proportion to the growth of Assamese nationalism. Government efforts to spread the teaching of Assamese in the schools, to increase the proportion of ethnic Assamese in the administrative services, and to press for job preferences for Assamese were intended primarily to strengthen the position of the Assamese in relation to the Bengali Hindu community, but they also sharpened the cleavages between the Assamese and other indigenous peoples in the state. The result was that by 1963 the rebellious Naga tribes had successfully persuaded the central government to grant them their own state of Nagaland. The Garo, Khasi, and Jaintia tribes were given autonomous status as Meghalaya, which was converted into a separate state in 1972. The Mizo hills district was separated from Assam in 1971 and was constituted as the union territory of Mizoram. And the NEFA was converted into a union territory, then into the state of Arunachal Pradesh in 1972.

Migrant Settlers: Public Assimilation. The indirect effect most welcomed by the Assamese has been the increasing identification of some migrant communities with the political interests of the Assamese. As we indicated earlier, there emerged a symbiotic relationship between Bengali Muslims and Assamese Hindus. Fearful of losing their land or even being repatriated, many Bengali Muslims sought political protection by allying themselves with the Assamese-dominated Congress party. This alliance was quite striking in view of the historic antagonisms between these two communities prior to 1947.

The Bengali Muslims provided more than political support in elections and in the legislatures. They also publicly embraced the Assamese language. Though the law provides for the creation of primary schools in the mother tongue of the students if requested by parents, Bengali Muslims did not object to the establishment of Assamese schools in their localities. Similarly, the tribal tea plantation workers who originated in southern Bihar and Orissa did not object to the government's school language policy. Even the adults in both communities asserted that they "switched" languages. The 1961 census reported an increase in the proportion of Assamese speakers, and a decline in the proportion of Bengali speakers and tea plantation laborers who speak either tribal languages or Hindi. According to census officials, almost all of the 2.2 million Muslims of Bengali origin reported Assamese as their mother tongue. And among the estimated 1.5 million tea plantation workers and their families, only 275,000 reported a tribal language as their mother tongue.[26] Both groups, however, apparently continue to speak their own languages at home and within their own community. By supporting the Assamese Hindus in their anti-Bengali Hindu policies, other migrant communities, especially Bengali Muslims, won protection from the government in the form of exemptions from potentially threatening policies.

The political support given by the Bengali Muslims to the Congress party in Assam was also a major reason why Congress consistently received a higher vote in Assam than in all but a handful of states. Even in 1977 when Congress won only 34.5 percent of the national vote and was overwhelmingly defeated in all the Hindi-speaking states, it won 50.6 percent of the vote in Assam. The alliance between Assamese Hindus and Bengali Muslims within the Congress party was the fundamental political arrangement which enabled the government to pursue its preferential policies for the Assamese.

Why, then, did the alliance appear to break up in 1979 with the emergence of an anti-Bengali movement that did not distinguish between the Bengali Hindu middle class and the Bengali Muslim cultivators and which, according to some observers, even took a "communal" (i.e., anti-Muslims) turn?

One element was the renewed evidence of an influx of Bengalis as indicated by the substantial increase in the electoral rolls. If the growth in the electoral rolls accurately reflects the population increases in the state, then Assam's population has increased by approximately ten percent more than that of the rest of India—a growth rate that may partially reflect a higher rate of natural population increase, but presumably also reflects continued migration into the state either from other parts of India or, illegally, from Bangladesh. That educated Assamese should be alarmed by this new evidence of a Bengali influx is not surprising.

But the political response to these demographic changes must be seen in the context of the breakup of the Congress party in Assam following the 1977 elections. In Assam, as elsewhere in India, the Congress party split into pro- and anti-Indira Gandhi factions, with the result that for the first time in post-independence India, the Congress party failed to win a majority of seats in the state assembly elections of March 1978. In an assembly of 126 seats, the Congress (I) won only eight seats, while the anti-Indira Congress won twenty-six.

The split within the Congress ended the postindependence coalition of Assamese Hindus and Bengali Muslims, for what attracted Bengali Muslims to the Congress was the certainty that the Congress would govern the state. Bengali Muslims subsequently shifted their votes to other parties; so, apparently, did many Bengali Hindus who had earlier supported Congress. Many Assam-ese assert that the Bengalis are voting for the Communist Party Marxist, a party which the Assamese regard as Bengali because of its dominant position in both West Bengal and Tripura. There was a substantial increase in the vote for the CPM in the 1978 state assembly elections when they won eleven seats. The Communist party of India won another five.

The All-Assam Student Union and the All-Assam Gana Sangram Parishad, the federation of organizations leading the anti-Bengali movement, have taken strong anti-Communist positions and attacked the left parties in Assam as "agents of the Bengalis."[27] There are reports too that many members of the Assamese urban middle class who own agricultural land leased to tenant farm-ers are hostile toward the Communist Party Marxist for its support of the demand by tenant farmers, many of whom are Bengali Muslims, that they be given title to land which they have cultivated for several years.[28]

There are thus a variety of political forces at work not only to prevent illegal aliens from voting, but to disenfranchise Bengali Muslims and to force many to leave the state or even the country. Both the Asom Jatiyotabadi Dal (Assam Nationalist Party) and the Purbanchaliya Lok Parishad (Eastern Peo-ple's Forum), the two prominent regional parties, explicitly seek to reduce the Bengali population within the state. Many of the former Jana Sangh mem-bers of the Janata party would like a cut-off date for revising the electoral rolls (1971) that would force many Muslims to leave, but permit Bengali Hin-dus to remain. And many opponents of Mrs. Gandhi would like to reduce the size of the Bengali Muslim electorate as a means of undermining what was once and could again become a major source of support for the Congress party.

The end of the alliance between Assamese Hindus and Bengali Muslims thus appears to result from a concatenation of developments: the continued influx of Bengali Muslims from Bangladesh; the split in the Congress party; the shift of some Bengali Muslims to the leftist parties; the opposition of As-samese Hindu middle class landowners to the demands of their Muslim tenants; and the efforts by political parties and groups opposed both to the leftist par-ties and to the Congress to reduce the size of the Bengali electorate.[29]

The agitation against "foreign nationals" has clearly created great anxieties among Muslim migrants, since they are the group most affected by any program of detaining and deporting foreigners. One result is a strengthening of the ethnic identity of the Bengali Muslims as indicated by the recent emergence of an All-Assam Minority Student Union. Mrs. Gandhi's Congress has been working with the AAMSU and other Muslim groups in the state in an effort to rebuild the old political alliance. But if the Bengali Muslims increasingly assert their Bengali identity and in the 1981 census (which has been postponed in Assam because of the antiforeign agitation) choose to report Bengali rather than Assamese as their mother tongue, then the linguistic composition of the state could be substantially modified—with dramatic consequences for politics in the state.[30]

Conclusion

Since the middle of the nineteenth century a continuous stream of migrants into Assam from other states and from Bangladesh has transformed its social structure and political life. The Assamese found themselves behind in the areas of education, urbanization, and employment in the modern sector. As Assamese nationalism grew before independence, one of their greater political problems was how to increase their numbers in the face of this influx. Since the Assamese could neither control the migration nor increase their own population, they looked upon boundary changes as a means of affecting their numerical ratio. Thus the redrawing of boundaries, in 1874, 1905, 1912, 1947, and in the early 1970s were critical events for the Assamese. Most crucial of all—a turning point in the political life of the Assamese—was the partition of Assam in 1947 at the time of independence, which reduced the Bengali population and thereby assured the Assamese Hindus of control over the government.

Once in political power the Assamese consolidated their control over the administrative apparatus, extended their domination of the educational system, and then sought to reach into the labor market for a larger share of employment in the modern, urban, organized sector.

Unable to close the borders and expel the migrants and their descendants as have many sovereign states, the government of Assam turned primarily to educational, language, and employment policies as a means of reversing the status of those groups, most especially the Bengali Hindus, who held a dominant position in the modern, urban, organized sectors of the economy.

In recent years the position of the Assamese has improved, but primarily in unskilled jobs and only secondarily in the clerical and managerial positions sought by the growing Assamese middle classes. To what extent these changes are more than marginally the effects of government policy is problematic, for there are also economic and educational forces at work shaping a larger role for the Assamese in the urban and industrial sectors. In any event the change in the *proportion* of jobs held by Assamese should be seen in the context of a low rate of investment in the state, only small increases in the size of the labor market, and growing overall unemployment. Government policy has affected —if it has had any effect on employment at all—only the *share* of jobs acquired by the Assamese within the organized sector. Unless the organized sector itself expands, the opportunities for an increasingly educated and urbanized Assamese labor force are likely to remain limited.

But perhaps the most important impact of the policies described here has been not on the migration process, or even on the economic opportunities of the nonmobile local population, but rather on the process of *incorporation*— of migrants, their descendants, and the non-Assamese local tribal people. The goal of these policies has been nothing less than that of transforming social relationships among ethnic groups so as to give the hitherto numerous but economically and socially subordinate Assamese a more important role in the economic order, the occupational structure, and the social hierarchy. The older notion of a social system made up of discrete ethnic groups, each functioning within its own economic sphere, each pursuing its own distinctive cultural life, in a hierarchical social order in which the local Assamese population was by no means at the top, has given way to the notion that the Assamese should be politically, economically, culturally, and socially elevated, and that other communities must modify their public behavior to accommodate themselves to the paramountcy of the Assamese. The policies described here are unmistakable signals to those who would migrate to the state, as well as to those minorities who reside in the state, that the Assamese have redefined the conditions under which they can remain.

Seven

Assessing Policy Consequences

Have the preferential policies of the Indian central and state governments increased equality among ethnic groups? Has there been an increase in equality in education, employment, and income? If so, to what extent is it the result of the preferential policies? And, whether or not the policies "work," what are the costs—for the migrants, for interethnic relations, and for economic growth? These are some of the questions one might ask in order to assess the effects of preferential policies.

But from the perspective of those who make policies, these are not the central questions. In each of the cases reviewed here it is clear that the primary concern of the policymakers was to generate political support or, at least, reduce political opposition. In Maharashtra, for example, the Congress government wanted to contain the Shiv Sena, a political party whose popularity rested upon its demand for protecting the interests of the local Marathi-speaking population, while at the same time it sought to encourage the Shiv Sena to undermine support for the Communist unions and the left parties. In Assam, the Congress government, recognizing that partition had changed the ethnic composition of the state, gave primacy to the demands of the majority Assamese over the minority Bengalis. And in Andhra, where the situation was more complicated because of the conflicting interests within the Congress itself, the objective of the central government, whose policy formula was ultimately accepted and enacted, was to keep the state intact as a single unit.

Given these political objectives, did the policies succeed? In Maharashtra, the protectionist policies of the state government helped to contain Shiv Sena's electoral power. The party continued as a major force in the politics of Bombay, but it did not do so well in 1973 as in the 1968 municipal elections; it did, however, continue to make inroads into some of the unions and to undermine the communists.

In Assam the political gains to the government were ambiguous. The pro-Assamese policies of the state government antagonized much of the non-Assamese electorate, but won it overwhelming support from Assamese voters. In the 1971 parliamentary elections the Congress party in Assam won 56 percent of the vote as compared with 43.6 percent nationally. Only in three other states (one of which was Maharashtra where Congress won 63.5% of the vote) did Congress do as well.[1] While it would be a gross oversimplification to assume that the overwhelming Congress victories in Assam and Maharashtra were the result of nativist policies, the victories reinforced the government's belief that nativist policies were politically profitable.

On the debit side, however, aggressive Assamese nationalism was a factor in the separatist demands of the tribal minorities, an element in the central government's willingness to carve the tribal areas out of Assam to form separate hill states, and, most recently, a cause of the breakdown of relations between Assamese Hindus and Bengali Muslims. Moreover, when the Congress party split in 1978, a large part of the electorate, particularly non-Assamese but Assamese as well, drifted away from the Congress party.

Finally, in Andhra the central government's objectives were to bring the agitation to an end, to dissolve the opposition Telangana Praja Samiti, and to maintain the state Congress party in power. In fact, these were the results of the government's Six-Point Formula. No small accomplishments!

From the policymaker's perspective, therefore, preferential policies, irrespective of whether they were effectively implemented, and irrespective of any change in the occupational structure of the local community, were politically successful. For policymakers, the electoral polls were a better indicator of policy success than any carefully developed set of statistical measures of policy impacts.

Moreover, since these particular policies were adopted in response to popular political demands, the government was acutely aware of the political costs of being unresponsive. In Bombay and Andhra the proposals for preferential policies were not initiated by those in power, but by their critics, and in Assam the government was fully aware of the strong popular feelings against Bengali Hindus and Marwaris. In all three cases the decisions to create preferences won immediate local approval. Whether they made a difference in employment was another matter.

Assessing the Benefits

Did the preferential policies actually create greater employment opportunities for the local population?[2] There are at least two ways we can deal with this issue. The first is by examining the census data to see if states or regions with preferential policies for local people have experienced a decline or slowing down in the migration rate. Has there, for example, been a decline in the number of Bengali-speaking migrants in the towns of the Brahmaputra valley in Assam, Tamil-speaking migrants in Bombay, and migrants from the Andhra delta in Hyderabad city? A corollary of this question is whether a decline in interstate migration is accompanied by an increase in intrastate migration as one group moves into the labor market when another is forced out. If so, it would suggest that preferential policies may be opening up employment op-

121

portunities not only for the "local" people in a very geographically restrictive sense, but for all the people within a state. Thus, a forced decline in the mobility of some ethnic groups may result in an increase in mobility on the part of others.

The second question is whether there is any evidence that employers recruit more actively among local people and less among migrants than was the case prior to the introduction of the restrictive policies. In other words, has the occupational structure of the local population begun to change as a result of new employment opportunities?

Before we turn to the evidence on these two questions, several caveats are in order. The first is that even if the policies have the intended effects, they may not be immediately apparent. In the past decade, the growth rate of the modern sector has been low. The changes, therefore, are likely to come slowly, since the policies affect only the annual increments in employment and the normal turnover resulting from resignations, retirements, and deaths. Moreover, since the policies are intended to affect the organized sectors of the economy and not the less-organized or informal sectors, only migrations to the organized sector might be affected.[3]

Then, too, a change in the patterns of employment in the modern sector need not be the result of preferential policies, but may be the consequence of the growing availability of skilled, educated, job-seeking individuals within the local community who are now better able to compete with migrants. The demand for preferential policies in itself reveals the growing availability of an educated local labor force.[4] So long as there is no discrimination, one would ordinarily expect this group to increase its share of jobs in the modern sector even in the absence of preferential policies.[5] The policies may simply be forcing some employers to do what they might voluntarily have done in any event.

During a period of rapid expansion in the modern sector, there might be an increase in both long-distance migration and local employment. And conversely, during a period of stagnation or slow economic growth, there might be a decline in migration and no substantial change in the composition of the local labor force irrespective of government policies. Thus, both migration and employment data must be interpreted with caution since change or lack of change does not necessarily indicate the success or failure of preferential policies.

Employment

In a survey of selected private and public sector firms in Bombay, we found that the employment of Maharashtrians in middle class white collar positions was increasing even before 1966, that is, prior to the formation of the Shiv Sena and the adoption of preferential policies by the government. The employment of Maharashtrians increased even more rapidly after 1966, but there was also a growth in the supply of educated Maharashtrians in the labor force as a consequence of the expansion of secondary schools and colleges in the city, as well as an expansion in the number of available white collar jobs as a result of economic growth.

Did the government's preferential policies result in a higher rate of increase in the employment of Maharashtrians in municipal, state, and central-government-run establishments, as against the private sector? The survey indicates that employment in central government establishments in the sample increased from 398 to 672 persons between 1962 and 1973, an addition of 274 workers; the number of Maharashtrians rose from 75 (19% of those employed) to 195 (29%), an increase of 120. In other words, of the additional 274 workers added during this period, 120, or 44 percent, were Maharashtrians. In the state and municipal establishments, 44 new positions were added and 49 more Maharashtrians were employed: Maharashtrians were thus evidently hired not only for new positions, but also as replacements for those who left. Finally, among top-level personnel in the private sector, 18 positions were added in 15 firms and 9 of these were Maharashtrians (see table 4.2).

One must be cautious in comparing public and private sector employment practices on the basis of data this limited, since the levels of the appointments are not comparable; the data do reveal, however, that the employment of Maharashtrians is accelerating in the senior levels of the private sector, and perhaps at an even faster rate among the middle-ranking positions in municipal, state, and central government employment. Here again, however, while there is some reason to believe that government policies are having an impact on employment practices, there is no way of ascertaining precisely what contribution government policies made or whether the impact is as great on the private sector as it appears to have been in the public, especially the state and municipal, sector.

In Andhra employment in the public sector is proportionally greater than in other states of India. In 1972, 71 percent of those who worked in the modern, organized sector of the economy in the state were employed by the central, state, and local governments, as against 62 percent nationally. Within the public sector the state and local government was the largest single employer. Approximately six hundred thousand persons worked for the state and local governments, and another 151,000 for the central government (see table 5.8). Between 1959 and 1968 92,000 persons were appointed to the state government within the Telangana region, presumably in accordance with the government's residential requirements that imposed restrictions on the number of non-Telangana persons that could be employed in the region. The rules, however, were not applicable to employment either in the private sector or in positions controlled by the central government. In other words, the *mulki* rules affected the appointment of ten thousand persons per year during this period. It was the decision of the courts to suspend the system of preferences for local people in state employment that transformed a demand for one or two thousand jobs per year in each district into a violent mass struggle for a separate Telangana state.

In Assam, however, as in Maharashtra, preferential policies were intended to regulate the private as well as the public sector. But Assam, like Andhra, is a predominantly agricultural state with only seventeen percent of the labor force employed in the organized sector of the economy, and of this, more than half in the tea plantations. The demand for preferences thus concerned state and local governments which employed 114,000 persons, the nonplantation private sector which employed 55,000 persons, and the central government services and public sector which employed 149,000 persons.

Our analysis of data produced by a study group for the Assam state legislature revealed that the centrally run public sector firms increased their employment of ethnic Assamese more rapidly than the private sector firms, but the increases were primarily in the employment of manual laborers. In fact the employment of non-Assamese white collar workers actually increased. In contrast, the private sector employed an increasing number of Assamese for white collar and managerial positions.

The employment gains for the Assamese, especially for middle class positions, were not particularly impressive. But this is largely because the growth in employment in the organized sector has been so small that hiring has largely been for replacements, not for new positions. The few new firms do tend to have a higher proportion of Assamese employees, possibly reflecting the preferential policies, but probably also reflecting the increasing supply of educated Assamese and of uneducated rural Assamese in search of urban employment.

Unfortunately, the survey does not report the changing pattern of employment in state and local government, but government officials report that for the past twenty-five years, preferences in these positions have been given to local Assamese. The expansion of the primary and secondary school system and the widespread use of Assamese as the medium of instruction in the schools—even in some of the non-Assamese areas—have provided new employment opportunities for Assamese graduates as teachers.

In none of the three cases studied are we able to distinguish between the effects of changes in the size and quality of the local labor supply and the effects of preferential policies.[6] Local people clearly are getting more and better jobs in state and local governments, and this presumably reflects both the changes in the labor supply and the government's policies. Local people are not doing so well in finding positions in public sector firms or in the administrative services of the central government where merit criteria remain paramount and where employment in white collar and technical positions is open to all without regard to place of birth or ethnicity. In Assam and Bombay—no comparable data were available for Hyderabad—local people are also finding more jobs in the private sector, but the slow growth of industry has limited the opportunities for employment.

In Assam, factory employment declined between 1961 and 1971. In Maharashtra there was a 26 percent increase during the decade, but most of the growth was before 1966. In Andhra Pradesh there was a 17 percent increase, also primarily before 1966. Everywhere the growth rate in employment was low after 1966. Nationally, employment in the privately owned manufacturing sector grew only 1 percent annually from 1966 to 1973, from 3.8 million to 4.1 million. Most of the increases in employment in the organized sector of the economy between 1966 and 1973, when employment rose from 16.2 million to 18.8 million, or 2.3 percent yearly, were in the public sector, and half of the increases were in direct central or state government employment. These numbers help explain why in most states the political struggle is over employment in the government or in the government-run public sector.[7]

Migration

If preferential policies had an effect and other determinants of migration remained constant, we might expect to see (1) a decline in the rate of migration from outside the state; (2) an increase in migration within the state as new opportunities for employment became available to people within the state; and (3) some emigration of the children of migrants belonging to nonlocal ethnic groups.

The census is the obvious source for examining these changes, but for a variety of reasons it has not proved to be satisfactory. For one thing, the decennial feature of the census makes it a poor instrument for measuring the short-term effects of internal migration policies. Since the census reports migration during the decade rather than yearly migrations, intercensus changes in migration that occurred after the passage of new laws and administrative regulations cannot be monitored. There are no annual reports on migration comparable to annual reports (for some localities) on changes in fertility behavior.

Second, the census reports where people came from, where they have moved, and many of their characteristics, but does not indicate the ethnicity of migrants. We cannot, for example, conclude that a growth in internal migration in Assam necessarily indicates that the Assamese have become more mobile, since the migrants may be Assamese-born Bengalis. Moreover, the absence of ethnicity data also precludes estimating income or educational differences between ethnic groups. In this respect, of course, India pursues a curious (non)-information policy common to many multiethnic societies in spite of the government's explicit commitment to greater ethnic equality.

Third, prior to the 1971 census, data were not provided on the educational level or occupations of migrants.[8] Though such information is provided in the 1971 census, no comparisons can be made with earlier periods. Since the object of policy is to *change* the educational and occupational characteristics of the migrants and local population, the absence of a time series precludes studying changes through census data.

These limitations are so great that one might conclude that there is no point in using the census data at all. Nonetheless, as we shall see, the census data do reveal at least one striking effect of the preferential policies. Again, we must be cautious about our finding, especially since we have been able to obtain detailed census data only for Assam and Hyderabad.

Assam has experienced a high rate of urban growth. From 1951 to 1961 the urban population increased from 346,000 to 816,000, an increase of 135 percent. In the next ten years the urban population rose to 1,327,000, a 62 percent increase.

According to the 1961 census, 298,000 migrants to the urban areas came from outside of Assam, and another 158,000 came from the rural areas of the state.

A decade later the census reported that 384,000 migrants to urban areas came from outside the state as against 294,000 from within the state.

If we assume these figures are correct, intrastate migration to urban areas has been increasing more rapidly than interstate migration.

But there are other data in the census that make this conclusion suspect. In 1971 the proportion of out-of-state migrants in Assam was 11.6 percent as against 14 percent ten years earlier. At the same time, curiously enough, the population of the state grew by 35 percent as against a national growth rate of 24.8 percent. For Assam to continue to have the highest population growth of any state in India while its migration from other states is declining seems most improbable.

Moreover, the migration data are not compatible with the data on urban growth. According to the 1971 census the urban areas added 507,000 persons by the end of the decade: 86,000 out-of-state migrants; 146,000 in-state migrants; and 275,000 in natural population increase. This means a natural population growth rate of 33.7 percent, but it seems unlikely that the natural population increase of Assam's urban areas should be so high, and even exceed, by 2 percent, the entire rural population growth rate in the state.

An alternative explanation is that interstate and international migration is underreported. The 1961 census director of Assam reported that many migrants from East Pakistan to Assam—mostly illegals—reported a local place of birth in order to avoid expulsion. Given the growing restrictions on the employment of out-of-state Indians in Assam, it seems quite plausible that in the 1971 census many Indian and Bangladesh migrants reported to the census enumerators that Assam was their place of birth. Fear of loss of employment may be leading many out-of-state migrants to misreport their place of birth.[9]

The 1971 census data from Hyderabad tend to support the hypothesis that restrictions on migration lead to misreporting place of birth. Here too the growth of the city appears to be disproportionately higher than can be accounted for by the natural population increase plus reported migration. The district of Hyderabad—which includes the city, suburbs, and some nearby rural areas—increased by 35% from 1961 to 1971, from 2,061,000 to 2,791,000, as against a state-wide population increase of 21 percent. The city itself grew by 43.8 percent from 1,248,000 to 1,796,000. Migration to Hyderabad city is largely from within the state (212,000, as against 123,000 from out of state). Surprisingly, however, the *increase* in migration into the district from 1961 to 1971 was only 71,000, quite insufficient to account for the growth in either the district or the city. The city itself, according to the census, had only 335,000 migrants in 1971. The city added 548,000 people during the decade, of which 262,000 can be accounted for through natural population increase. The difference, therefore, represents an *increase in migration* greater than the number of migrants living in the city in 1961. In short, the city probably added approximately 286,000 *new* migrants during the decade, far above the census figures. In other words, 200,000 migrants apparently claimed that they were born in the city.

The 1971 census reports that only 71,600 residents in the district of Hyderabad, or about 2½ percent of the population, were migrants from the delta region of Andhra. Few in Hyderabad would agree that the number of delta migrants could be so low. Some sections of the city—including one area known as the Andhra colony—are almost exclusively made up of delta migrants, and several of the suburban areas on the outskirts of the city are heavily populated by migrants. The number of migrants from the Andhra delta increased from 44,000 in 1961 to 71,600 in 1971, an increase of only 28,000. The increase seems implausibly low considering the influx that took place in the early sixties after the city was made the capital of a united Andhra and many Andhras moved there to take advantage of the public and private sector jobs.

As in Assam, it appears that the restrictions on the employment of migrants by the state government have led many migrants from the delta to report that they were born in the city. In short, there is no evidence that the laws regulating migration into Hyderabad city have actually resulted in any substantial decline in migration. But there is reason to believe that the laws and regulations induce people to lie to census enumerators. It seems appropriate to conclude, therefore, that attempts to reduce migration are merely reducing the reliability of the migration data produced by the census. In the future, researchers will have to be particularly cautious and take into account the possible effects of restrictive policies on the accuracy of the data they are interpreting.

Unintended Consequences

Thus far we have examined the effects of both the implicit and the explicit objectives of internal migration policies. It now remains for us to examine their unintended consequences. The unintended effects of governmental actions are often greater than the intended ones. Merely to consider whether a

127

government has achieved what it set out to achieve is to ignore the many effects which government policymakers did not intend, did not expect, and
often do not want. For this reason, policy assessments should always be made
without regard for policy intentions.

How did these policies affect relationships between the local population
and the migrants? Did they reduce or intensify tension, conflict, and violence
between local people and migrants? Do migrants and their children now learn
the local language and adopt local customs, or do they become more cohesive
and aloof from the local population?

What has been the effect on the economy? Do nativist policies discourage
outside entrepreneurs from investing in the region? Do local firms owned by
outsiders place new investments elsewhere? Are central government administrators and politicians less willing to expand public sector enterprises in a
region where there are strong pressures to hire only local people even for technical and managerial positions? In other words, do protectionist policies affect
the supply of jobs?

Do the policies in one state lead to countermeasures in other states? By
intervening to increase job and educational opportunities exclusively for its
own population, does a state government restrict their opportunities elsewhere
by provoking other states to pass protectionist policies of their own?

Do protectionist policies create anxieties and alienation among the local
ethnic minorities as well as among the migrants?

Within the local population, who gains from protectionist policies? Do benefits in education and employment go to those best able to compete against
migrants, while those least able to compete remain unaffected? How many of
the local people obtain jobs through protectionist policies who would not
have in open recruitment by merit?

What is the impact of the legislation on the children of migrants? Are their
employment opportunities restricted because of their ethnicity? Do they "return" to the land of their parents and grandparents? Are they embittered?
Are their talents lost by the society?

What is the impact of protectionism on relationships within the work place?
What is the attitude of those who hold their positions through open national
recruitment toward those in their own offices and factories who were hired
because they were local?

Simply to raise these questions suggests the complexity of assessing the
effects of government policy. Moreover, there is no logical method by which
one can create an analytically comprehensive checklist of possible consequences
of a government policy, especially since so many of the effects are not visible
and there are second-order effects that may not be felt for some time. Consider, for example, the British decision in the nineteenth century to incorporate
Assam into the province of Bengal: could anyone envisage then that the result
would be an ethnic division of labor with the Bengalis dominating the modern

sector of the economy while the Assamese remained in the traditional sectors? Or that the British decision not to incorporate the Nizam's province of Hyderabad into British India would create a schism within the Telugu-speaking population—with those living on the British side of the boundary having access to the new colleges and universities, while those remaining on the Hyderabad side having fewer educational opportunities?

These studies of Assam, Andhra, and Maharashtra reveal only some of the short-term effects, and even these are not easily verifiable.

The study of Assam suggests that preferential policies may have played a role in accelerating separatist sentiments among the tribal population, and may have been a contributing factor in the slow rate of private investment in the state. Protectionist policies also intensified the political cleavages between Bengali Hindus and the Assamese while temporarily bringing Bengali Muslims into an alliance with the Assamese.

In Andhra an assessment of unintended consequences is even more precarious, since there have been so many changes and reversals in policy. The revival of the *mulki* rules in 1972, which restricted job opportunities in the Hyderabad region for people in the eastern districts of the state, precipitated a separatist movement in the eastern region. Why, demanded the political elites in the eastern districts, should they remain in a state which denied them access to state employment on a competitive basis? A few years earlier, a court decision to revoke the *mulki* rules led to a similar separatist movement in the Telangana districts on the grounds that in the absence of preferential policies they would not be able to compete for state employment. In short, once preferences based upon geographic criteria became part of the law, their retention or suspension precipitated separatist sentiments on the part of the losers.

Other effects are less clear. Private investment in Hyderabad by entrepreneurs from the delta districts appears to have continued in spite of the *mulki* movement, but then the *mulki* rules did not affect employment in the private sector.

Fear and anxiety were evidently great among the migrants, and, given the proximity of the two regions, it was not difficult for each region to take retaliatory measures. When separatism erupted in the eastern districts, the people in these districts halted public and private vehicles and stopped the trains, thereby disrupting the movements of goods and people from north India to much of the south.

Finally, the political conflict was resolved through the Six-Point Formula which divided the state into seven employment zones for public employment. The policy thus arrested middle class spatial mobility within Andhra insofar as public employment is concerned, though it permitted mobility for private employment.

The much greater size of the private sector in Bombay, and the limited powers of the state government to enforce preferential policies on the private sector, have forced the Marathi population to give more attention to developing the skills with which to compete than appears to be the case in the other two states. In spite of the preferential rules, the Shiv Sena has urged its supporters to learn English and to study typing, accountancy, shorthand, and so on, so as to compete against the migrants for white collar positions. The fear of countermeasures by Tamil Nadu (especially against the Hindi film industry located in Bombay) has toned down some of the pressure for anti-Tamil migrant measures. Moreover, the continued expansion of industrial investment and of employment in Bombay has also reduced some of the tensions between the Marathis and the migrants: so long as employment expands, there is room for both. For these reasons preferential policies may have had fewer long-term indirect effects in Bombay than elsewhere.

In any event, it is not meaningful to measure the "success" or "failure" of these policies solely by scoring the demographic, economic, psychological, or social effects. "Success" ultimately remains a matter of perspective and values. A policy that increases support for the government on the part of the local population and expands their job opportunities, but which at the same time creates acute ethnic conflicts between the local population and the migrants or their descendants, may be viewed as successful by the state government, but unsuccessful by migrant minorities. A policy that succeeds in reversing the ethnic division of labor by providing more jobs and income for the local ethnic group may be judged successful to some observers even if the program is discriminatory against migrants, and some ethnic groups become alienated from the political system. The government and their nativist supporters may view the policy as successful even if it slows the rate of investment from outside and thereby reduces the overall rate of economic growth and expansion of employment—as long as the *share* of the labor market held by local people has increased. Any assessment of the bottom line in a balance sheet of costs and benefits must start with the notion that costs and benefits may be tallied quite differently by the government, by the local population, and by migrants.

Preferential Policies under Attack
India's state governments are in the main too partisan to take a broad view of the consequences of their preferential policies. They function in an environment in which the scale and volume of conflicts between various social and ethnic groups have been increasing, largely because social groups that were once low in status and wealth are now rising, or at least see the opportunity for social mobility. And, in turn, social groups once higher in power, status, and wealth now feel threatened. The result is that traditional rivalries are aggravated and new conflicts are created as social relationships change. These would be problems even if the economy were growing more rapidly and employment opportunities were expanding. But they are particularly acute in a society where social mobilization is stimulated by the educational and political system, but left unsatisfied by the economic order.

The middle classes that dominate India's state and central governments are committed to expanding higher secondary schools, colleges, and universities. As the middle classes—or, more precisely, the aspiring middle classes—have grown in numbers and political influence, they have successfully pressed for language, education, and employment policies to enhance the opportunities for the linguistic local majority, and particularly those who belong to its middle classes. They envisage the state not as an arbiter setting the rules within which social conflicts can take place, but as an active supporter of their group in relation to others. State governments have used their powers to support the demands of the local ethnic group to expand its middle class, that is, to make it commensurate in size, status, income, and occupations with the middle classes of groups against which it is competing. Thus, the government of Assam has sought to elevate the position of the Assamese middle class in relation to the local Bengali middle class; the government of Maharashtra wants middle class Maharashtrians to have jobs equal to those of the Tamils and other educated migrants communities; and the state of Andhra was politically torn because the local middle class in the Telangana region was fighting for control over the government to ensure that policies would be adopted that would protect its interests against those of the migrant middle classes.

For the achievement of this particular form of equality the middle classes and their state governments are prepared to incur many losses. Even if investments decline, tensions between the local population and the migrants grow, and opportunities for employment and education are taken away from the locally born descendants of migrants, the state governments are willing to pursue preferential policies. After all, the visible costs are largely borne by others, while some of the costs for the local population—declining private investment, for example—are invisible.

For these reasons it would be naive to expect state governments to monitor protectionist policies. Indeed, such monitoring would be perceived by the state governments and by the local middle classes as threatening. It is not in their interests that the social and economic costs of these policies and the effects on others be known. If India's preferential policies are to be fully assessed, it will have to be done by the scholarly community, by the courts, or by agencies of the central government, not by state government policymakers.

As preferential policies have been extended, there have been growing signs of protest against many of their features and even against the very principles which underlie them.

For one thing, the adoption of such policies has created a lack of national uniformity. Some states provide employment and educational preferences for local people against migrants while a few do not. Some define "local"in terms of state boundaries, others in terms of smaller geographic units. Some define "local" by place of birth, others by length of residence, and still others (in practice if not by law) by ethnicity. Some employ domicile requirements for education, others for employment. Similarly, definitions of "backward"

131

castes for inclusion in a list of preferences remain a matter of political pressure, with the result that the criteria and the numbers given preferences vary greatly from state to state, and members of scheduled castes and tribes given preferences in one state may find that when they or their children move to another state they are no longer entitled to benefits.

The sense of injustice has also grown among those young people who do not qualify for educational admissions or public employment under *any* preferential categories. Since there are reservations for government employment not only for members of scheduled castes, scheduled tribes, and backward classes, but also for ex-servicemen, the physically handicapped, and "dependents of freedom fighters," reservations often exceed fifty percent, a situation made more acute by the relatively limited number of employment opportunities for educated young people.

The population that has not been given any reservations is predominantly made up of "forward" or higher-caste Hindus who constitute approximately 30 to 35 percent of the population in most states. Since a large proportion of the forward classes are secondary school or college graduates, the competition among them for the remaining jobs is more acute than among other communities. Thus, as we have seen, where there are migrants from other linguistic regions also competing, it is typically the forward classes that have led the demand for preferential policies for sons of the soil. Since others are assured of a piece of the employment pie, the forward classes too seek some protection against competition.

The growth of economic and educational differences *within* the scheduled castes, scheduled tribes, and backward classes has called attention to the fact that the correlation between ethnicity and either education or income is neither perfect nor unchanging. Since members of the various backward communities have had preferred access to higher education some are now educationally equal to those who come from the forward castes. "Every caste," writes one critic of reservations, "is comprised of both the rich and poor. The poverty and backwardness are not the legacy of the so-called lower castes, and the upper castes are not equally opulent and developed. ... There are backwards in every caste."[10] Some Indians have questioned whether the children of these communities should be given preferences if their parents have college degrees and hold senior positions in the civil service. As preferential admissions and recruitment expand the size of the middle classes within protected communities, then preferences based upon ethnicity rather than upon, say, income create a new privileged class, with those least in need within these communities receiving the benefits.[11]

Cleavages thus grow within the backward communities as the children of those who have moved into middle class positions continue to receive benefits for which the children of the lower strata are unable to compete effectively.

In Bihar, for example, among the many castes that are listed as backward, four that are more affluent and more educated than the others—Kurmis, Koeris, Yadavas, and Baniyas—are in the best position to take advantage of job reservations, and there are similar divisions among the scheduled castes and scheduled tribes. There are thus "forward" castes among the backward castes, just as there are "forward" individuals within the backward communities, and "backward" individuals among the forward communities.

The appropriateness of caste as the *exclusive* criterion for job reservations became a politically controversial issue in Bihar in early 1978 when the state chief minister announced that 26 percent of all jobs in the state government would henceforth be reserved for members of backward classes, in addition to the 24 percent already reserved for members of scheduled castes and tribes. The state government said it was belatedly putting into effect the recommendations of the Backward Classes Commission headed by Kaka Kalelkar in 1955.[12] Similar reservations already exist in the southern states—Tamil Nadu, Andhra Pradesh, Karnataka, and Kerala; and in Uttar Pradesh, 16 percent of state government jobs are reserved for the backward classes. In caste conscious Bihar, the decision was greeted with agitation by castes not included in the reservations. The controversy was made even more acute by the fact that the chief minister of the state belonged to one of the backward castes, while his major rival within the governing Janata party belonged to a forward caste. The chief minister refused to budge on the questions of which castes would be listed as backward or the percentage of reservations, but he agreed that only those whose income did not exceed Rs. 1,000 per month (a middle class income in India) would be entitled to the benefits of reservations.[13]

Critics of reservations have also argued that the policy itself intensifies ethnic identifications, since politicians seek support by promising benefits to their caste, tribal, or linguistic constituents. And as politicians make these demands, and win support from ethnic groups, a struggle for benefits takes place which leads to a clash between backward and forward castes, Christian and non-Christian tribals, scheduled castes and caste Hindus, sons of the soil and migrants. Competition that might otherwise have taken place among individuals for education and employment now takes place among groups for political control as each group seeks to carve out a benefit for its exclusive use.

Moreover, the critics continue, once a caste, tribe or local group is given preferences, it will fight to retain reservations even if it is no longer backward in education and employment. In the name of seeking equality, reservations thus perpetuate caste and undermine efforts to create a casteless society.

Leftist critics further argue that policies which provide benefits along ethnic lines serve to encourage individuals to give primacy to their ethnic rather than their class interests. Class differences within ethnic groups are muted, and the opportunities for creating class-based political organizations that cut across ethnic lines are thus made more difficult. In Assam, as we have seen, leftists have argued (not without some evidence) that attacks against Bengalis are in part attempts to undermine the leftist parties.

More conservative critics have argued that reservations are detrimental to the functioning of the administrative system since jobs are given to those less qualified. Administrators, judges, engineers, doctors, and others appointed to government through reservations on the basis of ethnicity (either explicitly or indirectly through domicile requirements) may not be unqualified, but they are less qualified than those who would have been appointed had recruitment been through open competition without reservations.

Opposition to reservations in employment based upon ethnic or domicile criteria has also come from those who are excluded: Bengalis in Assam, Andhras in Telangana, Tamils in Bombay, and members of the forward castes in Bihar and in several of the southern states. But the larger the list of those who receive benefits, the smaller is the political clout of those who have been excluded. In Bihar, for example, where fifty percent of the population was excluded from benefits, the agitation was acute, but in Bombay the Tamil migrants were too few to resist.

In Andhra, domicile requirements for employment in Hyderabad city were made somewhat more palatable by zoning the entire state, and by assuring the people of the western districts that a share of senior positions in the civil service in the capital would be kept for open competition. Similarly, the decision of some states to restrict employment to sons of the soil has led other states to pass comparable legislation to protect their own populations. India is thus developing a kind of internal labor market protectionism comparable to international trade protectionism; less-developed, low-income groups seek protection, using a kind of infant industry argument, and this in turn provokes countermeasures by other states. Particularly disadvantaged are those states with a high emigration and low immigration rate, most notably the southern state of Kerala with its comparatively high level of education. It is not surprising, therefore, that educated people from Kerala have been seeking employment in the labor short countries of the Persian Gulf.

But whatever the economic and social costs of preferential policies for those who are excluded, the political costs of dismantling preferential policies are very high for both state and central governments. Once policymakers have redefined the disadvantaged to encompass the majority, the decision becomes virtually irreversible. Which majority is likely to give up benefits when it has the political clout to keep them? Why should the central government intervene in a state government policy that has widespread local popularity and thereby risk a politically costly clash between central and state authority? And what leverage do the excluded minorities have? They may seek loopholes in the laws, turn to the courts or to the central government, or appeal to the government of the states from which they come, but they do not have the political power to pressure the state governments to reverse the preferential policies.

A reversal of preferential policies by either central or state government would be politically costly. To terminate or in any way reduce the benefits provided scheduled castes, scheduled tribes, or backward castes would not only incur political losses from these communities but also generate ideological cleavages within any government or political party that appeared to be backsliding on its commitment to ethnic equality for the most deprived groups in the country. Similarly, the suspension of preferential recruitment in employment for local people not only would arouse local opposition to the state government but might even turn local people against resident migrants. A reversal of policy in this area might be politically possible, if at all, only if it were part of a national policy aimed at establishing reciprocity and uniformity among the states.

At present, however, it seems politically more likely that preferences will be extended than that they will be curtailed. So long as the educational system continues to expand the middle class more rapidly than the economy can provide it with employment, the middle class within each state and within each ethnic group will fight to carve out a protected niche in the labor market; a labor surplus middle class will want protection extended from the public to the private sector, from the state-run to the central-government-run public sector, from already included categories of employment to those that have thus far been excluded. Only if India's economy expands rapidly enough to meet the employment needs of the middle class does it seem likely that the demand for preferential policies will abate.

But in a deeper sense, the growth of preferential policies in India is more than simply the result of scarcity of employment or the consequence of uneven development, for what society has not experienced scarcity and unevenness? The notion of an open, free, competitive labor market in which individuals, irrespective of the linguistic, caste, tribal, or religious community to which they belong, can seek positions in the modern sector is not one with much support in India; that the state should regulate the modern labor market to provide some degree of equity—a share for the scheduled tribes, another share for the scheduled castes, still another share for a variety of backward castes, and shares for the local linguistic majority—is widely accepted. Indians may differ as to which groups are entitled to shares, how large these shares should be, what categories of jobs in the labor market should be reserved, and whether reservations should be extended from the public to the private sector; what is not at issue for most Indians is the conceptual basis on which these interventions rest.

Eight

India's Preferential Policies in Comparative Perspective

What can other multiethnic societies that are also committed to greater social and economic equality for disadvantaged ethnic groups learn from India's experiences with preferential policies? Not too many years ago it would have seemed farfetched to compare the ethnicity problems of the newly independent low-income societies of Asia and Africa with those of advanced industrial societies. In developing countries, ethnic attachments were so acute, the legitimacy of newly established regimes so precarious, and agreement upon procedures for dealing with political conflicts so limited that many were faced with prospects of civil wars and balkanization—while advanced industrial societies were not. But with the emergence of ethnic nationalism in Wales and Scotland, secessionist movements among the Basques and Quebecois, tensions between the Flemish and the Waloons, and racial violence in urban America, the differences no longer appear so great. Moreover, with the growth of migration from developing countries into Western Europe and the United States —e.g., Mexicans into the U.S., South Asians and West Indians into the U.K., Algerians into France, Indonesians into Holland, Turks into Central Europe— and with the newer Asian and African migrations into the oil-rich countries of the Mideast, the ethnic lines between the several worlds have, in fact, been crossed.

It is worthwhile reflecting for a moment on the question of why differences among ethnic groups have become a policy issue in so many countries. It was once widely accepted in advanced industrial societies that it did not make a great deal of difference if there was inequality among ethnic groups as long as the state endeavored to remove barriers to individual advancement, ensured a minimum standard of well-being for all its citizens, and removed great disparities in income. Since ethnic groups, it was assumed, differed in the attitudes and motivations that shaped the kind of education and occupations they sought and their ability to compete, there was no reason to expect that ethnic groups within the same society would have similar educational, occupational, or income profiles—at least not in the short run. It would not be expected, therefore, that X percent of each ethnic group would hold professional jobs or be in the top ten percent income bracket. In any event, there was no need for policymakers to make equality among ethnic groups an objective as long as they were concerned more broadly with increasing equality of opportunity and reducing income inequalities. In the long run, it was assumed, even the cultural differences might disappear and class would displace ethnicity as the basis of social division of advanced industrial societies.

In recent years these arguments have been eroded in advanced industrial societies. One reason is that disadvantaged ethnic minorities have almost everywhere organized to make demands upon government, and in some instances they have made their loyalty to the state and their willingness to act by democratic procedures contingent upon a commitment from government to strive for their advancement. It is now generally understood in most industrial societies that governments must be responsive to disadvantaged ethnic groups if political stability and social harmony are to prevail. Why there has been such a resurgence of ethnic identity and why ethnic groups now demand a larger share of the benefits of industrial societies than was the case earlier are the subjects of a growing scholarly literature; for our purposes it is important to note only that on this question of the equitable sharing of benefits there are many similarities in the demands made by disadvantaged ethnic groups in both developed and developing countries.

There are obviously enormous differences among societies in the character of their ethnicities, the intensity of ethnic conflicts, the degree of mobilization by groups along ethnic lines, the histories of group relations, the extent to which there are fundamental goals and values with respect to individual group rights that are widely shared, and, of course, the kinds of political systems they have. Some readers will find these differences so great as to make comparisons of any kind meaningless. The argument here, however, is that preferential policies, though adopted by countries that are different in so many respects, do have some similar effects and that however different the objectives of their advocates, such policies push societies in similar directions.

There is, for one thing, a similarity in the arguments employed by disadvantaged ethnic groups. The most common argument is that inequalities among ethnic groups are not simply the result of cultural differences but reflect the prejudicial action by social groups and/or by government itself favoring some ethnic communities over others. Members of disadvantaged groups may have been denied educational opportunities because of their race, caste, religion, or language; the state may have provided greater educational and employment opportunities to other ethnic groups; employers may have discriminated in their hiring; norms of subordination may have been created by racism, casteism, or religious communalism. In short, the ethnic group is disadvantaged, it is argued, not because of its cultural norms, but because barriers have been placed in the way of its advancement. Nor is it sufficient, the argument continues, merely to remove these long-established barriers, since disadvantaged groups would then start the competitive race with a handicap.

Government must provide disadvantaged ethnic groups with some special benefits or preferences to enable them to catch up.

Alternative Policies

In response to these arguments, many governments have designed a variety of policies aimed at the realization of greater income and occupational equality among ethnic groups. Preferential treatment (goals, quotas, or reservations for ethnic groups in jobs, university admissions, land ownership, licenses, housing, contracts, etc.) is simply one of several policies for dealing with ethnic inequalities. There are other policies, however, which also have as their objective the economic improvement of particular ethnic groups, but the means employed are more indirect. At least five other such indirect policies are now widely employed.

The first are regional and urban development programs. These are particularly suitable when the disadvantaged ethnic groups are geographically concentrated in a particular area of the country. Government may choose to develop an underdeveloped region, or a declining urban or rural area, in order to improve the economic well-being of the ethnic groups that live in that locale. Policies, for example, by India in the hill states of the northeast, Belgium in its Flemish-speaking area, Nigeria in its northern regions, Malaysia in its eastern regions, and the United States in its urban areas are intended to improve the economic position of one or more ethnic groups in relation to others. One limitation of such a policy, however, is that it does not ensure that local people will necessarily benefit, since a regional development program may attract migrants from other parts of the country.

Governments may also provide aid for selected sectors of the economy where disadvantaged ethnic groups are concentrated. When, for example, the ethnic group or a large proportion of it engages in agriculture, or fishing, or forest industries, then programs to develop these sectors serve to improve their position. Examples are the agricultural and plantation development programs in Malaysia intended to benefit Malays, and the forest development projects in some of the tribal areas of India. Since many multiethnic societies have an ethnic division of labor, sector development projects can sometimes be effective in improving the economic well-being of a disadvantaged ethnic group.

Social service programs to improve the health, education, and housing of low-income groups may yield greater benefits to disadvantaged ethnic groups because they are disproportionately poor. A compulsory education program, for example, may improve the capacity of young people in disadvantaged communities to compete more effectively in the modern sector. A youth employment program, though universalistic in name, may be intended to benefit minority youth. Similarly, nutrition programs, maternity programs, nurseries for the children of working mothers, and family planning programs can improve the position of disadvantaged groups by providing them with facilities that were hitherto available only to higher income groups.

Income and wealth distribution policies are another way to change the position of one ethnic community in relation to another. A land reform program to ensure security of tenure for tenant farmers, provide minimum wages to agricultural laborers, or transfer land from large landowners to the landless, for example, may primarily improve the position of one ethnic group at the cost of another. Similarly, policies to nationalize private companies, increase taxes on the wealthy, or restrict the expansion of the private sector may, intentionally or otherwise, hit one or more ethnic groups and thereby reduce inequalities. (Indeed, there are instances in which a motive behind socialism is a desire to undermine a particular ethnic group.)

Finally, in addition to these economic policies, there are also various measures to increase the political power of ethnic groups. Political boundaries may be redrawn or there may be a devolution of authority to smaller administrative units so as to alter the relative position of ethnic groups within the political system. Proposals for devolution in Scotland, creation of linguistic states in India, multiplication of states in Nigeria, and the move toward neighborhood-controlled schools in the United States in the 1960s are cases in point.

In sum, regional development plans, sectoral investment strategies, social service programs, income and wealth distribution policies, and devolutionary and other administrative reforms may all have as their objective the reduction of socioeconomic or political inequalities among ethnic groups, but these policies, whatever their intentions, do not *explicitly* allocate benefits on ethnic grounds.

In contrast, preferential policies make explicit use of ethnic as distinct from universalistic, nonascriptive criteria. Under preferential policies, individuals are given special benefits not because they live in underdeveloped regions, work in lagging sectors of the economy, or are educationally and economically disadvantaged, but because they belong to a particular ethnic category—a caste, tribe, religion, linguistic or cultural group into which they have been born and which, on the average, is less educated, earns less, and has lower-status employment than do other ethnic groups.[1] Preferences based on race, color, religion, caste, national ancestry, or place of birth are deemed more invidious than preferences based on class membership, residence, or occupation in part because the former attributes are ones over which the individual has no control. One advantage of policies which employ nonascriptive criteria for allocating benefits is their greater acceptability to those who are not beneficiaries. The result is that these policies are less likely to strengthen ethnic attachments and generate tensions between ethnic groups than appears to be the case with preferential policies.

There are nonetheless a number of reasons why preferences based upon explicit ethnic criteria have been adopted by both the United States and India, and by a number of other multiethnic societies. One is that the policy is *targeted* to meet the demands of a group that believes it has been unjustly treated. Unlike nonascriptive policies that are intended to improve backward regions or lagging sectors of the economy and that only indirectly benefit a targeted group, preferential policies provide *exclusive* benefits. Another argument is that inequalities cannot be reduced merely by policies to eliminate discrimination in education and employment since such policies are rarely effective in ending disguised and more subtle forms of discrimination. Group membership, it is argued, continues to be a determinant of an individual's place in multiethnic societies because of the hidden ethnic preferences of admissions officers, teachers, and employers—and these can be overcome only by government-mandated affirmative action programs, quotas, reservations, and the like.

A third argument, and to some the most critical, is that preferential policies rest upon the moral claim that the social or economic backwardness of a particular ethnic group results from a history of discrimination, either by the dominant ethnic groups or by the state, and that preferences are justified as a form of societal compensation for past actions.

Critics of preferential policies reject on moral grounds the substitution of group membership for individual merit as the basis for societal stratification. They argue that statistical evidence of group differences in education, income, and employment is not proof of discriminatory actions and that inequality is not necessarily the result of discrimination. They reject the notion that compensation or "reparations" on the part of the present generation for the behavior of previous generations are justified, or that some individuals should be asked to pay collectively for the injustices committed by others. And they object in principle to "affirmative" discrimination, refusing to allow that it is any more morally justified than other forms of discrimination based on group membership.

These arguments and their many variations are widely heard in the United States and to a lesser extent in India. Since many of these arguments rest upon moral positions that do not lend themselves to verification or refutation through empirical evidence, an examination of the Indian experience does not help clarify the American debate. The fact is that in both countries decisions concerning the formulation of preferential policies are largely made without benefit of knowledge concerning their consequences. Since, in India, ex-untouchables, scheduled tribals, backward classes, and, in some areas, local people—and, in the United States, blacks, Chicanos, native Indians, and women—are subordinate to others in education, employment, and income, and their subordination can in part be traced to a history of discrimination, moral authority for preferences is invoked in such a way as to make assessment of policy effects irrelevant.

Moreover, a judgment by politicians as to the political effects—both gains and losses—of preferential policies has been more important in guiding the future course of policy than the actual effects of the policies on the intended beneficiaries. Nonetheless, a considerable amount is known in both countries as to the impact of the policies on targeted groups. And though the evidence often remains inconclusive, the opportunities for scholarly input into the evaluation of policy effects in this field remain substantial. A review of the Indian experience suggests some striking similarities and differences—as well as some comparable problems in assessment—with the American experience.[2]

In order to make the two cases more comparable we shall consider the entire range of preferential policies in India, including those intended to benefit scheduled castes, scheduled tribes, and other backward classes, as well as those intended to benefit the local population in relation to migrants. Similarly, the appropriate item for comparison in American policy needs to be not domicile rules on employment and education, since these rarely relate to ethnicity, but affirmative action programs to benefit minorities and women.

Homo Hierarchicus, Homo Equalis?

That two countries with such divergent historical traditions and such divergent social norms should evolve a similar set of policies to deal with the problems of ethnic inequality is itself remarkable. On the surface at least there are probably no two societies which embrace such opposing values with respect to human equality and hierarchy. The classical Hindu tradition views inequalities of status and power as divinely prescribed; traditional norms of subordination and superordination sanctify the Hindu system of social stratification. Indians, the French anthropologist Louis Dumont once wrote, belong as it were to a breed apart, *Homo hierarchicus*.

An Indian anthropologist, Andre Beteille, has taken sharp issue with such attempts to distinguish between social systems on the basis of whether their "ultimate values" rest upon notions of either hierarchy or equality. "There is something of both in every human society and perhaps in every human individual," he writes.[3] Among Indian intellectuals and politicians, he argues, there is a commitment to a more equalitarian society, and the constitution itself calls for the creation of a "casteless and classless society." This commitment to equalitarianism, he says, may have grown out of India's exposure to the West (ironically, to the inequalitarian treatment which the British accorded the Indians), but it resonated within the Indian tradition. Buddha, for example, was opposed to caste, and Gandhi insisted that the Dharmasastra, a classical text devoted to the notion of the hierarchical ranking of castes, "did not represent the ultimate truth of Hinduism."[4] Beteille rejects these sweeping contrasts between the Western world and Asia, and particularly between the United States and India, as a form of self-congratulations on the part of Westerners.[5]

Beteille's caution against overgeneralizing, especially with respect to "ultimate values" (he recognizes the realities of the Indian system of hierarchy)

141

is well taken. Nonetheless, one cannot overlook the fact that since the eighteenth century, the American heritage has emphasized equality of opportunity and equality before the law, even if in reality there haye been barriers to mobility. With the aristocracy of Britain and Europe absent from American soil, and despite the existence of slavery in many of the American states, the popular belief prevailed that America offered opportunities for mobility rarely present elsewhere. The disenfranchisement of blacks and women notwithstanding, at the core of American political ideology was a belief in equal political rights and liberty for all.

In practice, of course, there was a divergence between the theory and the reality of social relations in both India and the United States. The caste system in India did not preclude the possibility of group mobility; and the principle of equal opportunity in the United States did not preclude the erection of institutional barriers to mobility. Still, in reality as well as in theory the two social systems diverged sharply in the kinds of opportunities provided for both individual and group mobility, as well as in the character of the prevailing ideology which provided the framework for such mobility.

In spite of these differences both countries chose to make some form of ethnic equality, or at least a reduction in the educational and occupational differences among ethnic groups, a public objective, and to do so through the use of preferential policies. For India, the adoption of such policies was earlier than in the United States, and, as we have seen, there were relatively few objections, initially at least, to the establishment of a system of quotas for specified ethnic groups. In the United States, on the other hand, where there has been a long political struggle for legislation to ensure equality of opportunity and the elimination of discrimination, the decision to pursue a preferential policy represented a change in policy, and stirred considerable controversy. But having adopted similar policies, the two countries offer striking parallels in the kinds of political consequences that have resulted—and, as we shall see, some differences as well. Let us first consider some of the similarities.

Similarities in Policies and Outcomes

In both countries the establishment of a system of preferencés for one group has generated claims on the part of others. A state policy to allocate benefits on the basis of ethnic group membership has stimulated the creation of political organizations in both countries along ethnic rather than class or occupational lines. In India, a system initially intended for scheduled castes and tribes has been extended to backward classes and sons of the soil, and there are now demands for the restoration of reservations for Muslims and other religious minorities. In the United States as well, policies intended to benefit blacks have been extended to other ethnic minorities and to women.

Each extension has been accompanied by protest from those who have been excluded. In India, upper castes who initially had willingly accepted reservations for scheduled castes and tribes have bitterly opposed their extension to backward classes, in large part because any further extension reduces the proportion of positions in educational institutions and in government employment that are accessible through competitive, merit-based recruitment. By the same token, criticisms of preferential policies have been met by countercritiques among actual and potential beneficiaries who fear a reversal or a dilution of these policies. Similarly, in the United States the extension of affirmative action programs to several different minorities and to women has catalyzed a variety of ethnic groups, professional associations, and labor and business groups either to support or to counter such policies.

Opposition to existing preferential policies has also grown with an improvement in the educational and occupational position of members of the ethnic group to which preferences have been given. Though some see this development as evidence that the policy is succeeding in reducing inequalities and hence should be continued, others have seen improvements as a reason for ending preferences or redefining them in such a way as to exclude some categories of beneficiaries. In the American debate over preferences, some have questioned the inclusion of Cubans—who are above the American average in education, employment, and income—in the preferential category of those with Spanish surnames, while others have questioned preferences to the children of parents with high education and income and who are presumed capable of making it in an open competitive system. These arguments, as we have seen, are also used in India where scheduled castes and tribes now include a middle class whose children have entered the educational system and the labor market. Why, some Indians have asked, should the son of an educated scheduled caste minister be given educational and employment preferences? And why should the member of an agriculturally prosperous backward class family be given preference over a poor youngster from an upper-caste family? Similarly, members of some of India's scheduled tribes have proposed that the Christian scheduled tribes be dropped from the preferential lists since such a substantial portion of this group has achieved higher positions. Opposition to preferences seems to increase in direct proportion to the success of the policy. With any substantial indication of progress for those who have received preferences the question of whether preferences should be continued has become a political issue.

In short, the establishment of preferential policies has spurred the mobilization of pro and anti forces in both countries. And in both countries, mobilized groups have sought to find allies, build coalitions, and, above all, establish an institutional base for creating political resources to extend, limit, or terminate the policies.

For India's scheduled castes, a key institutional base has been the scheduled caste representation in parliament and, to a lesser extent, the scheduled caste and scheduled tribe commissions of the central government. India's constitutional provision for parliamentary representation for scheduled castes and tribes assures these groups of political representation—and thereby guarantees that their claims for reservations in the educational system and in government employment will not be ignored.[6] Proponents of reservations for the backward classes have won the support of the Lok Dal party in northern India,[7] presumably in return for electoral support, while opponents of backward class reservations have looked to other political parties as well as to the courts for support.

In the absence of a system of assured legislative representation through reservations, American blacks and "Hispanics" have been underrepresented by members of their own communities in the legislatures. Proponents of minority claims have formed alliances with nonminority liberals and have sought support within bureaucratic agencies. A variety of such agencies—Justice Department, Equal Employment Opportunity Commission, Civil Service Commission, Civil Rights Commission, the Department of Health and Human Services and Education—have played a more visible role than departments and ministries in India, and in the process of lobbying for or against minority claims have gained reputations as being partisan to one position or the other. In both countries claimants have recognized the critical importance of placing supporters in those institutions which have the authority to implement policy.

Who are the beneficiaries of preferential policies is another contentious issue both in India and in the United States. In both countries preferential policies do not benefit all sections of the beneficiary group. They do not increase the educational opportunities of the poorest, or provide greater employment for the uneducated section of the targeted group. Their primary effect is to benefit the more-advantaged individuals within the disadvantaged ethnic group and thereby to enlarge the size of its middle class.

As we saw in earlier chapters, preferential policies in Maharashtra, Assam, and Telangana covered jobs in the organized industrial sector and in the bureaucracies. Preferential policies did not provide employment for those in the agricultural sector where most of India's poor are situated. Even within the occupations affected by these policies, the number of jobs at stake was generally small. In Bihar, for example, the demand by the backward classes for quotas in government employment was estimated to involve only two thousand jobs, out of a potential pool of some seventy thousand college students from the backward classes.[8]

In defense of the class-specific features of preferential policies, their supporters have argued that these policies have indirect benefits for the larger ethnic group from which the beneficiaries are drawn. The first is the familiar role model argument: high achievement by one sector of an ethnic group presumably raises the aspirations of young people who might otherwise have been contented with lower levels of education, employment, and income. The second argument is that the expansion of the middle class can increase the employment and income opportunities of those below since members of the middle class, especially those who obtain managerial positions, have the power to hire or can influence those who do. Moreover, the middle class can also play a role in influencing government officials to respond to demands by lower-income groups within the community, since the middle class can provide political leadership and exercise more political clout than the poor. The third argument is a psychological one: members of an ethnic group are more likely to be treated with respect if other communities recognize that they too can produce doctors, lawyers, journalists, professors, government officials, and managers. There can be, in other words, a diffusion of status respect if even only a small sector of an ethnic group has improved its socioeconomic position.

But the immediate beneficiaries of preferential quotas are certainly those to whom the coveted jobs or university admissions accrue, and those individuals are the ones with some education, some special skills, or some other advantage over others in the disadvantaged group to which they belong. In countries more industrialized than India, preferential policies may potentially reach a larger section of the population. Equal employment policies in the United States (Title VII of the Civil Rights Act and Executive Orders 11246 and 11375) cover industrial and tertiary sectors in which perhaps 70%–80% of the workforce is employed. But even in this case employment preferences can certainly not address the problems of those who are chronically unemployed, e.g., high school dropouts and welfare recipients. It would be a mistake therefore to judge the success or failure of preferential policies by their capacity or incapacity to redress poverty or to proffer immediate gains to the majority of a disadvantaged group. They are not a substitute for policies directly aimed at alleviating the problems of the poor.[9]

If preferential policies narrow disparities between ethnic groups, they do not reduce disparities within ethnic groups. To the contrary, preferential policies, by providing selective benefits in education and employment to the most advanced segments of an ethnic group tend to widen within-group differences. Such differences may of course grow even in the absence of preferential policies. It is well known, and by now well documented, that economic growth is often accompanied during its early stages by an increase in disparities between social classes and between regions. When region and occupation are, as is the case in India and in many other multiethnic societies, linked to ethnicity, then disparities between ethnic groups are likely to increase with economic growth. Even at relatively advanced stages of development, when ethnic and racial equalization seems to improve and income inequalities tend to narrow, disparities *within* as well as among ethnic groups may widen as some members of the ethnic group enter higher education, move into professional ranks, and achieve higher incomes, while other members of the same ethnic group remain behind. Preferential policies, to the extent that they succeed in making it possible for some members of the ethnic group to move up more rapidly than they might have in the absence of such policies, widen these disparities.

But if the targeted beneficiaries of preferential policies are the more advantaged, that is those who come from the better-educated and higher-income families within the preferred group, is there any evidence that even this segment actually benefits from preferential policies?

The previous chapter reviewed in some detail the inferences that can be drawn from employment and migration data on the impact of preferential policies in several regions of India. In Bombay, where the percentage of Maharashtrians employed in middle class positions increased, the changes appear to be part of a longer-term pattern of social and economic mobility that cannot be attributed to preferential policies alone. Similarly the number of Assamese employed in the organized section also increased, but changes in the number and quality of the labor force may have been responsible aside from preferential recruitment. In the absence of preferential hiring, would not other policies directed at increasing the number of trained and educated Maharashtrians and Assamese have resulted in increased employment for local persons?

A similar uncertainty exists with respect to the assessment of affirmative action programs in the United States. One well-known study of American affirmative action policies indicates that substantial minority gains in education, employment, and housing occurred before such policies were initiated and concludes that there is little evidence that minority groups actually benefited from preferential policies.[10] But other evidence suggests quite different conclusions.[11] Many university administrators have suggested that if special admissions programs for minority students were not employed, and if admissions standards were made uniform for white and black students, the percentage of minorities enrolled in professional schools would be severely reduced. In any event, since it can always be argued that even when the rate of minority advancement has been slow, it would have been slower in the absence of preferences, the controversy cannot easily be resolved through empirical studies.

The Indian government monitors the effects of reservations on the education of scheduled castes and tribes in reports that are annually published by the Ministry of Education, but data on employment among these communities are less rigorously collected. Nor are there any comparable data collected for backward classes—those numbers are in any event not recorded by the census —nor for the "local" population. As befits a more developed country, the United States does more systematically assemble data on its disadvantaged minorities, and there is a considerable amount of academic research on this data. But in both countries the monitoring itself is controversial, and the results of studies have been used both to support and to oppose the policies. In both countries, preferential policies are pursued with little regard for analyzing the ways in which these policies actually affect the education and employment of presumed beneficiaries.

The effect of preferential policies on the relationship between the preferred minorities and nonbeneficiaries is another source of controversy on which the Indian experience is as problematic as that of the United States. One purpose of preferential policies is to redress the grievances of an ethnic group, but the very measures adopted to achieve that objective—that is, the redistribution of resources preferentially—incur the high risk of aggravating interethnic relations. Supporters of preferences nonetheless are persuaded that even if providing socioeconomic advancement to disadvantaged groups may result in interethnic hostility, such hostility is a necessary price and may indeed be a measure of the success of such policies. Thus, the backlash to preferential policies in education and employment for blacks in the United States and ex-untouchables in India is interpreted by supporters of such policies as one indication that these disadvantaged groups are moving into positions hitherto denied them. They take the growing opposition as itself a demonstration that the policy is having an impact on improving the objective position of the minorities.

In the three Indian cases provided here on preferential policies it is clear that while the policies were a response to the political demands of one ethnic group, they resulted in angry responses on the part of other ethnic groups. In Bombay, Andhra Pradesh, and Assam each proposal for preferences for natives has engendered tension among the ethnic groups. Whether the conflict would have been greater had the government not responded favorably to demands for preferences is, of course, not an answerable question. But in some instances the initial proposal for preferential policies was made by politicians not as a response to popular demands, but as a means of mobilizing political support. Clearly, there are circumstances when the introduction of preferential policies can precipitate as well as mitigate ethnic conflict.

In many respects, then, there are similarities both in policies and in the political outcomes in the two countries. Policies which provdie benefits to disadvantaged groups through preferences based on ethnic criteria have been a stimulant to political mobilization by ethnic groups in both societies. In both countries preferences have worked to the advantage of the middle classes among the disadvantaged, but yet received popular support from the entire targeted ethnic group. In both countries the provision of preferences has stimulated a backlash among those who are excluded from the benefits. In both countries, proponents of preferences have sought allies either (in the case of India) within the political parties, or (in the case of the United States) within the government bureaucracy. In both countries opponents of preferences have turned to the courts to restrain administrators and politicians. And in both countries there is a continuous effort either to extend or to contract the system of preferences.

Differences in Policies and Outcomes

In India, however, the pressure for the extension of preferential policies has been far more intense than in the United States. In India preferences have been interpreted to mean precise statistical quotas, while in the United States preferences have been softened to less precise affirmative action programs. In India the system of preferences has been extended further than in the United States; there are reservations for parliamentary and state assembly representatives, and preferences are provided not only in employment but for promotions. And in India, the numbers of people who are covered by preferential policies are far greater than in the United States and in some states cover majorities as well as minorities.

The restraints on both claimants and policymakers have thus been far less in India than in the United States. There are several reasons. For one thing, as noted earlier, the longer tradition of preferential policies in India has given them a position of legitimacy and popular acceptability not found in the United States. Preferential policies in India were well established before independence. The British provided selected ethnic groups special rights in recruitment to the army, the bureaucracy, and the railway services, and they used reservations, as they saw it, to protect certain politically disadvantaged groups. The Nizam of Hyderabad and a number of provincial Congress governments used preferences to protect the employment interests of the local middle classes. The postindependence government of India also viewed some kinds of reservations as a legitimate instrument for policy. The principle was given legitimacy in the constitution itself which prescribed that the state not only could but should give preferences to scheduled castes and tribes. Higher castes accepted the principle that there ought to be preferences for these groups, for there was some feeling that reservations or protections were due to these communities in a society which traditionally prescribed disabilities. There was also some feeling among members of the Constituent Assembly that the belief in the social inferiority of the scheduled castes was so deeply engrained in Hindu society, and that discrimination was still so widely practiced, that nothing short of a state policy to provide preferences could overcome the handicaps they experienced.

Many Indians also argued that in any event the existing distribution of jobs within the "modern" sectors of the labor market, especially within government, was not the result of open competition, but reflected the division of labor prescribed by the Hindu social system, the differential access to education resulting from British policies, or the preferences the British gave to one group or another in employment. Why not, then, restructure the modern labor market in a more equitable manner to provide each community with its "share"? In contrast, while reservations or quotas were historically used in India to *benefit* one group in relation to another, quotas were historically employed in the United States to *limit access* by one or more groups to educational institutions and to social and economic positions. In short, historical and constitutional differences have contributed to the greater willingness on the part of Indians than of Americans to accept the principle of preferences.

Closely linked to these historical differences between India and the United States are divergent ideological perspectives as to the purpose of preferences. For most Indians the rationale for preferences is primarily the desirability of creating a social order in which inequality among ethnic groups is reduced; among Americans, preferential policies have been more closely tied to the issue of compensation for past discrimination.[12] In India, therefore, where inequality is the primary basis for preferential claims, a large number of ethnic groups can and do make a reasonable case for eligibility. Indeed, except for those at the very top, most ethnic groups are potential claimants with the result that demands for inclusion have proliferated. In the United States, by contrast, where the claims rest more explicitly on some plausible demonstration of group discrimination as well as inequality, only a few groups are plausibly able to present a case. Moreover, in the United States some ethnic groups believe that to seek preferential treatment is to admit that they are unable to compete, a position groups that no longer feel discriminated against are reluctant to adopt and which many believe runs counter to the American ethos of competition based upon individual merit. In India, on the other hand, groups more readily accept the argument that they could not win even if they had equal access to education and could openly compete for employment.

Moreover, Americans have tended to view inequality between individuals as the result either of individual performance or of discrimination rather than of some structural elements in the economy, whereas Indians tend to see individual differences as reflecting group differences that have in turn been shaped by the society, the economy, and control over the polity. Indians, therefore, have been less inclined to question the right of the state to influence (Americans would say "interfere in") group relations than have Americans.

The dual concern in the United States with utilizing quotas only as remedy to past discrimination while preserving the ethos of competition and meritocracy has therefore led to a more narrowly specified targeting of preferential claimants. Most quotas or race conscious recruitment policies in the United States use as the yardstick to measure appropriate goals either minority population figures or, more frequently, the more restrictive measure of "availability" which assesses the number of minorities qualified in the particular area for which recruitment or admissions are being undertaken. The University of California at Davis, defendants in the *Bakke* suit, set aside sixteen places out of one hundred for minorities in the incoming medical class. But in other situations, such as employment in skilled crafts, fire departments, or police forces, the courts have sanctioned higher percentages for minorities although it has usually been specified that these quotas are temporary and can be mandated by government only where previous discrimination has been demonstrated.

In India the percentage of places reserved for scheduled castes, tribes, backward classes, and other claimants can range as high as one-half of all positions, a figure identified as acceptable in a 1963 court decision (*Balaji* v. *Mysore*) and assumed to be law ever since. Subsequent to this case, it was deemed that reservations beyond this point would impinge on the rights of equality guaranteed by the constitution (to which preferential rights were seen as an exception) and would impair efficiency and productivity.[13] In India, then, where the goal of greater economic equality, rather than an end to discrimination, is the guiding norm pressures for an extension of preferential policies are considerably greater than in the United States.

Since some of the opposition to the extension of preferential benefits comes from those who believe that the efficiency of administration would be damaged by its extension, a statistical limit for some categories of university admission and employment has been an acceptable compromise. But in the United States where the attack against preferences (especially in the form of quotas) comes from those who believe that quotas by ethnic and racial criteria are morally wrong, statistical compromises have been unacceptable.

These historical and ideological considerations which make India more receptive than the United States to preferential policies are reinforced by the ethnic demography of the country. In India those who claim a right to preferential treatment, whether on the basis of backwardness or residence (or both), are proportionately a far larger section of society than in the United States. Scheduled castes and scheduled tribes together constitute 22.5 percent of the Indian population. In northern India, the backward castes are estimated at more than a quarter of the Hindi-speaking population. The Muslims, many of whom are now calling for reservations, form another 11.2 percent of the population. And sons of the soil claimants are typically majorities in the states in which they reside. In the United States, by contrast, minorities seeking preferences on the grounds of their disadvantaged status—blacks, persons of Hispanic origin, American Indians, and some Asian-American groups—taken together are more nearly 20% to 25% of the national population. The resurgence of ethnicity in America, and the very existence of policies and programs that provide benefits along ethnic lines, do of course enlarge the pool of potential claimants, and in some localities the claimants can even constitute a majority of the population; but still the potentially mobilizable population on behalf of preferences is not as great as in India where ethnic stratification is so pervasive and where all but a small proportion of upper castes can claim to be disadvantaged (and even the upper castes can claim to be disadvantaged by identifying themselves with sons of the soil claimants).

Finally, the issue of preferences is far more salient at the state than at the national level in India as compared with the United States. In India the selection of groups to be included in the system of reservations is made by state governments as well as, and in some instances instead of, the central government,[14] while in the United States it is primarily the federal government that has defined which groups are to be classified as "disadvantaged" minorities entitled to preferences. In India sons of the soil groups have thus been able to mobilize political support at the state level rather than at the national parliamentary level where their claims are more likely to be resisted. Similarly, the backward castes are sufficiently numerous in a few states to be able to marshall considerable electoral and party support for their preferential claims.

The result is that cleavages over preferential policies have been more acute in Indian than in the American states. Sons of the soil policies have been controversial issues in Assam, Maharashtra, Andhra, and Bihar; and backward caste claims have been issues in Karnataka, Bihar, Haryana, and U.P., among others. In some instances political movements have arisen that have made preferential claims the issue around which they sought to mobilize political support. There have been massive demonstrations, for example, in Patna, Gauhati, Hyderabad, Bombay, and Bangalore. In contrast, it has been Washington that has been the focal point for preferential claims in American society, where it is expected that the president, Congress, federal agencies, and the Supreme Court will decide how far to go and where to stop.

Conclusion: Divergences and Convergences

In both countries there is a tendency for each group to assert that it has rights, but its opponents merely have interests. Nevertheless, in both countries the central issue raised by any form of preferential policies is the question of competing rights. The difference lies in what rights are at stake. In the United States the claim by minorities that they have rights because of historical discrimination clashes with the claims of others that everyone should have equal rights to education and employment based upon merit and performance, without discrimination and without preferences.

In India the assertion that local people have a first claim to education and employment, and that they have the right to protect their own culture and way of life, is challenged by citizens in other parts of the country who claim the right to seek employment and live anywhere they choose in their own country.

In India there is widespread belief that the fundamental task of "integration" is to establish a relationship among the country's distinctive parts, a relationship based upon appropriate shares by each ethnic group in education and in employment. An integrated and harmonious social system in the Indian view envisages a place for each group in the social order, based upon mutual respect and proportionality in the distribution of society's benefits.

The American view of "integration" and equality has largely rested upon an image of a society based upon equality of opportunity for individuals—with individuals, not ethnic groups, having rights. "Equality" and "integration" have thus had very different meanings in the two countries.

But in recent years the differences between the two countries have become blurred. There is considerable concern in India over the impact of sons of the soil policies on the rights of Indian citizens; and there is a concern that reservations for backward classes are too destructive both to the claims of merit and performance, and to the interests of the remaining "forward" classes. The result has not been a reversal of policy, but a growing conflict over policies that, as applied to scheduled castes and scheduled tribes, were once widely acceptable.

Starting from a very different position, the United States has moved down the same road as India toward a system in which groups each have "shares" of public and private goods. The "rights" of minorities in the United States to preferential admissions in educational institutions and a proportional share of jobs rest upon many of the same arguments and assumptions as do similar policies in India. The view that ethnic groups have rights as ethnic groups is increasingly asserted in the United States: the demand, for example, by many "Hispanic" groups (a catch-all term for a wide variety of groups, not unlike the broad category in India of "backward" classes) for the "right" to use their own language in the schools has its parallels in India.

The United States is obviously far away from creating a social order in which ethnic groups are given exclusive rights over a fixed share of educational admissions, employment, and promotion. As we have seen, for reasons of history, ethnic demography, politics, and belief systems, such a social order is far more acceptable in India than in the United States. Still, the United States has taken steps in this direction in the past decade, and may take more steps in the next decade as Hispanics become a more organized political force.

An equalitarian ethos has become a typical attitude in both modern and modernizing states. But what is at issue is the question of what kind of equalitarianism. Equality of results is very different from equality of opportunity. A policy requiring that a fixed proportion of specified ethnic groups be hired is radically different from a policy that seeks to end discrimination in hiring. A more equitable distribution of income throughout the society is a very different kind of equality from one in which each ethnic group is proportionately represented within the middle class. The demand by one ethnic group that it ought to have exclusive rights to compete for jobs and buy and sell land within its own turf is at odds with the view that all the citizens of a country ought to have equal rights to compete for jobs and land anywhere they choose. In short, what appears to some as a policy aimed at the achievement of equality often appears to others as grossly inequitable and unjust.

Moral philosophers and policy analysts can make the distinctions clearer, specify the trade-offs, and indicate the consequences. But the choices made by different societies will be heavily shaped by the pervasiveness of these various ideas about equality, and by the extent to which particular groups are politically organized to claim "rights." What is also clear is that the policies themselves influence how people organize and what they demand. In both India and the United States, the adoption of preferential policies has generated demands for more preferential policies. Often the costs of such policies are indirect and invisible just as the benefits are long in accruing and difficult to measure. But the question of whether they work and for whose benefit is secondary to the political question of the "rights" of the claimants. For these reasons it seems unlikely that preferential policies will be ended in either country in the near future. Indeed, in both countries, it seems more likely that new claims and counterclaims will be made that will lead to more conflicts within the legislatures, universities, government bureaucracies, political parties, the courts, and in the streets. In both countries the clashes will be over conflicting "rights" and conflicting notions of "equality," though the rights that are asserted and the notions of equality that are employed may not always be the same in both countries. Can preferences once given ever be withdrawn? The political costs of terminating preferential policies may ultimately in both countries prove enormous. But for now the major unanswered policy questions are preferential policies for whom, to what extent, and in what form?

Notes

Chapter One

1. The terminology is, of course, intended to reveal the speaker's point of view. Marc Galanter of the University of Wisconsin, who has written more on the subject in India than any other scholar, employs the term "compensatory discrimination," but this too is hardly neutral. Throughout this book we shall use the words "preferences" and "reservations" because these seem to us to be judgment free terms.

2. There are a number of useful book-length studies of scheduled castes in India, but most only marginally deal with the impact of preferences and reservations. See Harold Isaacs, *India's Ex-Untouchables* (New York: John Day, 1964); Owen M. Lynch, *The Politics of Untouchability: Social Mobility and Social Change in a City of India* (New York: Columbia University Press, 1969); Michael Mahar, ed., *The Untouchables in Contemporary India* (Tucson: University of Arizona Press, 1972); Sachchidananda, *The Harijan Elite* (Faridabad: Thompson Press, 1977). Marc Galanter is currently completing a book entitled *Competing Equalities: The Indian Experience with Compensatory Discrimination.*

For an examination of the question of beneficiaries, see Parta C. Aggarwal and Mohammed Siddiq Ashraf, *Equality through Privilege: A Study of Special Privileges for Scheduled Castes in Haryana* (New Delhi: Shri Ram Center for Industrial Relations and Human Resources, 1976). For a particularly useful compendium of laws and court decisions on reservations, see G. P. Verma, *Caste Reservations in India: Law and the Constitution* (Allahabad: Chugh Publications, 1980). For a comparison of the politics of ex-untouchables in India and blacks in America, see Sidney Verba, Ahmed Bashiruddin, and Anil Bhatt, *Caste, Race and Politics: A Comparative Study of India and the United States* (Beverly Hills: Sage Publications, 1971).

Among the most useful articles on preferential policies are these: Karuna Ahmad, "Towards Equality: Consequences of Protective Discrimination," *Economic and Political Weekly,* January 14, 1978, pp. 69–72; Marc Galanter, "Who Are the Other Backward Classes?" *Economic and Political Weekly,* October 28, 1978, pp. 1812–28; Lelah Dushkin, "Backward Class Benefits and Social Class in India, 1920–1970," *Economic and Political Weekly,* April 7, 1979, pp. 661–67; Marc Galanter, "Equality and 'Protective Discrimination' in India," *Rutgers Law Review* 16(1961):42–74; Marc Galanter, "Group Membership and Group Preferences in India," *Journal of Asian and African Studies* 2(1967):91–124; Alan Gledhill, "Constitutional Protection of Indian Minorities," *Journal of the Indian Law Institute* 1(1959):403–15; Raj Kumar Gupta, "Justice: Unequal but Inseparate," *Journal of the Indian Law Institute* 11 (1969):57–86; Mohammed Imam, "Reservations of Seats for Backward Classes in Public Services and Educational Institutions," *Journal of the India Law Institute* 8(1966):411–46.

Chapter Two

1. Minorities need not, of course, be of migrant origin, but it is striking to note how often they are. It is this particular element, the ethnic minority as an outsider in the territorial as distinct from the cultural sense, that provides an important rationale for policies to give preferences to the local ethnic majority.

2. To take one of the many possible examples, the Hindu weavers of Saurashtra left Gujarat during one of the Islamic invasions and settled eventually in the southern city of Madurai where they have lived since the sixteenth century, practicing their ancient craft and speaking their native tongue.

3. The Muslim court in Hyderabad in the seventeenth and eighteenth centuries, for example, recruited their administrators from among the aristocratic Muslim classes in northern India and in Iran.

4. For an analysis of the ways in which migration has affected the ethnic composition and occupational structure of different regions of India, see Myron Weiner, *Sons of the Soil: Migration and Ethnic Conflict in India* (Princeton: Princeton University Press, 1978), chap. 2 ("Migration and the Growth of Ethnic Diversity"), pp. 19–74.

5. In 1971 the scheduled castes numbered 82.5 million or 15 percent of the population, and the scheduled tribals numbered 41.1 million or 7.5 percent. The scheduled castes are proportionately most numerous in Haryana, Punjab, Tamil Nadu, U.P., and West Bengal, and the tribals in Assam, Bihar, Gujarat, Madhya Pradesh, Rajasthan, Orissa, and Tripura. Four small states in the northeast—Mizoram, Arunachal Pradesh, Meghalaya and Nagaland—are predominantly tribal. Seventy-eight out of 542 seats in parliament are reserved for scheduled castes and 38 for scheduled tribes. The states with the largest combined proportion of reservations are Tripura (40%), Orissa (38%), Madhya Pradesh (33%), Himachal Pradesh (26.5%), West Bengal (25.9%), Rajasthan (28%), Punjab (24.8%), Bihar (23%), and U.P. (21.2%).

6. For a comprehensive legal review and history of the development of preferential policies toward the backward classes, see Galanter, "Who Are the Other Backward Classes?"

7. In the early sixties the Maharashtra state assembly did, however, extend preferences to neo-Buddhists for employment in the state government.

8. During the campaign for the 1980 parliamentary elections, the Imam of Jama Masjid, the leader of India's largest mosque, wrote a public letter to Mrs. Indira Gandhi demanding that twenty percent of government jobs should be reserved for Muslims, and that Muslims be given proportional representation in elected bodies and preferential treatment in commerce and industry. In her

reply Mrs. Gandhi avoided any commitment to reservations and preferences for Muslims but repeated the vague commitment of the Congress election manifesto that "we feel that in every field of national activity as also in the affairs of the government, the totality of the population should be properly and effectively reflected and represented in the interest of national integration." Letter published by All-India Congress Committee, New Delhi, Nov. 20, 1979. See also *Indian National Congress (I) Election Manifesto,* New Delhi, 1979.

Chapter Three

1. *New York Times,* June 9, 1980.

2. See the excellent article by Harry T. Edwards and Barry L. Zaretsky, "Preferential Remedies for Employment Discrimination," *Michigan Law Review* 74, no. 1 (November 1975):1–47.

3. *Defunis, et al.* v. *Odegaard, et al.* (416 U.S. 312, 1974). "The key to the problem," Justice Douglas wrote, "is the consideration of each application in a racially neutral way." This decision is a vivid contrast to that of the five-member majority that ruled in the Bakke case cited below that race-specific preferences under some conditions could be deemed constitutional.

4. *Regents of the University of California* v. *Allan Bakke,* 46 LW 4896 (1978).

5. The legality of the in-plant training program was considered in *U.S. Steel Workers of America* v. *Brian F. Weber, et al.* and two accompanying cases.

6. See account in *New York Times,* July 3, 1980, of *Fullilove* v. *Klutznick* that concerned a $4 billion public works program legislated by the U.S. Congress in 1977.

7. This clause, article 15(4), was adopted by the Constitution (First Amendment) Act, 1951.

8. *State of Kerala* v. *N. M. Thomas* 1976 (1) *Service Law Reporter,* p. 807.

9. There are other sections of the constitution, notably the sixth schedule, which regulates the sale of property in particular areas of India, that do restrict to some degree the freedom of movement of all persons throughout India.

10. *Report of the States Reorganization Commission* (New Delhi: Government of India Press, 1955) p. 230.

11. *Constituent Assembly Debates* (hereafter referred to as *CAD*), November 30, 1947, p. 676.

12. As Kartikeya Sarabhai has commented, it is ironic that this argument to accept residential requirements should have been enunciated by Ayyar and Rajgopalachari, two Tamil Brahmins, members of a community which in the 1960s was to become one of the chief targets of nativist protest in Bombay. "Unity among Diversity, Public Policies and the Evolution of India's Goal of National Integration," draft of a Ph.D. thesis, M.I.T., pp. 2–7.

13. *CAD,* April 30, 1947, vol. 3, p. 448.

14. Shiva Rao, *Framing of India's Constitution,* vol. 11, p. 186.

15. *CAD,* November 30, 1948, vol. 7, p. 700.

16. See speech by F. H. Mohsin, *Rajya Sabha Debates* 89:1–4 (July 25, 1974), p. 211. For other speeches by government spokesmen, see R. K. Khadilkar, Minister of Labour and Rehabilitation, in *Rajya Sabha* 80:10–18 (May 25, 1972), p. 88; Siddeshwar Prasad, Deputy Minister in the Ministry of Heavy Industry, in *Lok Sabha Debates* 29:6–10 (August 2, 1973), p. 191; M. H. Choudhury, Minister of Industrial Development, in *Rajya Sabha* 77:12–15 (August 9, 1971). Also see account by A. G. Noorani, "Legality of Local Recruitment," *Indian Express* (New Delhi), April 2, 1974.

17. *Lok Sabha Debates* 22:21–25 (December 13, 1972), p. 13. See also speech by F. H. Mohsin, n. 16, p. 213.

18. *Rajya Sabha Debates,* February 28, 1974, p. 93.

19. See *Lok Sabha Debates,* November 14, 1957.

20. See "Parochialism," *Times of India* (Bombay), October 15, 1973; Order No. ELP/Undertaking 7934, September 25, 1973, signed by Joint Director of Industries; and "Maharashtra Ticks but West Bengal Still Toys with Idea," *Hindustan Standard,* October 27, 1973.

21. See "Jobs for Local People," *Times of India* (Bombay), September 13, 1973; "Sons of the Soil?" *Finance,* June 7, 1975; and "Sons of the Soil: Report from the States," *Illustrated Weekly,* November 3, 1974, p. 22. The latter article reports that the West Bengal state assembly passed a resolution saying that anyone who had lived ten years or more in West Bengal should get preferential treatment in employment. It is interesting that one of the first actions of the present communist chief minister, Jyoti Basu, was to issue a statement repudiating policies of localism.

22. See "Jobs for Local People: T. Nadu Govt's Appeal to Employees," *The Hindu,* August 6, 1974; "DMK Demands 80 p.c. of Jobs for Locals," *Times of India,* July 8, 1974; and "Sons of the Soil," *Illustrated Weekly,* November 3, 1974. Another article in the same issue of *Illustrated Weekly,* "Who are the Sons of the Soil?" by K. P. Nayar, reports that legislation was passed in the state implementing the directive; however, there is no mention of such legislation in the other *Illustrated Weekly* article or in the newspapers or other periodical sources consulted.

23. See "Road to Ruin," *Times of India,* January 10, 1974, and editorial in *Statesman,* January 7, 1974. According to the *Statesman,* the restrictions do not apply to the cantonment and municipal limits of Shillong. In the rest of the state the law will prohibit a stay of longer than four months, without prior official permission, of anyone who has not already taken up fixed and permanent habitation in Meghalaya for twelve years or more. The article points out that the rules do not refer to buying land or to getting employment but simply to *being* in Meghalaya.

24. Shriram Maheshwari, "Regionalism in India: Political and Administrative Response," *Indian Journal of Public Administration* 19, no. 4, p. 457. See also Myron Weiner, "Changing Conceptions of Citizenship in a Multi-Ethnic Society," Migration Development Study Group Working Paper MDG/75-4, c/75-6, M.I.T., Cambridge, Mass.; and Hugh Gray, "The Failure of a Demand for a Separate Andhra State," *Asian Survey* 14 (April 1974):338–49. See also

K. V. Narayana Rao, "Mulki Rules in Telangana: A Study in Internal Migration Policy with Respect to Employment," Hyderabad, National Institute of Community Development, October 1975, unpublished.

25. See *Rajya Sabha Debates,* May 1, 1968, pp. 524–26.

26. In 1969–70, the State of Maharashtra medical colleges introduced a ruling that "in addition to the qualifying exam mentioned above (interscience) only those students will be eligible for admission to medical colleges who have passed also the SSC or Senior Cambridge of the Indian School Certificate . . . from any of the recognized schools in Maharashtra state." See "Medical Colleges of the Government of Maharashtra, Rules for Admission," 1973–74 (MO-A 0219-1), p. 2.

27. *Raghun Rao* v. *State of Orissa, A.I.R.* 1955 Orissa 113.

28. *Radha Charan* v. *State, A.I.R.* 1969 Orissa 237.

29. *AVS Narasimha* v. *State of Andhra,* decided by Supreme Court 28/3/69, 1970 *S.L.R.*

30. Terms used often in admission procedures are "lady students," "sportsmen," and "children of political sufferers." The Colombo Plan provides for the exchange of students among various "Third World Countries."

31. See *Gurinder Pal Singh and another* v. *State of Punjab and others, A.I.R.* 1974 Punjab and Haryana 125. The number of seats effectively if not officially reserved may go above 50 percent in some cases. A 1973 decision, *Subhash Chandra* v. *State of U.P.,* upholds a reservation of 49 percent in addition to the places reserved for nominees of the central government who qualify through a different examination system (*A.I.R.* 1973 Allahabad 295).

32. *D. P. Joshi* v. *State of Madhya Bharat, A.I.R.* 1955 S.C. 334, p. 334.

33. Some states had extremely restrictive requirement even earlier. *Sudhir Ch. Nag* v. *State of Assam, A.I.R.* 1958 Assam 25 concerns an Assam education department rule of the mid-1950s which made permanent residence in Assam a condition for scholarship eligibility.

34. Lawrence Ebb, "Inter-State Preference and Discriminations," in Lawrence Ebb, ed., *Public Law Problems in India: A Survey Report.* Proceedings of a conference held at Stanford Law School, July 15–August 16, 1957 (Stanford: School of Law, Stanford University, 1957).

35. See *A.I.R.* 1969 Orissa 80. The case, *Abodha Kumar* v. *State of Orissa,* involved the selection of candidates on the grounds of their district of birth. The court held the rule to be violative of article 15(1).

36. *N. Vasundara* v. *State of Mysore, A.I.R.* 1971 S.C. 1439, pp. 1440, 1443.

37. *A.I.R.* 1976 Karnataka 1974, p. 185.

38. Ibid., p. 178.

39. *Nookavarapu Kanakadurga Devi* v. *Kakatiya Medical College, A.I.R.* 1972 Andhra Pradesh 83, p. 90.

40. *Murlidhar* v. *State of Andhra Pradesh, A.I.R.* 1959 Andhra Pradesh 437; *Ramakrishna* v. *Osmania University, A.I.R.* 1962 Andhra Pradesh 120; and *N. K. Devi* v. *Kakatiya Medical College, A.I.R.* 1972 Andhra Pradesh 83. A number of decisions that will be discussed below sanction reservations for people from particular regions of a state (hill and rural areas and the Uttra-

khand division of Uttar Pradesh). These are not really analogous to the Andhra Pradesh cases since they involve regions outside the area where the university is located. Thus the issue is not one of "localism."

41. *I.L.R.* 1964(2) Ker. 53, rev'g *A.I.R.* 1964 Ker. 39; *A.I.R.* 1963 S.C. 1012; *Abodha Kumar Mohapatra* v. *State of Orissa, A.I.R.* 1969 Orissa 80; and *A. Periakaruppan* v. *State of Tamil Nadu, A.I.R.* 1971 S.C. 2303.

42. *A.I.R.* 1967 Mysore 67; *A.I.R.* 1971 S.C. 1762.

43. *A.I.R.* 1971 S.C. 1762, para 22.

44. *A.I.R.* 1973 Allahabad 295.

45. *Dilip Kumar* v. *State of Uttar Pradesh, A.I.R.* 1973 Lucknow 592. The decision upheld reservations for candidates from the Uttrakhand division.

46. Ibid., p. 595, para. 13.

47. *A.I.R.* 1975 S.C. 563.

48. Ibid., p. 569.

49. *A.I.R.* 1971 S.C. 2303.

50. Ibid., p. 2306, para 12.

51. *A.I.R.* S.C. 1762, p. 1769, para 22.

52. *Joshi* v. *Madhya Bharat, A.I.R.* S.C., p. 340, para. 15.

53. *N. Vasundara* v. *State of Mysore, A.I.R.* 1971 S.C. 1439, p. 1443, para. 8.

54. *A.I.R.* 1975 Allahabad 1 (full bench), p. 7, para. 13.

55. *Annual Survey of Indian Law, 1970* (New Delhi: Indian Law Institute, 1970), p. 70.

56. *Devi* v. *Kakatiya Medical College, A.I.R.* 1972 Andhra Pradesh p. 93, para. 17.

57. *A.I.R.* 1973, Uttar Pradesh, p. 592.

58. *Ramachandra Vishnu* v. *State of Madhya Pradesh, A.I.R.* 1961 Madhya Pradesh 247, p. 250, para. 8.

59. Ibid., para. 10.

60. Allan P. Sindler, *Bakke, Defunis and Minority Admissions* (New York: Longman, 1978), p. 285.

61. *Lok Sabha Debates,* November 14, 1957, p. 651.

Chapter Four

1. Shivaji was a seventeenth-century warrior hero whose campaigns enlarged the frontiers of the Maratha empire. The spacious Shivaji park in Dadar, a largely Maharashtrian neighborhood in central Bombay, and numerous statues of Shivaji mounted on horseback, are named after the Maratha hero.

2. For a discussion of the resurgence of ethnic movements in the West, see Milton Esman, ed., *Ethnic Conflict in the Western World* (Ithaca: Cornell University Press, 1977), and Nathan Glazer and Daniel Moynihan, *Ethnicity, Theory and Experience* (Cambridge: Harvard University Press, 1975).

3. Census of India, *Maharashtra,* 1961, vol. 10, pt. X(1-B) (Bombay: Government Central Press, 1964), p. 185.

4. For a further discussion of the origins of Shiv Sena, see Mary Fainsod Katzenstein, *Ethnicity and Equality: The Shiv Sena Party and Preferential Policies in Bombay* (Ithaca: Cornell University Press, 1979), chaps. 3 and 4.

5. *Shiv Sena Speaks* by Kapilacharya (Bombay: Marmik Cartoon Weekly Office, 1967).

6. Recounted in a Shiv Sena branch office in Parel, January 1971.

7. Recounted by a Shiv Sena municipal councilor, February 1971.

8. *Shiv Sena Speaks,* p. 47.

9. Signed by M. A. Dhumal, Industries and Labor Section, circular no. M.S.C. 2468-55003, February 4, 1968.

10. *Times of India* (Bombay), October 15, 1973.

11. See *Lok Sabha Debates,* March 5, 1974, pp. 175–93 and March 13, 1974, pp. 71–74.

12. *Times of India* (Bombay), April 24, 1974, p. 1.

13. These interviews were conducted in 1972 by Ritu Anand, a research assistant, then a senior at Wellesley College.

14. Interview in Municipal Corporation office of Shiv Sena, January 1970.

15. Proposal of W. Mahadik, April 10, 1969 (Municipal Agenda, p. 32).

16. See B. A. V. Sharma and R. T. Jangam, *Bombay Municipal Corporation: An Election Study* (Bombay Popular Book Depot, 1962), p. 116, and G. S. Badhe and M. U. Rao, *The Bombay Civil Election of 1968* (Bombay: All-India Institute of Local Self Government, n.d.), p. 131.

17. In its listing of private firms and government offices, the Bombay telephone directory includes the names, positions, and telephone exchanges of a firm or establishment's officers. From the names it is possible to identify quite accurately the linguistic background of the individual and thus to estimate the numbers of Maharashtrians and non-Maharashtrians employed. Some names are not readily identifiable. The surname Desai, for instance, could be either Maharashtrian or Gujarati. But when the identification is done by native speakers familiar with Maharashtrian names, there is probably a greater than 85 percent accuracy. This analysis was done by N. Kanodia and T.C. Daswani, research assistants, both natives of Bombay. For a fuller discussion, see Mary Fainsod Katzenstein, "Governmental Response to Migration," Migration and Development Study Group, M.I.T., C/76-11.

18. This study was done by a marketing research organization in Bombay, commissioned by the author and colleagues from the Migration and Development Study Group at M.I.T. in 1976.

19. These results are drawn from a survey conducted by the author and Kartikeya Sarabhai in Bombay in 1971. The survey included interviews with 479 Maharashtrian voters and an approximately equal number of south Indian voters living in Bombay.

20. Government of Maharashtra Education Department, *Educational Development in Maharashtra State, 1950–51 to 1965–66* (Bombay: Government Central Press, 1968), bar graphs following p. 90.

21. Mimeo, Education Department, Maharashtra State, 1971, p. 2.

22. Statistics taken from annual reports of the University of Bombay.

23. These calculations were made by examining Elphinstone enrollment rosters.

24. For data on economic growth in Bombay, see CIDCO, *New Bombay Draft Development Plan,* October 1973, Appendix S: Data Base, Diagram S-22.

Chapter Five

1. According to the Hyderabad state census of 1951, Muslims constituted 34 percent of the total urban population and 7 percent of the total rural population. The Muslim population of Hyderabad city was 22 percent of the total state population.

2. Abdul Waheed Khan, ed., *Brief History of Andhra Pradesh* (Hyderabad: State Archives, 1972), p. 62. Salar Jung became Dewan on May 31, 1855, at the age of 24.

3. Hyderabad State Committee Appointed for the Compilation of a Freedom Movement in Hyderabad, *The Freedom Struggle in Hyderabad* (Hyderabad State Archives, 1956), vol. 2, pp. 255-58.

4. In those days service as a profession was looked down upon. While Jagirdars and Mansabdars were referred to as "Bashars" in state documents, government servants were known as "Nafars," and sensitive Hyderabadis of those days were most reluctant to be styled as "Nafar" instead of "Bashar." This unfortunate tendency of the then *mulkis* was the principal cause of the non-*mulki* invasion and the subsequent capture by them of the entire administrative machinery. See Syed Abid Hasan, *Whither Hyderabad* (1938), p. 47.

5. For example, the work of one office would be split up into several branches. The partisans of the earlier officers would be retired with pay, and, in their place, the new officer would bring in his friends thus making it necessary for the government to pay two salaries to the same post.

6. Jiwan Yar Jung Bahadur, *My Life: Being the Autobiography of Nawab Server-ul-Mulk Bahadur* (London: Arthur H. Stockwell, 1932), p. 82.

7. *Mulkis* refer to the *ghair-mulki* officers as "imported" officers. In this connection, knowledgeable persons distinguish between Muslims belonging to the Shia and Sunni sects. The Nizams, with the exception of the last, and the bulk of the Muslim population of the city and the state belonged to the Sunni sect. The last of the Nizams was a Shia. The migrant *ghair-mulki* Muslims from the north were usually Shias and held top positions under the Nizams while the Sunni Muslims were to be found, by and large, in the lower ranks.

8. Bahadur, *My Life*, p. 98.

9. Aziz Jung, *Khazina-I-Finance Ja Hisab*, Hyderabad (1319 Fasli) 1909, pp. 35-73.

10. Fathullah Khan, *A History of the Administrative Reforms in Hyderabad State* (Secunderabad, 1935), p. 146.

11. *Report on the Administration of H.E.H. the Nizam's Dominions*, Hyderabad (1335 Fasli) 1927, pp. 72-73.

12. Leonard, K., *Hyderabad* (San Diego: U.C. San Diego Department of History, 1969), p. 3.

13. Salar Jung had said: "You Hindusthani people are not practised in speaking or writing Persian. The Persian language is a sign of the victory of Islam and points to our being a victorious people. You have effaced it in your country and are trying to reproduce the same effect here. We have conquered the country by the sword, and so long as I am living Persian shall also live." Bahadur, *My Life*, p. 22.

14. At almost the same time demands were made in some of the other

native states and British Indian provinces for jobs to be reserved for different linguistic groups. In the native state of Travancore in 1891 the Malayalee Memorial, signed by ten thousand persons, was submitted to the king. They complained that foreign Dewans-Tamil Brahmins were regularly introducing their relations, castemen, and friends into the state, thereby systematically excluding the native Malayalees from the higher ranks of the government (George Woodcock, *Kerala: A Portrait of the Malabar Coast* [London: Faber and Faber, 1967], p. 232). Similarly, the introduction of "Direct Recruitment by Interview" in 1891 led to Tamil occupation of all the important posts and created resentment among the inhabitants of the native state of Mysore. The latter began to press for their proper representation in the public services (K. V. Viswanathayya, "Public Personnel Administration: A Study of Its Origin and Growth in Mysore State up to 1967," *Indian Journal of Public Administration* 20, no. 1 (1974), pp. 191-92). In British India too the Biharis had been clamoring for the separation of Bihar from Bengal since the 1870s, because Bengalis were tending to monopolize the posts (see V. C. P. Chaudhary, *The Creation of Modern Bihar* [Patna: Yogeshwar Prakashan], 1964).

15. Sajanlal, K., "The Hyderabad Record," *Journal of Deccan History and Culture,* Quoted in *The Freedom Struggle in Hyderabad,* vol. 3, p. 37.

16. *The Mohammedan,* October 6, 1901.

17. *The Hindu,* December 6, 1899.

18. See Osmania University Charter.

19. This may be compared with the Aligarh Muslim University which since its inception in 1920 has used English as the medium of instruction. The Nizam College, an elite institution, established in 1878 and affiliated with Madras University, continued to teach in English. About 1949 it became affiliated with Osmania University, which switched to the English medium in that year.

20. Government of Hyderabad, *Report of the Reform Committee* (Hyderabad: Government Central Press, 1938), pp. 9-11.

21. Out of 999 gazetted officers in various departments in 1947-48, 754 were Muslims. Government of India, *White Paper on Hyderabad,* New Delhi, 1948, p. 20.

22. Quoted in Hyderabad Struggle Committee, *The Hyderabad Problem: The Next Step,* (Hyderabad: Socialist Party, 1948), p. 43.

23. Hanumantha Rao, *Telangana Andhrodyamam,* pt. 1 (Andhra: Andhra Chandrika Grandha Mala, 1948), pp. 81-85.

24. Elliot, C. M., "Decline of a Patrimonial Regime: The Telangana Rebellion in India, 1946-51," *Journal of Asian Studies* 34, no. 1 (1974):34.

25. Narayana Rao, K. V., *The Emergence of Andhra Pradesh* (Bombay: Popular Prakashan, 1973), pp. 270-73.

26. Narayana Reddy, M., *Facts about Mulki Rules* (Hyderabad, 1973), p. 3.

27. Elliot, "Decline of a Patrimonial Regime," pp. 32-37.

28. *The Freedom Struggle in Hyderabad,* vol. 4, p. 50. The first four conferences were held at Kakinada (Madras), 1923; Bombay, 1926; Poona, 1928; and Akola (C.P. and Berar), 1931. A brief review of the activities of the Nizam Andhra Mahasabha and its forerunner, the Nizam Rashtra Andhra Jana Sangham, formed in 1921, is given in Rao, *Emergence of Andhra Pradesh,* pp. 270-76.

29. *The Hyderabad Problem*, p. 54.

30. *Census of India, 1911*, vol. 19, Hyderabad, pp. 107–8 and *Census of India, 1931*, vol. 23, Hyderabad, pt. 2.

31. Hasan, *Whither Hyderabad?* pp. 44–47.

32. Reddy, *Facts about Mulki Rules*, p. 4.

33. *Report of the Reform Committee*, p. 136 ff.

34. Ahmed, Zahir, *Life's Yesteryears: Glimpses of Sir Nizamat Jung and His Times* (Bombay: Thacker, 1945), p. 257.

35. *Report of the Reform Committee*, p. 129.

36. *Report on the Administration of H.E.H. the Nizam's Dominions, Hyderabad* (1348 Fasli) 1941, p. 245.

37. Srikishen, C., *45 Years a Rebel* (1952), p. 158.

38. Government of Hyderabad, *Report: Inquiry Relating to the Firing in the City of Hyderabad on 3rd and 4th September 1952* (Hyderabad: Government Central Press, 1953), p. 20.

39. Srikishen, *45 Years a Rebel*, p. 108.

40. *Report: Inquiry Relating to the Firing in the City of Hyderabad*, p. 20.

41. *Golkonda Patrika*, July 16, 1952.

42. Ranga Reddy, K. V., *Sveeya Charitra* (Hyderabad, 1967), pp. 106, 107.

43. Government of India, *Report of the States Reorganization Commission* (New Delhi, 1955), p. 107.

44. For the text of the agreement, see Narayana Rao, *Telangana: A Study on the Regional Committees in India* (Calcutta: The Minerva Associates, 1972), pp. 82–84.

45. For the text of the order see ibid., pp. 393–406.

46. *Ibid.*, pp. 311–18.

47. *A.I.R. 1962* Andhra Pradesh, pp. 120–23.

48. *Census of India, 1951*, vol. 9, Hyderabad, pt. 1A, p. 86.

49. Kesava Iyengar, S., *Rural Enquiries in the Hyderabad State, 1949–51* (Hyderabad: Government of Hyderabad, 1951), pp. 116–17, 146–86.

50. *Golkonda Patrika*, July 25, 1954.

51. It then included the area now comprising the Andhra region of Andhra Pradesh as well as the present Tamil Nadu and some areas in Kerala and Karnataka.

52. A note prepared by Waheeduddin Khan for the metropolitan Hyderabad development project shows the number of immigrants by year as follows: before 1951:124,930; 1951–55:52,904; 1956–60:102,744; 1961:48,741.

53. *Statistical Abstract of Andhra Pradesh, 1968*, p. 242, and *Statistical Abstract of Andhra Pradesh, 1973*, p. 220.

54. Bureau of Economics and Statistics, Government of Andhra Pradesh, *Economic and Statistical Bulletin*, 16, no. 3 (1972):120.

55. For a detailed study of this aspect see Rao, *Telangana*, chap. 4.

56. Ibid., chap. 7.

57. Committee of Jurists, *Report on Telangana Safeguards (Public Employment)* (New Delhi: Government of India Ministry of Home Affairs, 1969), p. 4.

58. For the text of the agreement, see Rao, *Telangana*, pp. 380–85.

59. A division of the bench dismissed the appeal on March 7, 1969.

60. *Crisis in Andhra Pradesh: From Safeguards to Separation* (Hyderabad:

Pemmaraju Publications Private, 1973), contains the texts of the judgments of the Supreme Court of March 28, 1969, and October 10, 1972, and of the high court of Andhra Pradesh of December 9, 1970, and February 18, 1972. It also contains the text of the *mulki* rules, gentlemen's agreement (February 1956), All Party Leaders Agreement (January 1969), Eight-Point Formula (April 1969) and Five-Point Formula (1972).

61. The committee consisted of K. N. Wanchoo, former chief justice of India, M. C. Satalvad, M.P. and former attorney general for India, and Niren De, attorney general for India.

62. *Report on Telangana Safeguards,* p. 12.

63. *P. Lakshmana Rao* v. *State of Andhra Pradesh and others,* December 9, 1970.

64. *Andhra Pradesh Legislative Assembly Debates,* vol. 15(5), December 18, 1970, pp. 795-97.

65. *V. Venkata Reddy and others* v. *the Director of Industries and Commerce, Government of Andhra Pradesh,* Hyderabad, dated February 18, 1972 —Writ Appeal No. 633 of 1970.

66. *The Director of Industries and Commerce, Government of Andhra Pradesh* v. *V. Venkata Reddy and others* (C.A. No. 993 of 1972) dated March 10, 1972. See *Crisis in Andhra Pradesh,* pp. 148-50.

67. Janasambadha Sakha, Government of Andhra Pradesh, *Facts about Telangana* (Hyderabad, 1969), p. 5.

68. It is said that about 80 percent of the candidates study in Telugu, Hindi, Marathi, etc. Roughly 20 percent are permitted to continue in English language schools, based on their marks in English at the qualifying examination.

69. Andhra Pradesh Legislative Congress Party, *The Mulki Rules: Their Genesis and After* (Andhra Pradesh, 1973), p. 5.

70. For the text of the bill, see *The Hindu,* December 20, 1972.

71. There were a good number of students who had undergone the costly professional courses—medicine and engineering—even paying donations of thousands of rupees for admission to colleges. For them and for their parents, these restrictions were grating.

72. *Indian Express,* February 17, 1973.

73. There are three local areas, one comprising the districts in Telangana region, the other comprising Nellore and the four districts of Rayalaseema, and the third comprising the remaining seven coastal districts.

Chapter Six

1. East Bengalis who came to India before July 26, 1949, automatically became Indian citizens, and, under an agreement between India and Bangladesh, those who entered India between that date and March 25, 1971, could secure citizenship certificates, though few did so. However, the AASU and the All-Assam Gana Sangram Parishad (AAGSP), the council of Assamese organizations, viewed this latter agreement between Indira Gandhi and Mujib Rahman, the prime minister of Bangladesh, as illegal and unconstitutional.

2. For a vivid account of the movement, and photos of the anti-Indian

graffiti, see "The Danger of Secession: Assam and the North-East," *India Today* (North American Edition), vol. 2, no. 1, 1980, pp. 20–26.

3. The movement against outsiders also spread to Meghalaya, Mizoram, Arunachal Pradesh, and across the Indian border to the Chittagong Hill Tracts district of Bangladesh where the tribal population took arms against "Bengali expansionism." It should be noted that virtually every country of South and Southeast Asia, including Burma, Thailand, Laos, and Vietnam, has been faced with the political problem of integrating the tribal population living in their northern regions near the Chinese borders.

4. "The Danger of Secession," p. 24.

5. Cited by R. B. Vaghaiwalla, *Census of India, 1951, Assam, Manipur and Tripura,* vol. XII, pt. I-A, Report (Shillong, 1954), p. 72.

6. B. C. Allen, *Nowgong Assam District Gazetteer* (Calcutta, 1905), pp. 66–67.

7. For an account of the policies of the Muslim League governments toward migration and land settlement, see Amalendu Guha, *Planter Raj to Swaraj: Freedom Struggle and Electoral Politics in Assam, 1826–1946* (New Delhi: Indian Council of Historical Research, 1977). This fine book is the best account of the nationalist movement in Assam, and, while the focus is the conflict with the British, it pays considerable attention to Bengali-Assamese relations.

8. For a more detailed history of the various migrations into Assam, see Weiner, *Sons of the Soil,* chap. 3 ("When Migrants Succeed and Natives Fail: Assam and Its Migrants"), pp. 75–143.

9. Susanta Krishna Dass, "Immigration and Demographic Transformation of Assam, 1891–1981," *Economic and Political Weekly,* May 10, 1980, p. 855. Dass suggests that the substantial increase in the number of Bengali speakers between 1961 and 1971 (a 43.45% increase) was due to the migration of Hindu refugees from East Pakistan, particularly in 1965 when there were communal disturbances there. The Hindi growth (an increase of 54.1% in the decade) resulted from the migration of Biharis into the labor force in menial positions such as rickshaw pullers, brick makers, construction laborers, and porters.

10. The Assamese, it should also be noted, do not have much incentive to seek employment in other states either. According to the 1971 census of India only 0.6% of all Assamese-speaking people in India live outside of Assam.

11. Census of India, *Economic Characteristics of Population, Selected Tables, 1971,* Series 1-India, Paper 3 (1972).

12. Employment data from Assam Directorate of Employment and Craftsman Training, Research and Statistical Cell, *Employment Review, Assam State* (March 1974).

13. Letter to the editor, *Amrita Bazar Patrika,* November 4, 1972.

14. Government of India Ministry of Labour, Employment, and Rehabilitation, *Report of the National Commission on Labour* (New Delhi, 1969). The recommendations of the commission on the demands of "sons of the soil" can be found on pp. 74–78.

15. *National Integration Council Proceedings,* New Delhi, March 20, 1969.

16. According to figures published by the Labor Ministry, nearly 60 percent of the notifications of vacancies to the exchanges resulted in direct placements. In 1968, for example, 3,161,000 persons were registered in the country's 405 exchanges; 551,000 vacancies were notified; and 319,000 placements were effected. In Assam, however, only 3,751 placements were made for 8,623 vacancies, a placement/vacancy record of 43 percent. Only 6 percent of those registered found jobs through the exchanges in Assam that year, as compared with 10 percent nationally. *Report of the National Commission on Labour,* appendix 1.

17. *Report of the National Commission on Labour,* p. 78.

18. Assam, Assembly Secretariat, *Report of the Employment Review Committee, Third Report, 1973* (December 1973), p. 357.

19. Between 1951 and 1961 the population of Assam increased from 8 million to 10.8 million, an increase of 35 percent, but the number of Assamese speakers rose from 4.6 million to 6.7 million, an increase of 48.6 percent, suggesting the magnitude of language "switching" by the Bengali Muslims. No language figures are available for 1941, but in 1931 only 1.7 million people claimed Assamese as their mother tongue.

20. *Report of the Employment Review Committee,* vols. 1, 2, 3 (1st, 2d, and 3d Reports), 1973.

21. The high migration rate into Assam's urban areas is reflected in the sex ratio. The sex ratio of Assam's urban areas (in 1971) was 665 women per 1,000 males, while in Gauhati, Assam's largest city, only 39 percent of the population was female. Census of India, *General Population Tables,* series 3, Assam, pt. 2-A (1971).

22. The firms that were less than one-third Assamese were:

Assam Railways and Trading, founded in 1881, had the lowest percentage of Assamese (9%) of the twenty-eight companies. A large English-owned firm, employing 4,633 workers, it has traditionally recruited a substantial portion of its unskilled labor force from among Nepalis and Telugus (from Andhra). This pattern continues. During the year prior to the survey the firm hired 537 workers, of whom 447 were born outside the state. Its administrative personnel were almost all non-Assamese.

Woodcraft-Mariani employed 538 workers, all but a handful of whom (19%) were migrants. The workers came primarily from East Pakistan, Bihar, West Bengal, and U.P. (in that order). Thirty-six percent of the workers were Hindi speakers, 35 percent were Bengali, and only 18 percent were Assamese. None of its workers had been hired through the employment exchanges, though, like other companies, it notified the employment exchanges of openings.

Indian Airlines is one of a handful of public firms (apart from banks) that employ few Assamese. Only 11 percent of its small staff of 175 were Assamese. Forty-four percent were Bengali, many of whom were born in Assam, though the largest number were from East Pakistan. There are frequent transfers of employees to Assam from other states, following a practice of centralized recruitment and transfers. More than a fifth of the staff (22%) were neither Assamese, Bengali, nor Hindi speaking, having been recruited from all over the country.

Sarda Plywood employed mostly laborers from among the Hindi-speaking migrants from Bihar, U.P., and Rajasthan (59%), hired at the rate of Rs. 2.75 a day through labor contractors. The firm employed 190 workers and had a high turnover. The head office is located in Calcutta.

Assam Hardboards, with 359 workers, was another low-technology, traditional firm with a high turnover and a large migrant labor force. More than half of its employees (57%) had been in Assam less than five years; most came from Bihar or U.P. In the best-paid office jobs with salaries ranging from Rs. 500 to Rs. 749, only 25 percent were born in Assam.

Woodcraft Plywood–Joypore was another small factory with 346 workers, more than half of whom were drawn from Bihar and U.P. Like many plywood factories, it hired its workers through labor contractors. Some of its manpower needs are seasonal. Workers were paid a minimum wage of Rs. 2.75 a day. The government employment exchanges were not relied upon for hiring workers. Like Sarda Plywood, it has its head office in Calcutta.

Assam Oil, founded in 1900, employed 4,018 workers and had a low turnover rate compared with the companies thus far described. No contract labor was employed. However, more than half of the labor force were migrant, and of those who were born in Assam (44%), only a little more than half (56%) were Assamese. Nearly a third (31%) of the labor force in this company was Bengali, half of whom were locally born. A substantial portion of the labor force was also imported from Nepal.

India Carbon, a small, private firm employing 267 persons with its head office in Calcutta, largely employed Hindi-speaking workers from Bihar and U.P. Originally the manual laborers were engaged through labor contractors, but this practice was no longer followed. The firm had a low labor turnover rate, even, surprisingly, among the unskilled laborers where sixty-five percent had held their jobs for five to ten years. The firm reported that none of its employees from outside Assam was recruited by direct advertisement, or through the employment exchanges.

United Bank of India, a nationalized bank employing 857 workers, with its head office in Calcutta, had comparatively few migrants (30%), but most of its locally recruited labor force (61%) were Bengalis. Many of the migrants were Bengalis, born in East Pakistan but long-time residents in Assam, who often worked elsewhere before joining the bank. Of its 857 employees, only 25 were recruited through the employment exchanges.

Everest Cycles is another firm hiring unskilled manual workers from Bihar, U.P., and Rajasthan. Sixty percent of its labor force were migrants, almost all from the Hindi-speaking states. The director reported that the casual and unskilled labor were recruited at the gate. "Local people do not want to stick to such jobs," he said, explaining why the unskilled workers were not Assamese.

Steelworth-Gauhati is one of the three branches of this firm in Assam, the others being in Tezpur and Tinsukia. They each employed a few hundred workers (255 at Gauhati), with their unskilled workers from the Hindi-speaking states. Almost all of the Assamese-speaking workers were paid under Rs. 250 a month. The Bengali workers, many of whom had the higher-paid jobs, tended to be hired locally (19 out of its 22 Bengali workers).

Associated Industries, a company with a chemical unit and a textile-spinning mill, employed 717 workers in its two plants. Two-thirds of its workers (66%) were migrants. The migrants appeared to be hired locally "at the gate." The firm hires workers as apprentices. They were paid Rs. 1.50 per day for three months, then Rs. 2 per day, and, after six months, Rs. 2.50. Few Assamese apply. Among the skilled workers, too, migrants predominated (72%).

Punjab National Bank, a nationalized bank with regional headquarters in Calcutta, employed only 101 workers. Its national headquarters used to be in Lahore, but it subsequently moved to Delhi. It is an old bank, having been founded in 1896. Its staff, mainly clerical and administrative people, were about half from Assam and half from outside. Nearly a third (32%) was Assamese, about another third (31%) were Hindi speakers, mainly from Bihar, and about a quarter (26%) were Bengalis, more than half of whom were locally born. It is interesting to note that this was the only bank with a large Hindi-speaking staff. Most of the other banks had a larger Bengali staff, and a correspondingly smaller Hindi staff (usually less than ten percent Hindi mother tongue), reflecting their closer connections with Calcutta.

Assam Match Company, another lumber-based industry, also employed Hindi-speaking manual laborers, had its head office outside Assam, and had few Assamese-speaking people in the top pay scales. An unusual feature of this firm, however, was that it employed a large locally recruited Bengali labor force. More than a third of its 1,790 workers (35%) were Bengali speakers, and the bulk of these were from Assam. The remaining Bengalis were largely migrants from East Pakistan. This firm did no labor contracting, but it had a continuous stream of workers from Bihar who constituted nearly a quarter of the work force.

Assam Cotton Mills employed migrants for two-thirds of its 750 workers. The firm also uses an apprenticeship system. New workers were paid Rs. 1.54 a day for three months, with increases thereafter. Workers were recruited directly from Bihar or U.P., rather than through employment exchanges. About a third of the workers were local born, almost all Assamese. The Bengalis who held the higher-paid clerical and administrative jobs were almost all from West Bengal. It should be noted that all four of the company directors lived in Calcutta.

23. The public sector firms that employed Assamese were:
Oil and Natural Gas Commission, with 3,788 workers, recruited 68% of its labor force locally, almost all (96%) being Assamese. But of those born in Assam, ninety-five percent were in the lowest wage categories, earning less than Rs. 250 per month.

Regional Research Laboratory, under the Council of Scientific Industrial Research, recruited 59 percent of its small staff of 259 locally, and of these 95 percent were Assamese, but again almost all were in the lowest wage group. Only 18 percent of its executives were born in Assam.

Fertilizer Corporation of India, an employer of 2,035, was 62 percent locally recruited, 88 percent Assamese. This firm had made a special effort to hire its technical work force locally. More than half of its technical personnel (52%) were Assamese. At the managerial level, however, the staff was still predominantly nonlocal. Only 22 percent of the class 1 (managerial) jobs were held by personnel born in Assam, 16 percent recruited in the last year of the survey, and only 6 percent who had been with the firm for two to four years. Again, Assamese predominated at the lowest income positions.

Food Corporation of India was more than half Assamese (52%) and a quarter (26%) Bengali, with a comparatively small Hindi labor force (11%). The reason for the high proportion of Bengalis and Assamese is that more than two-thirds of its labor force (68%) were recruited locally. While much of the senior staff was recruited outside of Assam, the middle-level staff was predominantly from Assam. One reason is that many were on deputation from the state government; state government employees are recruited locally, and are more likely to be Assamese than Bengali. Ninety-seven percent of the locally recruited staff was either Assamese (75%) or Bengali (22%).

24. Data from Department of Economics and Statistics, *Statistical Outline of India, 1975* (Bombay: Tata Services Limited, 1976), table 90, p. 96.
25. Ibid., p. 92.
26. The 1891 census reported 1.4 million Assamese speakers in the state. In 1961 there were 6.7 million. Had the Assamese-speaking population increased at the same rate as the Indian population as a whole, in 1961 it would have been 2.8 million. The difference—3.9 million—represents a crude figure as to how many people (or their ancestors) may have switched to Assamese, if not at home, at least for public purposes. According to Dass, the original Assamese Muslims, who were a small but important landed class in Assam, played an important role in persuading Bengali Muslims that it was in their interest to become Assamized by adopting Assamese as the "mother tongue." Dass, "Immigration and Demographic Transformation of Assam," p. 858.
27. *Statesman* (Calcutta), January 15, 1980.
28. Yogi Aggarwal, "Left in Waiting," *Economic and Political Weekly,* June 14–21, 1980, p. 1046.
29. For alternative Marxist explanations, see the articles by Hiren Gohain in *Economic and Political Weekly*, February 23 and May 24, 1980, and Ghan-

shyam Pardesi, "Internal Colony in a National Exploitative System," *Economic and Political Weekly,* June 7, 1980. For an analysis by an Assamese who believes that the left has underestimated the importance of the demographic changes resulting from an influx of Bengalis, see Sanjib Kumar Baruah, "Cudgel of Chauvinism or Tangled Nationality Question?" *Economic and Political Weekly,* March 15, 1980.

30. Muslims constituted 24.6 percent of the population of Assam in 1971. They form 40 percent or more of the population in the districts of Cachar, Goalpara, and Nowgong. It was these last two districts that experienced a major increase in Assamese-speaking population after 1951. For a particularly useful description of the demography of India's Muslims see Nafis Ahmad Siddiqui, *Population Geography of Muslims of India* (New Delhi: S. Chand, 1976). For a specific analysis of the linguistic and religious composition of Assam, see Susanta Krishna Dass, "Immigration and Demographic Transformation of Assam," *Economic and Political Weekly*, May 10, 1980.

Chapter Seven

1. In the 1977 parliamentary elections Congress won 50.6 percent of the votes in Assam, 47.0 percent in Maharashtra, and 57.4 percent in Andhra, as compared with a national vote of 34.5 percent.

2. The focus here, as elsewhere in this book, has been on preferential policies affecting the employment of local people in relation to migrants. Regrettably, there is little research on the impact of preferential policies on the employment of scheduled castes and scheduled tribes. Of particular interest is a paper by Barbara R. Joshi, "Scheduled Caste Political Reservations: Who Benefits?" Annual meeting, Association for Asian Studies, Chicago, 1978, which reports a substantial increase in the employment of untouchables in public sector industries between 1971 and 1974, particularly in the class III (clerical) posts and class IV (blue collar, excluding sweepers). Among the higher grades, she reports, there has also been a substantial increase, though the proportion of scheduled castes in these positions still remains well below their proportion in the population.

3. However, to the extent that wages and employment opportunities in the modern sector of an economy are determinants of rural to urban migration even for those who enter the unorganized informal sector, we might expect the overall migration rate to the urban centers to slow down if entry into the modern sector is restricted.

4. For succinct accounts of the expansion of education in India since independence, see J. P. Naik, *Policy and Performance in Indian Education, 1947–74* (New Delhi: Orient Longman, 1975) and J. P. Naik, *Equality, Quality and Quantity: The Elusive Triangle in Indian Education* (New Delhi: Allied Publishers, 1975). The number of students in Indian universities grew from 362,000 in 1950 to 3,262,000 in 1971, nearly a tenfold increase in a little over two decades.

5. One of the arguments for preferential policies in India is that employers and personnel officers are themselves of immigrant extraction who discriminate in favor of outsiders in spite of the increased availability of locally educated and skilled manpower.

6. The relationship is somewhat more apparent in the case of scheduled tribes and scheduled castes since there are several studies that report the impact of preferential recruitment on the educational achievements of these groups. See: Agarwal and Ashraf, *Equality through Privilege* and Vimal P. Shah and Rara Patel, *Who Goes to College?* (Ahmadabad: Rachna Prakashan, 1977). For a review of the recent literature, see Ahmad, "Towards Equality." See also Kusum K. Premi, "Educational Opportunities for the Scheduled Castes: Role of Protective Discrimination in Equalisation," *Economic and Political Weekly*, November 9, 1974, pp. 1902–10. For a quantitative analysis of educational performance, see J. P. Naik, *Education of the Scheduled Castes 1965–66*, Occasional monographs, no. 6 (New Delhi: ICSSR, 1971). None of these studies, however, systematically relates educational achievement of the scheduled castes and scheduled tribes with their changing patterns of employment.

7. Department of Economics and Statistics, *Statistical Outline of India, 1974* (Bombay: Tata Services Limited, 1975), pp. 94–95.

8. The Bombay city census for 1961 does provide some data on the education and occupation of migrants, but comparable city-wide tables for 1971 have not been published.

9. The 1971 census reports that the migrants continue to be better educated than the local population. Twelve percent of the interstate migrants and 14 percent of the migrants from Bangladesh were matriculates or had higher education, as against 7 percent of the nonmigrant local population. The census also reported that 41,100 persons holding the better-paying jobs as professionals, administrators, and clerical and sales personnel came from other states, as against 35,700 who had migrated to the urban areas from within Assam.

10. Verma, *Caste Reservations in India*, p. 117.

11. Kusum Premi, in her study of scheduled caste education cited above, provides evidence that there are large educational inequalities within the scheduled castes in the Punjab. The small amounts paid as stipends, she believes, make it possible for those Harijans from higher-income families to go on to higher education, but it is insufficient to support those from the lowest income groups. The result, she argues, is that inequalities among scheduled castes are growing since the lowest income groups are unable to take advantage of the benefits provided by the government. She concludes that "children of Class I and II categories of scheduled caste officials (higher ranking civil servants) should not be accorded any preferential treatment" ("Educational Opportunities for the Scheduled Castes," p. 1909). Evidence of educational inequalities is also reported by Suma Chitnis, "Education for Equality: Case of Scheduled Castes in Higher Education," *Economic and Political Weekly*, Annual Number (1972) pp. 1675–81. The Mahars, in Maharashtra, though 35.1 percent of the scheduled caste population obtain 85.8% of the scholarships, while the Mangs, though 32.6 percent of the scheduled caste population, receive only 2.2 percent of the scholarships.

12. K. K. Katyal, "The Politics of Job Reservations," *The Hindu* (International Edition), April 1, 1978, p. 4.

13. "Income Base for Bihar Job Quota," *The Hindu* (International Edition), April 1, 1978, p. 5.

Chapter Eight

1. One recent example of a policy which distinguishes citizenship rights on the basis of ethnicity comes out of Burma. According to a report in the *New York Times* (Henry Kamm, "Proposed Law to Create Two Kinds of Burmese Citizenship Worries Millions," August 13, 1980, p. A 14), the Burmese government proposes to enact a citizenship law which would deny equal employment rights to "the millions of people in this nation who are not native-born citizens of ethnic groups recognized as indigenous." The proposed law would give local bodies authority to make citizenship decisions. The major targets of the law apparently are the Bangladeshis who have been migrating into Arakan state in western Burma for several decades, and the long-time Chinese and Indian residents, many of whom were born in Burma.

2. There are a few comparisons of the American and Indian legal approaches to preferences. See Alan Katz, "Benign Preferences: An Indian Decision and the Bakke Case," *American Journal of Comparative Law* 25 (1977): 611–40. An excellent early essay on residence requirements in India and the United States is Lawrence F. Ebb's "Interstate Barriers in India and American Constitutional Experience," *Stanford Law Review* 2, no. 1 (December 1958): 37–93.

3. Andre Beteille, "Homo Hierarchicus, Homo Equalis," *Modern Asian Studies* 13, no. 4 (1979):534.

4. Ibid., p. 547.

5. Ibid., p. 548. In a similar vein Edward Said denounces attempts to contrast East and West as a subtle and disguised way of undervaluing non-Western societies. Said puts his argument starkly: "Can one divide human reality ... into clearly different cultures, histories, traditions, societies, even races and survive the consequences humanly? ... For such divisions (between Westerners and Orientals) are generalities whose use historically and actually has been to press the importance of the distinction between some men and some other men, usually towards not especially admirable ends" (*Orientalism* [New York: Random House, 1978], p. 45). Because some have used such comparisons to diminish other societies and to congratulate themselves on their own does not mean that comparisons cannot be used for nonjudgmental scholarly and scientific purposes to understand the differences between societies, the reasons for these differences, and their consequences for human behavior.

6. See Joshi, "Scheduled Caste Political Reservations: Who Benefits?"

7. The Lok Dal, a party with support from among the backward classes in Uttar Pradesh, Bihar, and Haryana, called for reservations in its election manifesto for the 1980 parliamentary elections. "While the socially and educationally backward classes (other than Scheduled Tribes and Castes), both Hindu and Muslim, constitute more than half of our people, they have little place in the administrative map of the country and are, therefore smarting under a sense of injustice and deprivation. While the Lok Dal regards that reservations cannot be a permanent feature of our arrangements, in an unequal social order that obtains today, there is no alternative to the policy of preferential opportunities. At least 25 percent of Group A and B jobs in the

central Government services will, therefore, be reserved for young men and women, coming from these classes, as recommended by the Backward Classes Commission appointed in the fifties by the Union Government itself, under Article 340 of the Constitution."

8. The estimate is made in a paper by Harry W. Blair, "Rising Kulaks and Backward Classes in Bihar: Social Change in the Late 1970s," Center for International Studies, Cornell, April 1979, pp. 11–12. Professor Blair estimates that government posts created in Bihar each year number 9,000 of which 20 percent would be reserved for backward classes under the formula proposed by the chief minister, Kapoori Thakur. Blair estimates that of the approximately 210,000 college students in Bihar, 30 to 40 percent are from backward classes.

9. The charge that preferences for scheduled castes are largely ineffectual and have become a substitute for policies is forcefully made in a document prepared by a group of Delhi-based intellectuals on the eve of the 1980 parliamentary elections, entitled, "An Agenda for India" (*Seminar*, no. 245, [January 1980], pp. 74-85). "It is time," they write, "to examine carefully the appropriateness and adequacy of measures adopted so far to ameliorate the conditions of Harijans. The nation's responsibility towards them does not end with the enactment of constitutional and legal provisions for compensatory discrimination, especially since there is no evidence of such steps having produced any significant differences in the lives of the vast majority of the socially oppressed and deprived sections of the community. Reservations and related concessions are hardly the answer to the problems of the Harijans for such provisions cannot be a permanent feature of a just and equitable social system. This was indeed the premise on which the Founding Fathers had acted. If we still pursue a policy of preferential treatment through a routine extension of reservations we probably do so more to salve our consciences than out of a genuine concern for the existential problems of the Harijans." The "Agenda" was prepared by Romesh Thapar, Rajni Kothari, Bashiruddin Ahmed, George Verghese, Kuldip Nayar, and Mrinal Datta-Chaudhuri and signed by fifty other prominent intellectuals.

10. Nathan Glazer, *Affirmative Discrimination: Ethnic Equality and Public Policy* (New York: Basic Books, 1975).

11. See Nijole V. Benokaitis and Joe R. Feagin, *Affirmative Action and Equal Opportunity: Action, Inaction, Reaction* (Colorado: Westview Press, 1978), and "Evaluating the Impact of Affirmative Action: A Look at the Federal Compliance Program: A Symposium," *ILR Review* 29 (July 1976): 485-584. See also Richard A. Lester, *Reasoning about Discrimination* (Princeton: Princeton University Press, 1980); John E. Fleming, Gerald R. Gill, David H. Swinton, *The Case for Affirmative Action for Blacks in Higher Education* (Washington: Howard University Press, 1978).

12. This ideological distinction has made the adoption of preferential policies easier in India. But two recent (Bakke and Weber) judicial decisions in the United States held that past discrimination need not be found in order to employ race conscious policies and thus moved the United States markedly down the path toward an acceptance of preferential policies meted out

on the principle of achieving ethnic equality. Neither case undermined the broader argument that the historic presence of discrimination within American society justified preferential policies even if specific institutions themselves never engaged in discrimination.

13. Since the mid-1960s this arbitrary fifty percent figure has become widely though by no means universally accepted. Many Indians now argue that the principles of equality and efficiency are violated only if reservations exceed fifty percent; the principle is obviously not accepted by supporters of sons of the soil movements.

14. A number of central government commissions have attempted to specify criteria for defining "other backward classes" as a category for preferential treatment, but without success. The central government therefore declined to use caste criteria (other than with scheduled castes and tribes) for providing government benefits, with the result that it was left for the state governments to develop their own criteria and for the courts to unify and limit them. For an excellent review of these efforts see Galanter, "Who are the Other Backward Classes?"

Index

175

75-76; education policy, 35, 38, 74, 76; migration to, 76-80; public employment in, 75-76, 80-81, 82-83; regional committee, 72-73; separatism in, 30, 83-85, 129; Six Point Formula, 86-88. *See also* Andhra Pradesh; Gentlemen's agreement; Hyderabad; *Mulki* rules; Telangana Praja Samiti
Telangana Praja Samiti, 13, 18, 84, 88, 121
Telugu (language), 58, 69, 100, 105. *See also* Telangana
Thackeray, Bal, 45, 46
Times of India (newspaper), 47
Title VII (U.S.), 145
Tokenism in Bombay, 53
Tribal people: *See* Hill tribes; Separatism
Tripura (state), 26, 42, 91, 102
Tyagi, Mahavir, 24

Uganda, 7, 8
Union Public Service Commission, 100, 101, 109

University admissions, 32-35, 74. *See also* Education policy; Medical schools
University of Hyderabad Act, 87
Urbanization, 126-27, 138; in Andhra Pradesh, 76-80, 85-86, 127 (*see also* Hyderabad); in Assam, 95-96, 113. *See also* Bombay
Urdu (language), 59, 60, 71, 72
U.S.A. and India compared, 21-22, 136-53 *passim*
Uttar Pradesh (state), 29, 35-36, 38, 64, 133
Uttrakhand (region), 35, 36, 38

Vidarbha (region), 83
Vietnam, 8
Voltas, 52

Wanchoo Committee, 28
Warangal (region), 69
West Bengal (state), 26, 27, 30, 91. *See also* Assam; Bangladesh; Bengalis; Pakistan
Woodcraft Plywood Factory, 104